VISUAL QUICKSTART GUIDE

iPHOTO 6

FOR MAC OS X

Adam C. Engst

 **Peachpit Press**

eet • Berkeley, CA 94710

 • 800/283-9444 • 510/524-2221 (fax)

 the Web at www.peachpit.com.

rt errors, please send a note to errata@peachpit.com.

pit Press is a division of Pearson Education.

Editor: Nancy Davis
Production Coordinator: Lisa Brazieal
Copyeditor: Tonya Engst
Compositor: Adam C. Engst
Indexer: Rebecca Plunkett
Cover Design: Peachpit Press

ISBN 0-321-42331-3

9 8 7 6 5 4 3 2

Printed and bound in the United States of America

Dedication

To my son, Tristan Mackay, subject of so many of my photo...

About the Author

Adam C. Engst is the publisher of *TidBITS*, one of the oldest and largest Internet-based newsletters, and the Take Control electronic book series (with print collections published by Peachpit Press), both of which have helped many thousands of readers (find them at `www.tidbits.com`). He has written numerous computer books, including the best-selling *Internet Starter Kit* series, and many articles for magazines, including *Macworld,* where he is currently a contributing editor. His photos have appeared in juried photography shows.

His indefatigable support of the Macintosh community has resulted in numerous awards and recognition at the highest levels. In the annual MDJ Power 25 survey of industry insiders, he consistently ranks as one of the top five most influential people in the Macintosh industry, and he was named one of MacDirectory's top ten visionaries. And how many industry figures can boast of being turned into an action figure?

Please send comments about this book to Adam at `iphoto-vqs@tidbits.com`.

Other Books by Adam C. Engst

Take Control of Your Wi-Fi Security

Take Control of iKey 2

Take Control of Buying a Mac

The Wireless Networking Starter Kit

Internet Starter Kit for Macintosh

...ks

...rk of a single person, and ...elped with this one, including

...Engst (not only my wonderful ...but also a great copyeditor)

Nancy Davis (an excellent editor and an almost geographically suitable friend)

◆ Lisa Brazieal (spotter of wayward pixels!)

◆ Nancy Ruenzel (for giving me the nod on this book)

◆ Scott Cowlin (for marketing wizardry)

◆ Chris Engst (for watching Tristan!)

◆ Glenn Fleishman, Marshall Clow, Fred Johnson, and David Blatner (without whose help I could never have explained color management and resolution)

◆ Keith Kubarek, Sandro Menzel, Cory Byard, and Laurie Clow (for their photography knowledge and tips)

◆ Jeff Carlson, Geoff Duncan, Glenn Fleishman, Joe Kissell, Matt Neuburg, and Mark Anbinder (for helping keep *TidBITS* running)

Technical Colophon

I wrote this book using the following hardware and software:

◆ A dual-processor 1 GHz Power Mac G4 with a pair of 17-inch Apple Studio Display monitors, Canon PowerShot S100 and S400 digital cameras, and an Addonics Pocket DigiDrive card reader

◆ Mac OS X 10.4 Tiger, iPhoto 6, Adobe InDesign CS2 for layout, Snapz Pro X 2.0 for screen shots, and the Peachpit VQS template

Featured Photographers

I took most of the photos in this book, but I also included some pictures from my sister, Jennifer Upson, and my father, Chris Engst. And of course, any photos that I'm in were probably taken by Tonya Engst or Tristan Engst (who is now 7 years old and loves to take pictures with my older camera).

CONTENTS AT A GLANCE

TABLE OF CONTENTS

Chapter 5: Showing Photos Onscreen 95

Chapter 6: Printing Photos 123

1

GETTING STARTED

In late 2001, Apple realized the immense popularity of digital cameras meant that millions of Mac owners now use digital cameras in lieu of their traditional analog counterparts. And yet, the camera is only part of the equation, and the other part, the software, is often incomprehensible to the average user.

Enter iPhoto, which helps users perform tasks never before possible in a photo management program, such as ordering prints from an online service and building and printing photo books—essentially customized hardcover photo albums. At the same time, iPhoto is easy to use, thanks in part to a simple interface, but also thanks to the fact that it doesn't attempt to compete with the big boys of the image-cataloging and image-editing worlds.

If iPhoto is so easy, why write this book? Even though iPhoto 6 improves on previous versions, it still doesn't entirely demystify the process of importing a digital photograph, editing it, and presenting it on paper or on the computer screen. And iPhoto comes with no documentation beyond minimal and incomplete online help.

Read on, then, not just for the manual iPhoto lacks, but also the help you need to take digital photos and make the most of them.

Get the Electronic Version!

I make an electronic version of this book available for free to anyone who's bought the paper version. Why might you want to read the book in PDF format onscreen?

◆ It's completely searchable.

◆ It takes up only a few megabytes of space on your hard disk and thus doesn't weigh down your bag like the paper book when you're traveling.

To find out how to get it, send email to get-iphoto6-vqs@tidbits.com.

Hardware and Software Requirements

Although iPhoto 6 is a simple program, it has fairly significant system requirements thanks to the difficulty of working with large digital images.

To run iPhoto, you need:

◆ A Macintosh with a PowerPC G4, PowerPC G5, or Intel Core processor with 256 MB of RAM (though 512 MB of RAM is better). Realistically, the more CPU power and RAM you can throw at iPhoto, the better its performance. You'll also find a large monitor extremely helpful.

◆ Mac OS X. Specifically, Mac OS X 10.3.9 or 10.4.3, but Apple recommends Mac OS X 10.4.4 and QuickTime 7.0.4 (which is included with iLife '06).

◆ An optical drive that can read DVD discs, since iLife '06 comes on DVD. Burning DVDs directly from iDVD requires a drive that can write to DVD as well, such as an Apple SuperDrive or a third-party DVD burner.

◆ A source of digital images, which could be an iPhoto-compatible digital camera, scanned images, Photo CDs, or a service that provides digital images along with traditional film developing. Apple maintains a list of cameras and card readers that are supposedly compatible with iPhoto at www.apple.com/macosx/upgrade/cameras.html. Take that list with a grain of salt; some devices on it may not work entirely, and some devices missing from the list work fine with iPhoto.

✔ Tips

■ To be able to use iDVD for creating and burning slideshows to DVD, you need at least a 733 MHz PowerPC G4-based Mac.

■ iPhoto can import photos in RAW format, which is an uncompressed image file format used by some high-end cameras. However, there are multiple flavors of RAW, and iPhoto does not support all of them.

Acquiring iPhoto

Apple offers several methods of getting iPhoto, although it's worth noting up front that iPhoto is no longer a free download, as it was before iPhoto 4.

Ways to get iPhoto:

◆ Look in your Applications folder. If you purchased your Mac since January 2006, iPhoto 6 may already be installed.

◆ Buy a $79 copy of Apple's iLife '06, which is a CD/DVD package containing all five of Apple's digital hub applications: iPhoto 6, iMovie HD 6, iTunes 6, iDVD 6, GarageBand 3, and iWeb. Although these applications come free with new Macs, the iLife package is the only way for current owners of iPhoto, iMovie, iDVD, and GarageBand to get updates for those products. Visit www.apple.com/ilife/ for details.

◆ Buy a new Mac, which will come with iPhoto pre-installed. Steve Jobs thanks you.

✔ Tip

■ Rather than buy multiple copies of iLife '06, you can buy a $99 family pack that's licensed for up to five users.

Installing iPhoto

Installing iPhoto from the iLife '06 package requires almost no effort at all.

To install iPhoto:

1. Insert the iLife CD or DVD.

2. In the Install window that appears after mounting the CD or DVD, double-click the iLife 06 icon (**Figure 1.1**).

3. Click through the Introduction (**Figure 1.2**), Read Me, License, Select Destination (select your hard disk here), Installation Type, Install, and Finish Up steps.

   When you're done, you end up with iPhoto (and the rest of the iLife applications) in your Applications folder.

✔ Tips

■ The iLife installer won't allow you to install if any of the iLife applications are currently running; you must quit them before installing.

■ If you don't want to install some of the iLife applications (iDVD and GarageBand take up a lot of disk space), click Customize in the Installation Type screen and select only the applications you want (**Figure 1.3**).

■ The installer calculates whether or not you have enough disk space; if you're on the edge, install only iPhoto.

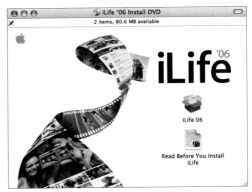

Figure 1.1 Double-click the iLife 06 icon to start the installation process.

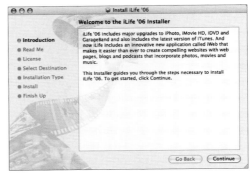

Figure 1.2 The Introduction screen describes the iLife applications briefly.

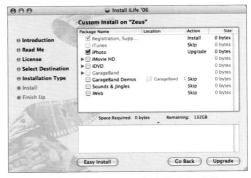

Figure 1.3 If you don't want to install all the iLife applications, click Customize in the Installation Type screen and select only those you do want.

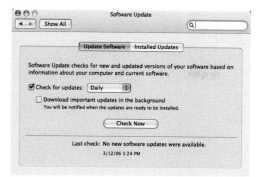

Figure 1.4 Click Check Now to make Software Update look for iPhoto updates.

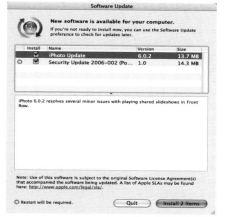

Figure 1.5 To install an update, select the checkbox next to its name, and then click the Install button.

Watching for Updates

I recommend setting Software Update to check for updates automatically, and iPhoto can do so itself too (select Check for iPhoto Updates Automatically in the General pane of iPhoto's Preferences window). You can also visit Apple's iPhoto Web pages at www.apple.com/iphoto/ every so often for news about iPhoto or updates that might not have been released via Software Update.

Updating iPhoto via Software Update

Although you can't get iPhoto 6 for free via Software Update, Apple will release minor revisions via Software Update.

To update iPhoto via Software Update:

1. From the Apple menu, choose System Preferences.

2. To display the Software Update pane, choose Software Update from the View menu.

3. To check for updates, make sure you're connected to the Internet, and then click the Check Now button (**Figure 1.4**).

    If Software Update finds any updates, it launches another application that displays updates that make sense for your Mac, including iPhoto, if any exist.

4. Select the checkbox next to the update you want to install (**Figure 1.5**).

5. Click the Install button, and when the installer prompts you for it, enter your administrator password.

    Software Update proceeds to download and install the update with no more input from you.

✔ Tips

■ Choose Check for Updates from the iPhoto application menu at any time to see if you have the latest version of iPhoto.

■ To set Software Update to kick in on its own, select the Check for Updates checkbox, and from the pop-up menu choose how often you wish it to check.

■ When Software Update fails to find updated software appropriate for your computer, it tells you none are available.

Updating to iPhoto 6

In theory, updating from an earlier version of iPhoto should be merely a matter of installing iPhoto 6 and letting it upgrade your iPhoto Library. However, a few simple actions can prevent future problems.

Tips when updating to iPhoto 6:

◆ Make sure to back up your iPhoto Library folder (located in your Pictures folder) before installing iPhoto 6. Then, if something bad happens, or if you need to revert to your earlier version for some reason I can't imagine, you won't lose all your photos. I'm sure you have a backup anyway, but another one can't hurt.

◆ Run Software Update and download the latest version of iPhoto 6 before updating your iPhoto Library.

◆ If you have installed third-party export plug-ins (see the "Export Plug-ins" sidebar on "Exporting to Web Pages" in Chapter 5, "Showing Photos Onscreen"), it's best to remove them before updating (and to install new versions that are confirmed to work with iPhoto 6). To find them, (Control)-click iPhoto's icon in the Finder, choose Show Package Contents, and navigate to the PlugIns folder. Drag any third-party plug-ins to the Desktop.

◆ For a clean installation, move the com.apple.iPhoto.plist file and the iPhoto application to the Trash, but leave your iPhoto Library folder alone. Then install iPhoto 6.

◆ If you have trouble immediately after updating, delete the files mentioned in the previous tip, then reinstall iPhoto 6.

New Features in iPhoto 6

iPhoto 6 came out at the very beginning of 2006; a year after iPhoto 5 and two years after iPhoto 4 (see the pattern?). iPhoto 6 offers a number of welcome enhancements that are covered throughout this book. Here are my favorite new features:

◆ Full-screen mode for editing photos at the largest possible size

◆ Comparison of up to eight photos in full-screen mode

◆ Photocasting of albums for sharing your photos with others, whether or not they use iPhoto

◆ The addition of professionally designed and printed calendars and cards alongside iPhoto's books

◆ Integration with Apple's new iWeb, replacing the HomePage button

◆ An Effects panel that enables you to apply common effects to your photos, replacing the B&W and Sepia buttons

◆ The capability to leave photos imported from your hard disk in their current folders

◆ Better support for RAW files

◆ A pop-up panel that displays film roll names and dates as you scroll through your library

◆ The capability to print photo titles on contact sheets

◆ Automatic zoom and crop for full-page and standard-sized prints

◆ A functional Check Spelling As You Type command, finally!

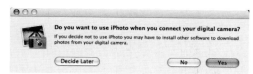

Figure 1.6 Select whether or not you want iPhoto to launch automatically when you connect your digital camera or insert a memory card into a card reader.

Launching iPhoto

Once you have installed iPhoto, the next step is to launch it. The first time you launch iPhoto differs from subsequent launches.

Ways to launch iPhoto:

◆ Double-click the iPhoto icon in your Applications folder.

◆ If iPhoto's icon already appears in your Dock, click the Dock's iPhoto icon.

◆ Drag the iPhoto icon to your Dock to add it to the Dock permanently, and then click the Dock's iPhoto icon.

iPhoto's initial launch

The first time iPhoto ever launches, it gives you a choice of what happens when you connect your camera to your Mac (**Figure 1.6**). The choice you make here sets your "Hot Plug Action."

Hot Plug choices:

◆ Click Yes to set iPhoto to launch automatically when you connect your camera.

◆ Click No to leave your Hot Plug Action setting the way it is right now (probably set to launch Image Capture).

◆ Click Decide Later to have iPhoto ask you this question again on the next launch.

✔ Tips

■ You can reset the Hot Plug Action in the preferences of Apple's Image Capture application.

■ iPhoto 6 upgrades your iPhoto Library on the first launch; to avoid causing problems, don't interrupt the relatively slow upgrade process or work in other iLife applications while it's upgrading.

Recovering Photos on Upgrade

When iPhoto 6 upgrades your iPhoto Library, if it finds photos that aren't properly tracked in iPhoto's database, it offers to recover them. I strongly encourage you to agree to the recovery, since it's a fast way of getting all those lost photos back. When it's done, iPhoto puts the photos in an album called Recovered Photos.

In some cases, the recovered photos may actually be duplicates, at which point you can easily delete them. To figure out which are duplicates, search on the filename of the photo (it's usually the sequential number assigned by your camera). If only the recovered photo appears in the search results, you know it's unique and should be kept; if two or more photos that are obvious duplicates show up, you can probably delete any extras.

iPhoto's Modes

When you use iPhoto, you'll find yourself in one of five modes at all times. The rest of the book looks at these modes, focusing on the tasks you perform in each mode. Here's a quick summary of the modes.

Import mode

To add photos to your photo library, you import them, either from files or directly from a digital camera. There isn't much to do in import mode, since iPhoto 6 still lacks selective import, but at least you can keep working while iPhoto imports photos.

Organize mode

Once you have images in iPhoto, you'll want to organize them into albums, assign them keywords, and delete the lousy ones. All that and more happens in organize mode, where you'll probably spend the bulk of your time.

iPhoto's organize mode also provides tools for exporting photos, printing them, ordering high-quality prints online, printing books, running slideshows, creating Web pages, setting your screen saver and Desktop picture, emailing photos, and much more.

Edit mode

Even the best photographers edit their images. iPhoto provides a few simple image-editing tools so you can crop pictures, enhance colors, remove red-eye, retouch unsightly blemishes, and apply a variety of effects. iPhoto 6 provides some more advanced editing tools that let you adjust brightness and contrast, play with the colors in your photo, and change the exposure, among other things. If you need even more advanced tools or tools that let you work on only selected portions of a photo, iPhoto can work with another image editor like Adobe Photoshop Elements.

Slideshow mode

With iPhoto's powerful slideshow tools, you can create highly customized slideshows containing music, elegant transitions, per-slide timings, and of course, the Ken Burns Effect for panning and zooming photos. Once you create the slideshows, you can replay them as many times as you like, or even export them to QuickTime movies that you can share with your friends and relatives.

Book/calendar/card mode

One of iPhoto's great strengths is the way it helps you design and print professional-looking photo albums. Book mode provides the tools you need to lay out these books and order copies from Apple for your friends and relatives. New in iPhoto 6 is the capability to create equally gorgeous calendars and cards—both folded greeting cards and postcards.

Interface Overview

Before we dive into the specifics of using iPhoto in the upcoming chapters, let's take a bird's-eye view of the main window so you can orient yourself and get a feel for the program's primary functions (**Figure 1.7**).

I assume here that you already know about standard Mac OS X window widgets like the close, minimize, and zoom buttons, the scroll bars and scroll arrows, and the resize handle in the lower right. If not, let me recommend that you check out a copy of Robin Williams's *Mac OS X 10.4 Tiger: Peachpit Learning Series,* also from Peachpit Press. It will help you with the basics of Mac OS X.

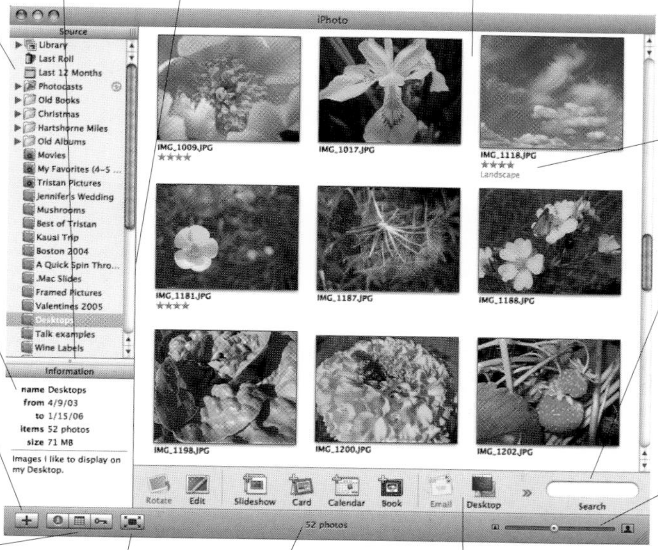

Source pane. Create and work with photocasts, albums, folders, books, calendars, cards, and slideshows here. Cameras and card readers also appear here when importing.

Drag to resize the Information pane.

Drag to resize the Source pane.

Display pane. Your images show up here in a variety of sizes, as do thumbnails of book pages you create.

Information pane. Info about your images and albums shows up here.

Photo titles, ratings, and keywords appear below the images.

Click to add an album.

Search field. Type text here to display photos whose names, captions, or keywords match the search term.

Click to hide or show the Information pane, the Calendar pane, and the Keywords pane.

Figure 1.7

Click to enter full-screen mode.

Number of photos in the current set.

The controls available here change with your current mode (organize mode shown).

Size slider. Adjust this slider to resize the contents of the display pane. In organize mode, the slider displays more or fewer thumbnails; in edit and book mode, it zooms in or out.

Importing and Managing Photos 2

The first thing to do in iPhoto is import some photos. iPhoto provides a number of ways you can import photos, including the most obvious: from a digital camera. You can also import files that you downloaded from your camera previously, acquired on a CD, scanned in from prints, or received from a photo-processing company that provides digital images along with traditional prints. It's also possible to use a card reader—a USB device into which you put the memory card from your camera and which presents the contents of your memory card as files on a disk—with the twist that iPhoto recognizes some card readers and can import from them just as though they were cameras. And lastly, you can copy photos that other iPhoto users make available to you on disc or over a network.

In this chapter, we'll look at all the ways you can import pictures into iPhoto and manage them afterward, including such tasks as trashing and recovering photos, making and switching between different iPhoto Library folders, backing up your images to CD or DVD, and learning exactly how iPhoto stores images on your hard disk.

Multitasking While Importing

Although you may not realize this fact, you can work in other parts of iPhoto while it is importing images. Although this is worth keeping in mind, it's not always as much of a help as you might think, since you usually want to work with the images that are being imported.

Entering Import Mode

It's easy to bring your photos into iPhoto no matter where they may originate because iPhoto offers four different importing approaches, all of which switch you into import mode automatically. The only time you need to switch into import mode manually is if you switch modes after connecting a camera but before clicking the Import button to start the actual import.

Ways to enter import mode:

◆ Connect your digital camera to your Mac's USB port and turn the camera on. iPhoto need not be running; it launches automatically if necessary (**Figure 2.1**).

◆ Insert your camera's memory card into the card reader. iPhoto need not be running; it launches if necessary.

◆ From iPhoto's File menu, choose Import to Library (Cmd Shift I). iPhoto displays an Import Photos dialog from which you can select a file, a folder, or multiple items before clicking Open.

◆ From the Finder, drag and drop one or more files or an entire folder of images into the iPhoto window or onto the iPhoto icon in the Dock.

✔ Tips

■ The Last Roll album remembers the last set (or sets, if you wish; see iPhoto's Preferences window) of images you imported. Click it to see just those images (**Figure 2.2**).

■ iPhoto tracks every import as a separate film roll (choose Film Rolls from the View menu if you're not seeing them). Film rolls are a useful automatic organization tool, but appear only in the Library album.

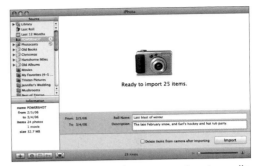

Figure 2.1 After you attach a camera or insert a media card, it shows up in the Source pane automatically.

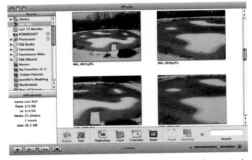

Figure 2.2 To see the last set of images you imported, click the Last Roll album.

Launching Automatically

iPhoto launches automatically only if you allow it to do so. The first time iPhoto runs, it asks if you want it to launch automatically from then on. If you agree, iPhoto takes over for Image Capture as the application that launches when you connect a camera; see "iPhoto and Image Capture," in this chapter, for more details.

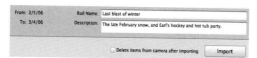

Figure 2.3 Enter a name and description for the roll that will be created; you can do this later, of course, but this is a handy way to label your photos.

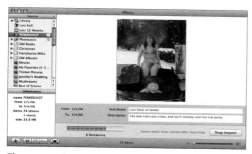

Figure 2.4 While iPhoto imports photos, it displays the image being downloaded along with a progress bar. To stop the process before it completes, click the Stop Import button.

Supporting More Cameras

Although iPhoto supports a large number of cameras, some extremely inexpensive cameras still lack support from Apple. Luckily, a small firm of driver gurus called IOXperts has stepped up to the plate. To add support for many cameras with similar guts, download a copy of the USB Still Camera Driver for Mac OS X Driver from www.ioxperts.com/products/usbstillcamera.html. That page links to the full list of supported cameras.

Importing from a Camera

If you use a digital camera, it's easiest to import photos directly from the camera.

To import from a digital camera:

1. Connect your camera to your Mac using the USB cable included with the camera.

2. Turn on the camera. Make sure the camera is set to view pictures.

   iPhoto automatically switches into import mode (**Figure 2.1**, opposite).

3. If you wish, enter a name and description for the new film roll that will be created by the import (**Figure 2.3**).

4. To have iPhoto erase the contents of your camera after importing, select Delete Items from Camera After Importing.

5. Click the Import button.

   iPhoto starts importing the photos, showing thumbnails and a progress bar. If you've made a mistake, click Stop Import (**Figure 2.4**). When the import finishes, the photos appear in the display pane.

✔ Tips

- To be safe, **never** select the Delete Items from Camera After Importing checkbox. Instead, erase the card in your camera after verifying the import.

- If you want to import only selected photos into iPhoto, see "Importing Only Selected Photos," in this chapter.

- iPhoto warns you if you're about to import duplicate images and asks if you want duplicates or only new images.

- Some cameras mount on your Desktop like a hard disk. Eject the camera using the eject button next to its name in the Source pane before disconnecting it!

Importing from a Card Reader

Importing images via a memory card reader works almost exactly like importing from a digital camera.

To import from a card reader:

1. Connect your card reader to your Mac using USB or FireWire, as appropriate.

2. Insert your memory card.

   iPhoto automatically launches and switches into import mode.

3. If you wish, enter a name and description for the new film roll that will be created by the import. You can also do this later.

4. To have iPhoto erase your card after importing, click the Delete Items from Camera After Importing checkbox.

5. Click the Import button.

   iPhoto starts importing the photos, showing the images and a progress bar. Click Stop Import to stop if necessary.

6. To remove the memory card from the card reader, first click the eject button next to the card's name in the Source pane, and then eject the card from the card reader (**Figure 2.5**).

✔ Tips

■ When using a card reader, you may be able to preview your pictures in the Finder's column view (**Figure 2.6**). You can also drag files from the card into iPhoto to import them manually.

■ If you delete pictures from the memory card before importing into iPhoto, eject and reinsert the card before importing to avoid confusing iPhoto.

■ Never eject the card while importing!

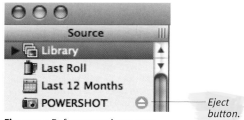

Figure 2.5 Before removing a memory card from your card reader, click the eject button next to the card's name in the Source pane.

Eject button.

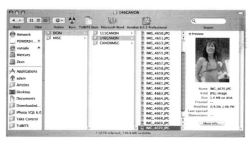

Figure 2.6 For a quick look at a photo on a memory card, make sure you're in column view (the rightmost of the View buttons), navigate to where the images are stored, and select one to see a preview.

PC Card Adapters

If you use a PowerBook with a PC Card slot, you can buy an inexpensive PC Card adapter for your memory cards. Then, instead of mucking about with a bulky USB card reader, you can insert your memory card into the credit card-sized PC Card adapter, and then insert the PC Card adapter into the PowerBook to import the photos on the memory card.

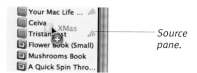

Source pane.

Figure 2.7 The easiest way to import files into iPhoto is to drag the desired files or folders into the display pane or the Source pane, as I've done here.

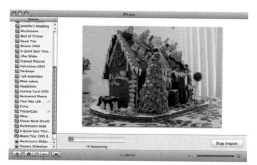

Figure 2.8 iPhoto shows the photos being imported during the import.

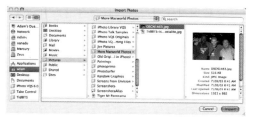

Figure 2.9 To import existing image files into iPhoto, choose Import to Library from the File menu, navigate to your images, select the desired files, and click Import.

Supported File Formats

iPhoto can import images in any file format supported by Apple's QuickTime technology, including BMP, GIF, FlashPix, JPEG, MacPaint, movies (read-only), PICT, PNG, Photoshop, RAW (at least some flavors), SGI, Targa, and TIFF.

Importing from Files

If you used a digital camera before you started using iPhoto, you probably have a collection of photos already on your hard disk. iPhoto can import these files in several ways.

Ways to import files into iPhoto:

◆ From the Finder (or some photo cataloging applications), drag the desired files or folders into iPhoto's display pane or Source pane (**Figure 2.7**).

iPhoto starts importing the images. If you want to halt the import, click Stop Import (**Figure 2.8**). When the import finishes, the photos appear in the display pane.

◆ From the File menu, choose Import to Library ([Cmd][Shift][I]). In the Import Photos dialog, navigate to your images, select the desired file(s) or folder(s), and click Import (**Figure 2.9**).

✔ Tips

■ Hold down [Shift] or [Cmd] to select multiple files in the Import Photos dialog.

■ By default, iPhoto copies the files you import, so make sure you have enough hard disk space before starting.

■ If you drag a file or folder into the Source pane, iPhoto imports the photos *and* creates an album, but you must drag into just the right spot below most of the albums, such that a thick line surrounds the Source pane. You can also drag photos into a specific album to import and add the photos to that album.

■ iPhoto retains the EXIF camera information stored with images along with filenames you've given the images.

■ If you import folders, iPhoto creates and names a new film roll for each folder.

Importing from a Kodak Photo CD or Picture CD

One way to get digital images from a film camera is to order a Kodak Photo CD or Picture CD (Photo CDs have higher resolution scanned images than Picture CDs) when you have your film developed. If you do that, you can import pictures from those CDs directly into iPhoto.

To import from a Photo/Picture CD:

1. Insert the Photo or Picture CD into your Mac's optical drive.

   iPhoto should launch and switch into import mode automatically.

2. Click the Import button (**Figure 2.10**).

   iPhoto starts importing the photos, showing pictures and a progress bar. Click Stop Import to halt if necessary.

✔ Tips

- iPhoto imports images from Photo CDs at the highest resolution available on the disc (usually 3072 x 2048).

- You can't erase the contents of the CD after importing, because Photo CDs and Picture CDs are read-only.

- You can also import files from Picture CDs manually by importing files from the Pictures folder on the disc. Don't try to import the entire disc or you'll end up with many unwanted files to delete.

- It's possible to copy files from Photo CDs for manual importing, but you can't see the necessary Photos folder on the disc in Mac OS X. Certain Mac OS X utilities may also be able to see the folder.

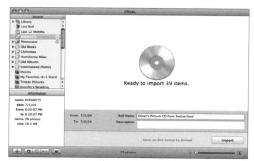

Figure 2.10 To import photos from a Kodak Photo CD or Picture CD, insert the disc and click the Import button.

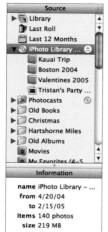

Figure 2.11 iPhoto discs appear in your Source pane with any albums on the disc showing up under the disc name.

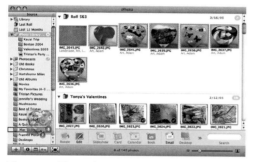

Figure 2.12 The easiest way to import pictures from an iPhoto disc into iPhoto is to drag the desired photos into an album, as I've done here.

No Keywords from iPhoto 5

Unfortunately, iPhoto 5 did not save keywords when burning to an iPhoto disc, which makes importing from an old backup disc less desirable if you've put much effort into keywords. Luckily, iPhoto 6 fixes the problem, including keywords on iPhoto discs and importing them along with photos.

Importing from an iPhoto Disc

iPhoto helps you protect your photo collection by making backup copies to CD or DVD (see "Backing up Your Photos," later in this chapter). Should something go wrong with your main iPhoto Library, you can restore your photos from these backup discs.

Also, friends or relatives who use iPhoto might send you discs of photos; although you can view photos from the disc, if you want to edit a photo or create a book, you must first import the desired images.

To import from an iPhoto disc:

1. Insert the iPhoto disc into your Mac's optical drive and switch to iPhoto.

   iPhoto displays the disc in your Source pane (**Figure 2.11**).

2. Select one or more photos or albums, and then drag them to your Library album to import them just into the Library, into an album to import them and add them to that album (**Figure 2.12**), or to the bottom of the Source pane to import them and create a new album.

   iPhoto starts importing the photos, showing the images and a progress bar. Click Stop Import to halt if necessary.

✔ Tips

- Importing from an iPhoto disc works almost exactly the same as copying photos from a shared photo album.

- iPhoto should perform duplicate checking, just as with the other import methods, though it often fails.

- Dragging a disc's album to the bottom of the Source pane copies the album to your iPhoto Library.

Importing Only Selected Photos

When you import photos from a camera, USB card reader, or Kodak Photo/Picture CD, iPhoto tries to import every photo. But since importing can be slow, at times you may want to import only a few photos.

Ways to import only selected photos:

◆ If you have imported from a camera or memory card once, and added photos, it's easy to import just the new ones. Import as you would normally but when iPhoto asks about importing duplicates, select Apply to All Duplicates and click the Don't Import button (**Figure 2.13**).

◆ Use Image Capture to download selected images from your camera to your hard disk (**Figure 2.14** and **Figure 2.15**), and then import those files by dragging them into iPhoto.

◆ If you're importing from a memory card reader, view the contents of the card in the Finder in icon view and drag just the desired images into iPhoto.

✔ Tips

■ Relying on iPhoto's duplicate checking capability to import only new images on a camera or memory card is slow because iPhoto looks at each photo in turn. If you want to import just a few selected photos quickly, choose one of the other methods.

■ If you import a photo, delete it in iPhoto (but don't empty iPhoto's Trash), and then import again, iPhoto still sees the deleted image as a duplicate.

■ If you want to see selective import in a future version of iPhoto, tell Apple via the Provide iPhoto Feedback command in the iPhoto menu.

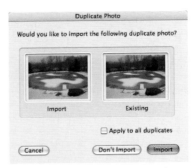

Figure 2.13 When iPhoto prompts about duplicates, tell it not to import duplicates. iPhoto will import only the new images on the camera or card.

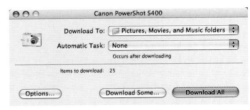

Figure 2.14 To download selected images in Image Capture, connect your camera or insert your memory card, open Image Capture, and click Download Some to see a thumbnail list of available images.

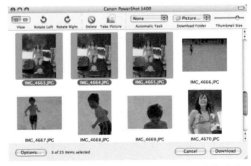

Figure 2.15 After clicking Download Some, Shift-click to select a range of desired images (Command-click no longer seems to work) in Image Capture's thumbnail listing, and then click the Download button.

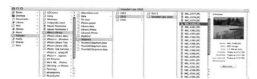

Figure 2.16 iPhoto uses a film roll-based directory structure that starts in your Pictures folder.

iPhoto Directory Structure

iPhoto creates its entire directory structure in the Pictures folder inside your user folder, starting with a folder called iPhoto Library. Inside it, iPhoto creates three special folders: Originals, Modified, and Data. Inside each are folders for years; inside those are folders corresponding to film rolls, and inside those film roll folders you finally get to the actual image files (**Figure 2.16**).

The top-level Originals folder contains your original photos. The Modified folder contains, in its film roll folders, modified versions of your photos. Until you make a change to an original image, there won't be a corresponding file in the Modified folder. The Data folder holds thumbnail images of your photos; they look the same in the Finder's preview, but are much smaller in size.

✔ Tips

- Other than the items mentioned in "Old Stuff That Can Go," do **not** move, rename, or delete anything inside the iPhoto Library folder in the Finder because you'll risk confusing iPhoto and corrupting your library!

- If you ever have to recover your photos from a corrupted iPhoto Library folder, look in the Originals and Modified folders. Originals contains the photos as you imported them and Modified contains the versions that you edited.

- To locate a file corresponding to a photo in iPhoto, ⌃Control⌄-click it in iPhoto and choose Show File. If you have edited the file, you can instead choose Show Original File to display the original file in the Finder.

Old Stuff That Can Go

Although you shouldn't mess with files and folders in the iPhoto Library folder generally, there are a few items you can delete without harm—if they're present—because they're relics from previous versions and are no longer used. You likely won't save much disk space by deleting these unused items, but sometimes it's nice to have things be a bit more tidy.

With iPhoto 6, the structure of the iPhoto Library folder changed significantly. Previous versions of iPhoto used a year/month/day hierarchy of folders, storing originals and modified images separately within the final day folder. If there were errors in upgrading your library when you first launched iPhoto 6, those year folders may still exist at the top level. As long as you allowed iPhoto 6 to recover the photos nested inside, you can delete all the year folders with impunity (it's worth checking inside each one first, of course!).

Other items you can delete include the Desktop, iDVD, and Screen Effects folders. These folders merely contain aliases used by previous versions of iPhoto for your Desktop picture, iDVD, and the Mac OS X screen saver.

Leaving Photos in Place

Perhaps the most significantly hidden new feature in iPhoto 6 is the capability to import photos into iPhoto *without* bringing the original files into the iPhoto Library folder. The lack of this feature in early versions of iPhoto drove users nuts, since people weren't sure they trusted iPhoto to manage all their laboriously arranged photos.

iPhoto 6 introduces a simple checkbox in the Advanced pane of its Preferences window: Copy Files to iPhoto Library Folder When Adding to Library. Uncheck this checkbox (**Figure 2.17**), and iPhoto will create aliases to your original photos in the Originals folder, leaving the original files wherever they're located on your hard disk.

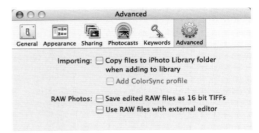

Figure 2.17 Uncheck Copy Files to iPhoto Library Folder to leave photos imported from your hard disk in their original locations.

✔ Tips

■ Turning off Copy Files to iPhoto Library Folder has no effect on photos imported from cameras.

■ When you edit a photo, iPhoto stores the edited version in the Modified folder, just as you'd expect. But the changes you make are not reflected in the version stored outside of your iPhoto Library folder.

■ To locate a file corresponding to a photo in iPhoto, Control-click it in iPhoto and choose Show File. If you have edited the file, you can instead choose Show Original File to display the original file in the Finder.

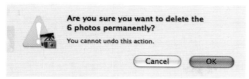

Figure 2.18 iPhoto checks to make sure you really want to delete photos from your hard disk before doing so.

Deleting Photos

Many of the pictures any photographer takes are lousy, and you need to cull the ones of your spouse wearing a stupid expression. Believe me, you really do. But that's the best part of digital photography; there's no cost to taking a photo and trashing it immediately.

You can trash photos only if you're currently in the Library, Last Roll, or Last 12 Months album.

Ways to trash photos:

◆ In one of those three albums, select one or more photos (see "Selecting Photos," in Chapter 3, "Organizing Photos"), and press ⟨Delete⟩, drag one or more images to the Trash album, or ⟨Control⟩-click one or more photos and choose Move to Trash from the contextual menu that appears.

◆ While viewing a photo from the Photo Library, Last Roll, or Last 12 Months album in a basic slideshow or in edit mode, press ⟨Delete⟩.

To delete photos for good:

1. Choose Empty Trash from the iPhoto application menu.

   iPhoto asks if you really want to remove the pictures (**Figure 2.18**).

2. Click OK to delete the photos.

✔ Tips

■ Deleting a photo from a normal album you created does not delete the original image but removes it from that album.

■ The only way to remove a photo from a smart album is to change the photo's criteria so the smart album doesn't see it.

■ Dragging a photo to the Trash icon on the Dock does nothing.

■ Remember, backups are your friends!

DELETING PHOTOS

Culling Photos Quickly

Now that you know how to delete photos, you need to learn how to delete them as quickly and effectively as possible. There are four ways to cull photos, but the best approaches aren't necessarily the most obvious. In order of worst to best...

Ways to cull imported photos:

◆ In organize mode, make your thumbnails large enough to see either one or two photos at a time, then click each one you want to delete and press ⌊Delete⌋. Because this method requires so much clicking and scrolling, it's slow and clumsy.

◆ Select the photos you want to check out (see "Selecting Photos," in Chapter 3, "Organizing Photos"), click the Play button, and in the Slideshow dialog, click the Play button. Once you're in the slideshow, press ⌊Delete⌋ or move the cursor to display the slideshow controls, and then click the Trash button. Unfortunately, deleting from slideshows is slow, and you can't undo mistakes; you must instead recover the photo from the Trash.

◆ Select up to eight photos and click the full-screen button to enter full-screen mode with all the photos showing at the largest possible size (**Figure 2.19**). Click a photo in full-screen mode to select it, and press ⌊Delete⌋ to trash it. Cycle through more photos by pressing the arrow keys. This method works well for comparing similar photos but doesn't display the photos as large as when you view them one at a time.

◆ In editing mode, either full-screen or in iPhoto's display pane, cycle through the photos with the arrow keys, pressing ⌊Delete⌋ to trash those you don't like (see full instructions in the sidebar).

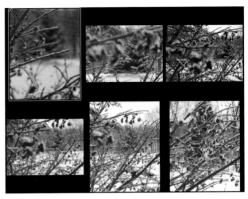

Figure 2.19 In full-screen mode, you can compare up to eight photos; click any one to select it, and send it to the Trash by pressing Delete.

The Best Way to Cull Photos

So you've just imported a bunch of photos and you want to get rid of the ones that are fuzzy or otherwise worthless. Here's my favorite method, which can be done entirely from the keyboard and shows each photo at full size, which helps when deciding which should bite the bit bucket.

1. Switch into full-screen mode by selecting the first photo in the film roll you want to clean up and clicking the full-screen button.

2. If necessary, rotate the image to the correct orientation with ⌊Cmd⌋⌊R⌋ or ⌊Cmd⌋⌊Option⌋⌊R⌋. You could also do other minor edits at this point, but don't get bogged down.

3. If you like it, press ⌊→⌋ (the right arrow key) to move on to the next photo.

4. If you don't like it, press ⌊Delete⌋ to move it to the Trash and move on to the next photo automatically. If you delete a photo accidentally, press ⌊Cmd⌋⌊Z⌋ to bring it back.

5. Repeat steps 2–5 as necessary.

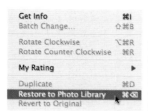

Figure 2.20 To remove photos from the Trash, select them and choose Restore to Photo Library from the Photos menu.

Recovering Photos

iPhoto sports a special Trash album that holds all your deleted photos, just like the Finder's Trash. And like the Finder's Trash, you can pull mistakenly deleted photos out.

Ways to recover photos:

◆ Select one or more photos in the Trash album and choose Restore to Photo Library ((Cmd)(Delete)) from the Photos menu (**Figure 2.20**).

◆ Select one or more photos in the Trash album, (Control)-click the selection, and choose Restore to Photo Library from the contextual menu that appears.

◆ Drag one or more photos from the Trash album into the Library album or to the bottom of the Source pane.

✔ Tips

■ You can't edit photos stored in the Trash, nor can you create a book, calendar, or card using the Trash album. Well, duh!

■ You can't drag a photo from the Trash album into another album without first restoring it to the Library album.

■ iPhoto doesn't move the actual image files when you put them in the Trash; it merely tracks which ones are in the Trash album. Only when you empty the Trash are the actual files deleted.

Use Your Trash!

I strongly recommend that you make full use of iPhoto's Trash and empty it only occasionally. The whole point of having a Trash is to save you from mistakes, and you never know if you'll realize a mistake right away. Instead, let photos sit in the Trash for a while before deleting them for good. Or wait until you feel like you need the disk space they take up before deleting them.

Creating Multiple iPhoto Library Folders

Although there's little outward indication of this, iPhoto lets you create and maintain multiple iPhoto Library folders.

Reasons to create multiple iPhoto Library folders:

◆ You might want to keep two different types of photos completely separate, such as personal snapshots and location shots for your real estate business.

◆ You might want different iPhoto Library folders for different purposes. For instance, I have a special iPhoto Library folder that holds just a few images that I use when giving presentations.

◆ You might want an iPhoto Library for miscellaneous photos sent to you by other people that you don't want cluttering your main collection.

To create an iPhoto Library folder:

1. Quit iPhoto.

2. Hold down Option and click iPhoto's icon in the Dock to launch it.

   In the Choose Photo Library dialog, click Create Library (**Figure 2.21**), and in the New Photo Library dialog, enter a name and select a location for your new iPhoto Library folder (**Figure 2.22**).

✔ Tip

■ If you want a second iPhoto Library folder to contain all your photos to start with, select the original iPhoto Library folder in the Pictures folder in the Finder and choose Duplicate (Cmd D) from the Finder's File menu.

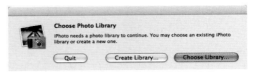

Figure 2.21 Create a new iPhoto Library folder by holding down Option while launching iPhoto and then clicking Create Library in the Choose Photo Library dialog.

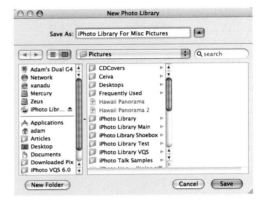

Figure 2.22 Name and save your new iPhoto Library folder however and wherever you like.

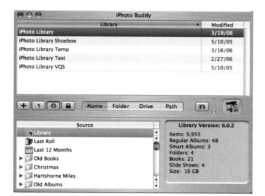

Figure 2.23 Use iPhoto Buddy to switch among multiple iPhoto Library folders.

Switching between iPhoto Library Folders

So you now have two (or more) iPhoto Library folders. How do you switch between them?

Ways to switch between iPhoto Library folders:

◆ Hold down (Option) and click iPhoto's icon in the Dock to launch it and display the Choose Photo Library dialog. Click Choose Library (**Figure 2.21**, opposite), and locate the desired iPhoto Library folder.

◆ With iPhoto not running, manually rename or move your main iPhoto Library folder, then rename or move the desired iPhoto Library folder so it's called just "iPhoto Library" and is located in your Pictures folder.

◆ When iPhoto is not running, rename or move the iPhoto Library folder, launch iPhoto, and, when prompted, click Choose Library and locate the desired iPhoto Library folder (**Figure 2.21**, opposite).

◆ Use the free iPhoto Library Manager from http://homepage.mac.com/bwebster/iphotolibrarymanager.html.

◆ Use Rick Neil's free iPhoto Buddy (www.iphotobuddy.com), which gives you a simple interface for switching quickly among multiple folders (**Figure 2.23**).

Backing Up Your Photos

The most important thing you can do when managing your photos is to make a backup.

To back up photos:

1. Select the items you want to back up, which is best done by selecting entire film rolls, folders, albums, books, or slideshows in the Source pane (**Figure 2.24**).

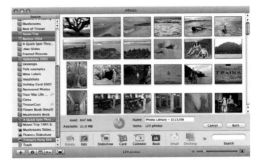

Figure 2.24 To get started, select the items you want to burn in the Source pane, choose Burn from the Share menu, and then insert a blank disc.

2. From the Share menu, choose Burn, insert a blank disc if prompted, and click OK.

   Below the display pane, iPhoto shows the name of the disc and information about how much data will be burned to the disc (**Figure 2.25**). The disc's icon will be red if it can't hold the selected photos.

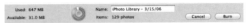

Figure 2.25 Once you've inserted the disc, iPhoto lets you name your disc and gives you information about how much data will be burned to it.

3. Select fewer or more photos to use the space on your destination disc as desired.

4. Change the name of the disc if you want.

5. When everything looks right, click the Burn button to start the burn, and when iPhoto asks you to confirm one last time and lets you set additional burning options, click Burn (**Figure 2.26**).

   iPhoto creates a disk image, copies the selected photos to it, and burns the disc.

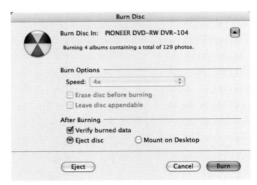

Figure 2.26 iPhoto verifies that you really want to burn a disc with one last dialog that also provides additional burn options if you click triangle the button in the upper-right corner (for more information, see the sidebar "Burn Options," opposite).

✔ Tips

- Don't believe the Information pane; the only numbers that matter are those that iPhoto reports in step 2 above.

- On the disc, your photos are stored in an iPhoto Library folder like the main one. If you want to give the disc to someone who doesn't use iPhoto, see "Sharing Photos on Disc with Windows Users" in Chapter 8, "Sharing Photos."

A Proper Backup Strategy

I'll be honest. I think backing up just your photos by burning them to CD or DVD is only a small step above useless. If you value the contents of your Mac, and if you value having a working Mac as a communications device for email and iChat, you need a real backup strategy. To learn more, I recommend Joe Kissell's *Take Control of Mac OS X Backups* ebook (`www.takecontrolbooks.com/backup-macosx.html`). It's only $10 and will help you figure out exactly what hardware and software you need and how to set it up.

Burn Options

I recommend that you select Verify Burned Data for safety; if you have trouble burning, try reducing the burn speed.

The options for erasing media and leaving a disc appendable apply only to rewritable media like CD-RW (but iPhoto won't erase no matter what; use Disk Utility).

The choice of ejecting the disc after burning or mounting it on the Desktop is minor, though I recommend a quick visual inspection of the contents of the disc in iPhoto after burning.

True Archiving

If you want to archive photos, that is, burn them to disc and then remove them from your hard disk, I recommend the following:

- Make at least two copies and store one off-site, like at a friend's house.

- Work methodically by making albums from film rolls to retain organization and by selecting *everything* in order.

Other Backup Options

What if you don't have a writable optical drive or don't want to end up with your photos existing only in an iPhoto Library? You have a few options.

Other backup options:

- Copy your iPhoto Library (remember that it's in your Pictures folder) to an external hard disk.

- Use a dedicated backup program, such as EMC Insignia's Retrospect Desktop (`www.emcinsignia.com`), to back up your iPhoto Library folder (and while you're at it, I recommend backing up your Home folder, or even your entire Mac).

- Export photos to folders in the Finder, then manually burn them to CD or DVD to back them up with your desired organizational approach. It's more work, but you get exactly what you want at the end.

✔ Tips

- No matter which backup method you choose, I recommend having more than one backup copy and storing one of them off-site. That way, should your house or office burn down or be burglarized, your backup would remain safe.

- To reduce media usage (though CD-R discs are awfully cheap), buy the more expensive CD-RW discs and erase them in Disk Utility between uses.

- Don't use CD-RW discs for true archiving, since anything that can be erased is a lousy permanent medium.

- Don't assume that any backup media will last forever. Every so often, check to make sure your backups are readable, and it wouldn't hurt to recopy them every few years, just to be safe.

Merging iPhoto Library Folders

If you have two Macs, you may want to merge the contents of two iPhoto Library folders, one from each computer.

To merge iPhoto Library folders (I):

1. Network your Macs via AirPort, Ethernet, or even FireWire (using IP over FireWire, which you can enable in the Network preference pane).

2. On both Macs, turn on photo sharing in iPhoto's Preferences window (**Figure 2.27**). For more information, see "Network Photo Sharing" in Chapter 8, "Sharing Photos."

3. Drag the desired photos or albums from the source Mac's shared album to the Library album of the destination Mac.

To merge iPhoto Library folders (II):

◆ If one of your Macs has a writable optical drive (CD-R, CD-RW, or DVD-R), burn a disc containing all the photos you want to transfer from the source iPhoto Library folder. Then import them into the destination iPhoto Library folder as explained in "Importing from an iPhoto Disc," earlier in this chapter.

To merge iPhoto Library folders (III):

1. From the source iPhoto Library, export the desired images by album or film roll into folders (see "Exporting Files" in Chapter 8, "Sharing Photos").

2. Copy those folders to the Mac with the destination iPhoto Library folder via a network or FireWire Target Disk Mode.

3. Drag the folders into iPhoto to import their photos (see "Importing from Files," earlier in this chapter).

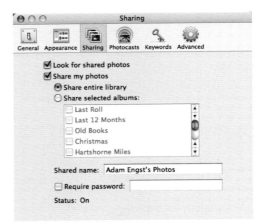

Figure 2.27 To turn on photo sharing, select Look for Shared Photos and Share My Photos in the Sharing pane of iPhoto's Preferences window.

To merge iPhoto Library folders (IV):

◆ Use Brian Webster's $19.95 iPhoto Library Manager, which claims to be able to merge iPhoto Library folders automatically, retaining all titles, keywords, ratings, and albums. Find it at: `http://homepage.mac.com/bwebster/iphotolibrarymanager.html`.

✔ Tips

■ If you're burning to disc, use CD-RW media if you want to reuse that disc; use CD-R media if you want a backup.

■ When exporting via the third method, I recommend using the photo title as the filename or else you'll lose any work you put in titling your photos.

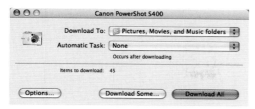

Figure 2.28 Use Image Capture if you want to download photos to a folder in the Finder, rather than straight into iPhoto.

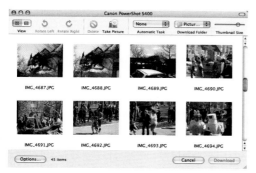

Figure 2.29 To download only some images, click Download Some in the main Image Capture window, select the images to download, and then click the Download button.

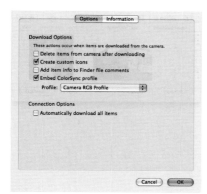

Figure 2.30 Image Capture has some options that may be useful; access them by clicking the Options button.

iPhoto and Image Capture

Before Apple released iPhoto, the way you transferred images from a digital camera to a Mac running Mac OS X was with an included utility called Image Capture (found in your Applications folder). Image Capture is still useful for downloading selected images from your camera.

Image Capture functions:

◆ Using Image Capture, you can download photos to any folder. Choose one in the Download To pop-up menu, and then click the Download All button (**Figure 2.28**).

◆ You can also download only selected images in Image Capture. Click the Download Some button in Image Capture's main window, select the images to download, and click the Download button (**Figure 2.29**).

◆ Although Image Capture offers some options for making a Web page from the images you download and formatting them to different sizes, it's easier and more reliable to do this in iPhoto.

◆ If you want to download images using Image Capture, and then import them into iPhoto, it might be easiest to set the "When a Camera Is Connected, Open" pop-up menu in Image Capture's Preferences window to launch Image Capture rather than iPhoto.

◆ To adjust Image Capture's options, click the Options button in Image Capture's main window. In particular, make sure it doesn't delete after downloading so iPhoto can download the images as well (**Figure 2.30**).

ORGANIZING PHOTOS

There are two types of people when it comes to photos. First are the Martha Stewart types who manage to organize every picture into precious handmade albums constructed of used tissues and old grocery bags. Then there are the rest of us, who dump our pictures in a box, and that's if we remember to develop the film in the first place. We in the second group hate those in the first group (though we're sure you're actually very nice people).

For me, the promise of digital photography was a way not just to join that first group, but to beat them at their own game. I'm constitutionally incapable of cutting a print to crop it, and my miserable handwriting makes captions painful. I figured I could do it all on the computer with no trouble and make prints to boot. Unfortunately, it was just too hard—until iPhoto.

iPhoto's editing tools are covered in a future chapter, so here we're going to focus on iPhoto's organizational features. Some require a little effort, but even with no work, your digital photo collection will be far better organized than the box in the closet.

And if you're one of those people who put together handmade photo albums before digital photography, well, you're still going to love what iPhoto can do for you.

Switching to Organize Mode

Whenever you're not importing photos, editing photos, creating a slideshow, or making a book, iPhoto ensures you're in organize mode. Thus, there are only two basic ways to return to organize mode from another mode:

- In the Source pane, click the Library, Last Roll, or Last Months album, or any regular album or smart album to switch to organize mode and display the contents of the selected album.

- When you have switched into edit mode from organize mode but are not using the Retouch or Red-Eye tools, double-click the picture (outside of a selection, if you've made one) to switch back to organize mode.

What's New in Organize Mode

If you've used previous versions of iPhoto, you'll want to pay attention to the new features iPhoto 6 brings to organize mode.

New features in organize mode:

◆ The new cards and calendars are, like books, independent entities that are parallel to albums, smart albums, and slideshows in the Source pane.

◆ When you scroll through your photos in organize mode using the scroller in the scroll bar, iPhoto displays a translucent pop-up containing the date of the visible photos and, if you're in the Library album, the name of the current film roll (**Figure 3.1**). Unfortunately, it doesn't work if you use a scroll wheel to scroll.

◆ You can now include EXIF data when defining smart albums, which enables you to create smart albums containing images selected by aperture, camera model, flash, focal length, ISO, or shutter speed.

◆ When filtering the contents of the display pane by keywords, you can now choose whether selecting multiple keywords presents photos matching *any* of the selected keywords or only those photos that have *all* the selected keywords.

◆ Performance is distinctly better.

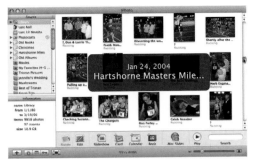

Figure 3.1 As you scroll, iPhoto 6 now displays a translucent pop-up that helps you figure out where you are in the album.

Albums and Books and Slideshows, Oh My!

Versions of iPhoto before iPhoto 5 put only albums in the Source pane. In fact, because of that, I called it the "album pane" in earlier editions of this book. However, in iPhoto 5 and later, other types of items can appear in the pane— albums, smart albums, books, cards, calendars, slideshows, and folders—so I'm following Apple's lead in calling them "sources" and the pane itself the "Source pane." In most cases, things you can do to one type of source (like delete it, move it around, or add photos to it), you can do to all the types of sources. When that's the case, I'll use the term "sources"; when there are exceptions, I'll use the specific term or call out the exception.

Organize Tools Overview

iPhoto's interface changes depending on what mode you're in, and some controls even offer different functions depending on mode. Here's a quick reference to the controls available in organize mode (**Figure 3.2**).

A folder containing other collections. Click its triangle to open and close.

A folder containing albums, smart albums, books, a calendar, a card, and a slideshow.

Information pane. Info about the selected item(s) shows up here. Modify titles, dates, and comments.

Click to add a new item to the Source pane.

Currently subscribed photocasts. Click the refresh button to check for updates.

Source pane. Create and work with collections of photos here.

Film roll, showing import date and roll name. Click its triangle to open and close.

Selected picture (note the frame around the image).

Photo title.

Rating.

Keywords assigned to this photo.

Search field. Enter text here to find matching photos.

Size slider. Adjust this slider to display more or fewer thumbnails. Drag the slider or click the desired location. Click the end icons for smallest and largest sizes.

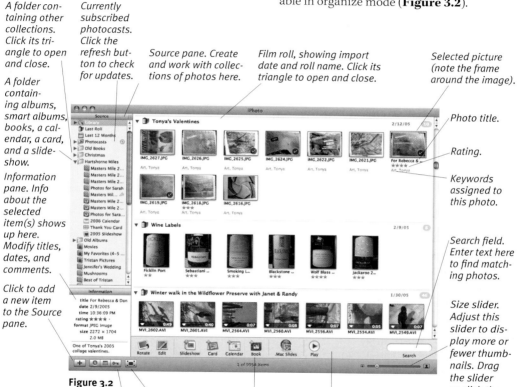

Figure 3.2

Click to switch between showing the Information pane (currently showing), the Calendar pane, and the Keywords pane.

Click to enter full-screen mode.

This indicator shows the number of photos selected (1) in the current set (9954).

The buttons in the organize mode's toolbar help you switch between modes and offer different methods of sharing photos.

Changing the Display Pane's Layout

One of iPhoto's slickest features is the slider that enables you to change the size of the thumbnails, but you can do other things to change the way the display pane looks.

To change the display pane layout:

◆ Move the size slider (or click in the desired location) to adjust the size of the thumbnails from a single image (which automatically hides titles and keywords) at the largest (**Figure 3.3**) all the way down to as many photos as fit in the window at postage stamp size (**Figure 3.4**).

◆ To show or hide titles, ratings, keywords, and film rolls (**Figure 3.5**) (film rolls only when in the Library album), choose the desired item from the View menu.

◆ To add or remove a sharing tool from the toolbar, choose the item from the Show in Toolbar menu in the View menu (**Figure 3.6**).

✔ Tips

■ You can shrink the Source pane by dragging its handle (next to the word "Source") to the left. Expand it by dragging back to the right.

■ Viewing titles in the display pane isn't useful when you use smaller thumbnail sizes, but remember that the current photo's title is in the Information pane.

■ Film roll separators help show where you are in the Photo Library, so I recommend leaving them showing and giving them names. (Option)-click a film roll expansion triangle to hide or show all film rolls.

■ Play with different settings for the size slider to find a setting that fits your monitor size and working style.

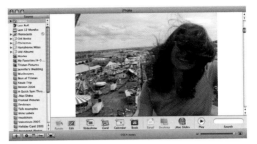

Figure 3.3 To view one image at a time in organize mode, move the size slider all the way to the right, or press the 1 key.

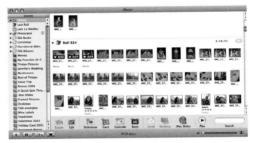

Figure 3.4 To view as many thumbnails as possible, move the size slider all the way to the left or press the 0 (zero) key.

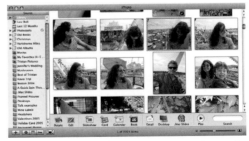

Figure 3.5 Turn off display of titles, ratings, keywords, and film rolls in the View menu for an uncluttered look.

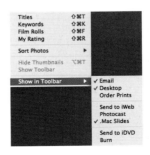

Figure 3.6 Choose which sharing tools you want in the toolbar using the Show in Toolbar menu.

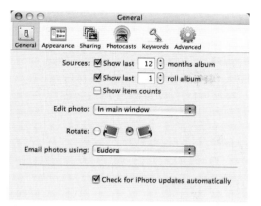

Figure 3.7 Use the Sources settings in iPhoto's General preference pane to control the Last Months and Last Rolls albums, and the display of the item count next to source names.

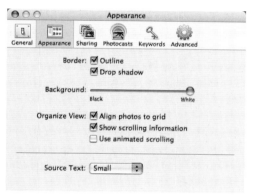

Figure 3.8 The Appearance pane of iPhoto's Preferences window provides settings that control how iPhoto draws and scrolls through photos, and the size of source name text.

Most Recent Photos Checkbox

A long-standing preference has disappeared in iPhoto 6: the Place Most Recent Photos at the Top checkbox. Now, to change the order in which photos appear, use the Ascending and Descending items in the Sort submenu of the View menu.

Other Display Preferences

You can also set options in iPhoto's Preferences window that affect how the display pane looks.

From the iPhoto application menu, choose Preferences (Cmd ,) to open the Preferences window; you can find display preferences in both the General and Appearance panes (**Figure 3.7** and **Figure 3.8**).

Display preferences you can change:

◆ In the General pane, use the Sources controls to manage which of the Last Roll/Months albums appear and how many rolls or months they contain.

◆ Select Show Item Counts to append the number of photos in each album, smart album, folder, book, card, calendar, and slideshow after its name in the Source pane.

◆ In the Appearance pane, select Outline and/or Drop Shadow border styles, and use the Background slider to change the darkness of the background.

◆ To align all your photos to a regular grid in which the width of the widest picture sets the width for all photos, check the Align Photos to Grid checkbox.

◆ Use the Show Scrolling Information checkbox to toggle whether the translucent information pop-up appears when scrolling.

◆ The Use Animated Scrolling option makes scrolling via the Page Up and Page Down keys smoother.

◆ If you have many albums, set Source Text to Small so you can see more at once.

OTHER DISPLAY PREFERENCES

Contextual Menu Shortcuts

iPhoto isn't great about letting you edit information about a photo—title, date, and keywords—directly "on" the photo. Instead, you must select the photo and then make your changes in the Information or Keywords pane. However, you can (Control)-click (or, if you have a two-button mouse, right-click) a photo to bring up a contextual menu that lets you perform a number of actions directly on the photo you clicked (**Figure 3.9**).

Contextual menu shortcuts:

◆ You can cut, copy, or paste photos, but only within iPhoto. Cutting a photo removes it from the current album and pasting a photo adds it to the current album (other than the Library).

◆ The Edit commands are particularly useful for opening photos in alternative ways without switching iPhoto's preferences.

◆ Show File and Show Original File switch you to the Finder. Show File selects the original file if no changes have been made; the edited version otherwise. And if changes have been made, Show Original File selects the original.

◆ The rest of the commands—Rotate, Show Info, Batch Change, Duplicate, My Rating, Delete from Album, and Revert to Original—are like those in iPhoto's Photos menu, but using the contextual menu to apply them may feel more intuitive.

✔ Tip

■ Although you can't copy a photo from iPhoto and paste it into another application, you can often drag photos from iPhoto to other applications.

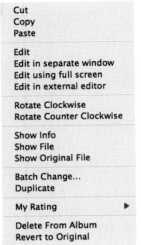

Figure 3.9 Control-click one or more selected photos to display iPhoto's contextual menu shortcuts.

✔ More Tips

■ The Show Info command in the contextual is the same as Get Info in the Photos menu. No idea why it has a different name.

■ Some of the menu items become unavailable when they don't make sense (for example, you can't paste into the Library album, and Revert to Original doesn't apply to original photos).

■ Delete from Album changes to Move to Trash when you're in the Library.

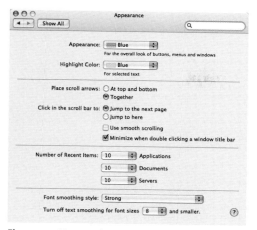

Figure 3.10 You can change Mac OS X's scrolling behavior in the Appearance preference pane.

Moving Around in iPhoto

Obviously, you can move around in iPhoto using the scroll bars, but knowing a few tricks and techniques can make navigating through your photos easier.

Ways to move around:

◆ Click or drag in the scroll bar, just as you would in any other Mac application.

◆ (Option)-click the scroll bar to jump to the particular spot you clicked.

◆ Click a photo to make sure the display pane is active; then use the arrow keys to move around.

◆ With the display pane active, use (Page Up) and (Page Down) to scroll through your photos one screen at a time.

◆ With the display pane active, use (Home) and (End) to move to the top and bottom of the current album.

✔ Tips

■ The (Option)-clicking (Jump to Here) behavior actually applies to Mac OS X in general, and you can make it the default behavior by selecting the Jump to Here radio button in Mac OS X's Appearance preference pane (**Figure 3.10**). I find the Jump to Here setting disconcerting, since it's counter to the way I've used scroll bars on the Mac forever.

■ If you're having trouble scrolling to a desired location, it might help to reduce the thumbnail size so you can see many more thumbnails on the screen at once.

■ Hold down (Option) when scrolling to scroll smoothly. This feature may not help many people, but it made arranging the iPhoto window (to take nicely aligned screen shots) a lot easier for me while I was writing this book.

Editing Film Rolls

You can change the titles and dates of film rolls in the Library album. This capability proves to be extremely useful, since film rolls with a title are much easier to identify, and by changing the film roll's date, you control where it appears in the Library album when it's sorted by film roll.

To change the title of a film roll:

1. Make sure you're in the Library with film rolls and the Information pane showing, and then click a film roll in the display pane to select it.

2. In the Information pane, enter a new title in the Title field (**Figure 3.11**).

   iPhoto changes the title of the film roll in the display pane to match.

To change the date/time of a film roll:

1. Make sure you're in the Library with film rolls and the Information pane showing, and then click a film roll in the display pane to select it.

2. In the Information pane, enter a new date and time for the film roll in the Date and Time fields (**Figure 3.11**).

   iPhoto changes the date and time of the film roll in the display pane and re-sorts the film rolls to put the one you edited in the proper order.

✔ Tips

■ Although iPhoto recognizes a large number of date formats, it ignores improperly formatted dates, so to avoid confusion, it's easiest to edit the date using the same date format iPhoto uses.

■ After you change the date of a film roll, iPhoto sorts it according to the new date, so it will probably move to a new location in the display pane.

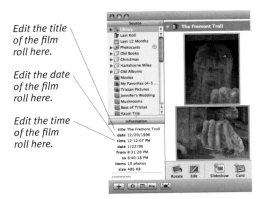

Edit the title of the film roll here.

Edit the date of the film roll here.

Edit the time of the film roll here.

Figure 3.11 Use the Title, Date, and Time fields in the Information pane to change the details of the selected film roll in the Library.

Other Date and Time Fields

So what the heck is that second Date field in the Information pane? You can't change it, and it may not appear at all or may be different from the first Date field, even before you've changed anything.

The top Date field reflects the date you created the film roll; in other words, the date you imported your photos. The second, lower Date field is the date the photos were created. And the From and To fields list the times between which the photos were taken.

What if not all the photos in the film roll were taken on the same day? Then iPhoto eliminates that second Date field entirely and changes the From and To fields to list the dates between which the film roll was taken.

There is a quirk associated with these date fields. If you drag a photo in from the Finder, the first date field for its film roll is not the imported date, but the date the photo was last modified (or created, if it hasn't been modified).

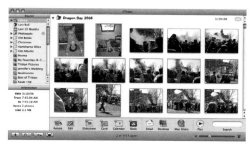

Figure 3.12 Select some photos, as I've done with the first two of Tristan; then choose Create Film Roll from the File menu.

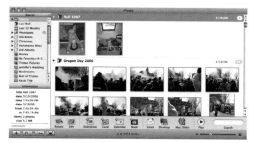

Figure 3.13 iPhoto creates a new film roll using the selected photos and organizes it according to the dates of the photos.

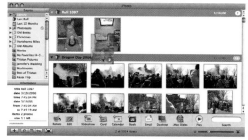

Figure 3.14 Drag photos from one film roll to the name of another to move them.

Creating and Modifying New Film Rolls

Whenever you import photos into iPhoto, it creates a film roll to hold them, and in early versions of iPhoto, that was that. Now, however, you can create new film rolls and move photos between film rolls.

To create a new film roll:

1. In the Library, select one or more photos (**Figure 3.12**).

2. From the File menu, choose Create Film Roll.

   iPhoto creates a new film roll using the selected photos (**Figure 3.13**).

To move photos between film rolls:

◆ Select one or more photos and drag them on top of another film roll's name. iPhoto moves the photos to the destination film roll (**Figure 3.14**).

✔ Tips

■ Creating new film rolls is a great way to break up a too-large import into groups of related photos.

■ By default, the new film roll picks up the dates of the photos you've added to it, which may mean that it sorts higher or lower in your Library than you expect.

■ You must drop the selected photos on the film roll's name, which highlights as your pointer moves over it. Dropping the photos inside the film roll won't work.

■ Although you might think otherwise, you can't use the Edit menu's Cut or Copy command with the Paste command to move photos between film rolls.

■ If you drag all the photos out of a film roll, it disappears entirely.

Creating and Working with Folders

iPhoto 6 provides folders into which you can organize multiple albums, along with books, cards, calendars, saved slideshows and even other folders. Folders are a great way to tuck away older items you don't want to see all the time.

To create a folder:

1. From the File menu, choose New Folder.

   iPhoto creates a new untitled folder with the name selected so you can name it.

2. Enter a name for the folder.

To move items into and out of folders:

◆ Drag one or more items (albums, books, saved slideshows, or other folders) into or out of the folder.

   iPhoto moves the items, giving the folder an expansion triangle if necessary so you can open and close it (**Figure 3.15**).

To duplicate a folder and its contents:

◆ Control-click a folder and choose Duplicate from the contextual menu that appears.

To delete a folder:

◆ Select one or more folders and press Delete, or Control-click a folder and choose Delete Folder from the contextual menu that appears.

   iPhoto prompts you to make sure you know what you're doing; click Delete to delete the folder and all its contents. (**Figure 3.16**).

◆ Select one or more folders and press Cmd Delete to delete them and their contents without being prompted for confirmation.

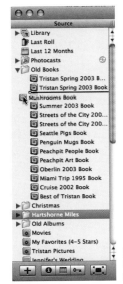

Figure 3.15 Drag items into or out of a folder to add or remove them from the folder.

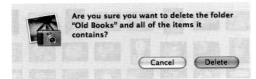

Figure 3.16 Confirm that you really want to delete both the folder and its contents.

Facts about Folders

Folders can take a bit of getting used to:

◆ When you select a folder in the Source pane, the display pane shows all the photos from all the albums, slideshows, books, cards, and calendars inside that folder.

◆ When you delete a folder, you delete the items (albums, books, and so on, though not the original photos, of course) inside it as well. Be careful!

◆ All items in the Source pane, including folders, must have unique names, so you can't have both a saved slideshow and a folder with the same name.

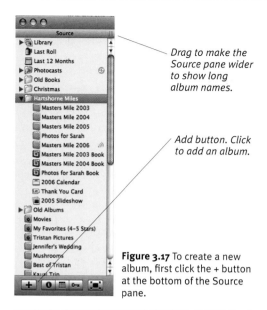

Drag to make the Source pane wider to show long album names.

Add button. Click to add an album.

Figure 3.17 To create a new album, first click the + button at the bottom of the Source pane.

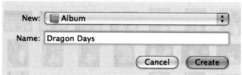

Figure 3.18 Next, choose Album from the New pop-up menu, name the album, and click Create.

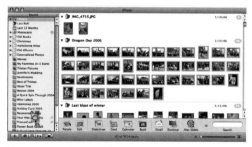

Figure 3.19 When you drag photos into the Source pane to create a new album containing them, notice how the entire Source pane gets a thick black border.

Creating Albums

iPhoto provides "albums" to help us categorize photos—these were from the Fiji trip, those were from Joe's birthday party, and so on. Albums are also useful starting points for saved slideshows, books, and calendars.

To create an album:

1. Click the Add button (+) at the bottom of the Source pane (**Figure 3.17**) or choose New Album (Cmd N) from the File menu. iPhoto displays a dialog asking what type of item you want to create and what you want to call it (**Figure 3.18**).

2. Choose Album from the New pop-up menu, enter a name, and click Create to add it to the Source pane.

Other ways to create an album:

◆ Select some photos before following the steps above, or just choose New Album from Selection (Cmd Shift N) from the File menu.

◆ Drag one or more photos, or an entire film roll, into the Source pane, but *not* onto any existing album (**Figure 3.19**).

◆ Drag one or more photos, or a folder of photos from the Finder into the Source pane, but *not* onto any existing album.

✔ Tips

■ When the Source pane is full, the only "empty" spot is just above the second-to-last album (and above any books).

■ Use albums for categories of pictures that appear once in your photo collection. Use keywords for categories that recur throughout your collection. Albums work well for a specific trip's photos; keywords work better for identifying pictures of your family members, landscapes, or recurring events.

Creating and Editing Smart Albums

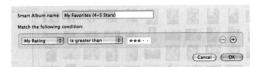

Figure 3.20 Name and configure your smart album in the dialog that appears after choosing New Smart Album from the File menu.

You may find yourself adding photos to an album over and over again. There's a better way: smart albums. Unlike normal albums, which you must maintain manually, smart albums use a set of rules that you create to maintain their contents automatically.

To create a smart album:

1. Click the Add button (+) below the Source pane, choose Smart Album from the New pop-up menu, and click Create. Better yet, either Option-click the Add button or choose New Smart Album (Cmd Option N) from the File menu.

   iPhoto displays a dialog for you to name and configure your album (**Figure 3.20**).

2. Enter a name for the new album.

3. From the first pop-up menu, choose a criterion that photos must match to be included (**Figure 3.21**).

4. From the second pop-up menu, choose how that criterion should be evaluated (**Figure 3.22**).

5. Enter a condition against which the criterion is to be evaluated (**Figure 3.23**).

6. If you want your smart album to have multiple criteria, click the + button and repeat steps 3–5.

7. When you're done, click the OK button.

   iPhoto looks at all your photos and adds those that match to the smart album.

To edit a smart album:

1. Control-click an album and choose Edit Smart Album from the contextual menu.

2. Follow steps 2–7 above to change the smart album's name or configuration.

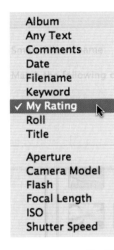

Figure 3.21 Smart albums can match photos based on numerous criteria, shown here. In this case, I'm looking for photos with a specific rating.

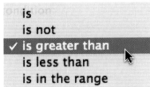

Figure 3.22 Once you've chosen a criterion, you must determine how it should be evaluated. The second pop-up menu changes dynamically to match the selected criterion. Here, since I'm matching on rating, and I'd like the smart album to find only photos with 4 or 5 stars, I've selected Is Greater Than.

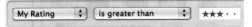

Figure 3.23 Lastly, enter the condition against which your criterion will be evaluated. To finish the smart album that matches my 4- or 5-star photos, I've clicked the field to select 3 stars. Read as a whole, my rule says, "Select all photos whose rating is greater than 3 stars."

Smart Album Ideas

It may be hard to think about the types of smart albums you can create, so use these ideas to get started.

Smart album ideas:

◆ By matching on ratings, you can easily create a Favorites smart album that contains just your top-rated photos.

◆ By looking for the filename extensions `.avi`, `.mov`, and `.mpg` at the end of an Any Text or Filename criterion (there's a bug with Filename such that it doesn't always find as many items as Any Text), you can create a smart album of movies.

◆ Since iPhoto 6 adds Camera Model to the list of criteria for smart albums, it's easy to create a smart album that contains photos taken by cameras *other than* yours—in other words, photos that were taken by other people and sent to you. Of course, this doesn't work if one of your friends or family uses the same camera as you do.

◆ To create an album that contains all the photos of a certain person, use the Any Text criterion matching that person's name. It won't be perfect, but if you give your photos descriptive titles or comments, it's a good start.

✔ Tip

■ You can't remove photos from a smart album manually; the only way to take them out is to change either the photo or the criteria so they no longer match.

Duplicating Sources

Anything you can create in the Source pane—be it an album, smart album, a card, a slideshow, a calendar, or a folder—you can duplicate. Duplicating isn't something you'll use every day, but it can be useful.

Ways to duplicate a source:

◆ Control-click an item in the Source pane and choose Duplicate from the contextual menu that appears (**Figure 3.24**).

◆ Select an item in the Source pane, and then choose Duplicate from the Photos menu (Cmd D).

iPhoto duplicates the album, appending "2" to its name (**Figure 3.25**).

Reasons to duplicate sources:

◆ If you're making picture books for two sets of grandparents, for instance, you might want to use a very similar set of photos with different text. Lay out one book, then duplicate it to eliminate the effort of arranging photos again.

◆ If you want make differently themed books or calendars with the same set of images, create one, then duplicate it and change the theme of the duplicate.

◆ If you've put quite a lot of work into a book, calendar, or slideshow, and you want to try something without potentially messing up your work, make a duplicate first.

◆ If you've constructed a complex smart album and want to make another that's only slightly different, duplicating the first one and modifying the duplicate is easier than making a new one.

✔ Tip

■ Remember that duplicating a folder also duplicates everything inside it.

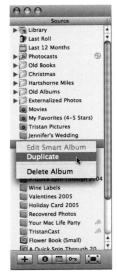

Figure 3.24 To duplicate a source, Control-click it and choose Duplicate from the contextual menu.

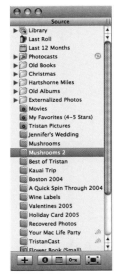

Figure 3.25 iPhoto appends a number to the name of the duplicate.

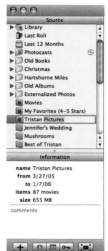

Figure 3.26 To rename a source (such as one you just duplicated), double-click its name and edit it, or select it and edit the name in the Name field in the Information pane.

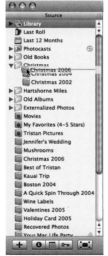

Figure 3.27 To move an item in the source list, drag it to the desired location.

Renaming and Rearranging Sources

You'll undoubtedly want to rename everything in the Source pane to give the items descriptive names. Plus, since iPhoto initially lists sources in the order you created them, you'll probably want to move them around in the list.

Ways to rename a source:

◆ Double-click the source's name, and then edit the name (**Figure 3.26**).

◆ Select a source, and then edit its name in the Name field in the Information pane (**Figure 3.26**).

To rearrange the source list:

◆ Drag a source to the desired location in the list. Note the black bar that indicates where the item will appear when you drop it (**Figure 3.27**).

✔ Tips

■ All names must be unique.

■ Each type of source—folders, albums, smart albums, books, cards, calendars, and saved slideshows—sorts together (both in the Source pane and inside folders), and you can rearrange items only within each type.

■ You can also enter comments about the source in the Comments field of the Information pane.

■ You can use iPhoto's spelling tools while editing names and comments. See "Checking Spelling as You Type" in Chapter 7, "Cards, Books, and Calendars."

■ You can Cmd-click or Shift-click to select and move multiple sources at once.

Deleting Sources

It's easy to create items in the Source pane, and luckily, if you decide you don't want one cluttering your list, they're even easier to delete.

Ways to delete a source:

◆ Select one or more items and press [Delete].

iPhoto prompts you to make sure you know what you're doing; click Delete to delete the source (**Figure 3.28**).

◆ [Control]-click an album and choose Delete Album from the contextual menu that appears (**Figure 3.29**).

iPhoto prompts you to make sure you know what you're doing; click Delete to delete the album (**Figure 3.28**).

◆ Select one or more items and press [Cmd][Delete].

iPhoto deletes the items instantly, without asking for confirmation.

✔ Tips

■ Deleting an album (or anything else in the Source pane) doesn't affect the original photos in the Library since the album merely contains pointers to the originals.

■ Deleting a folder deletes albums, slideshows, and books inside it. Be careful!

■ Don't feel that albums must be created carefully and then kept forever. It's totally reasonable to group a bunch of photos in an album, work on them for a little while, and then delete the album. I do that often to avoid scrolling around my entire Library.

■ On the other hand, if you think you might want to use an item again, store it away inside a folder for future reference.

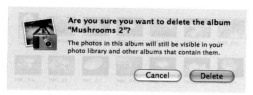

Figure 3.28 iPhoto prompts to make sure you want to delete the selected item. Click Delete if you do.

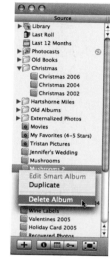

Figure 3.29 You can Control-click an item in the Source pane and choose Delete to delete it, though that's harder than just pressing Delete or Command-Delete.

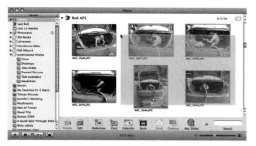

Figure 3.30 To select multiple pictures by dragging, click in an empty area of the display pane, and then drag a selection rectangle over the desired photos.

Selecting Photos

Throughout the rest of this chapter, I tell you to select photos before performing some task. I'm sure you have figured out the basic ways of selecting and deselecting images, but some others aren't so obvious.

Ways to select photos:

◆ Click a photo to select it.

◆ Click one photo to select it, hold down Shift, and then click another photo to select it and all the intervening pictures.

◆ Click one photo to select it, hold down Cmd, and then click additional photos to add them to the selection individually.

◆ Click in an empty area of the display pane, then drag a selection rectangle over the photos you want to select (**Figure 3.30**). If you drag to the top or bottom of the display pane, iPhoto scrolls the pane and keeps selecting additional images.

◆ With the display pane active, choose Select All (Cmd A) from the Edit menu to select all the images in the current album.

◆ In the Library, use the View menu to make sure film rolls are showing, and then click a film roll separator to select all the images in that film roll. This works only in the Library because film rolls don't show in other albums.

Ways to deselect photos:

◆ To deselect one of several selected images, Cmd-click it.

◆ To deselect all photos, click in the empty area surrounding the photos or choose Select None from the Edit menu (Cmd Shift A).

Select Multiple Albums

Don't assume you must work with only the photos in a single album at a time. You can select multiple albums at once by Cmd- or Shift-clicking album names, and when you do that, the photos from all the selected albums show in the display pane.

Similarly, if you select a folder, the display pane shows all the photos in all the items inside that folder.

Adding Photos to Sources

Even after you've made an album, book, calendar, or saved slideshow, you can add photos to it (smart albums populate themselves).

Ways to add photos to sources:

◆ Select one or more photos in the display pane and drag them onto a source other than a folder, which can hold only other sources. Note the thick black border that appears when you drag over a source (**Figure 3.31**).

◆ From the Finder, drag one or more photos, or an entire folder of photos, to a source. iPhoto imports the photos and then adds them to the source. Note that the photos will appear in the Library also, not just in the source.

◆ Drag photos from the display pane into the Source pane, but not onto a specific source (just below the second-to-last album or just below the Trash). This technique creates a new album and adds the images to it (**Figure 3.32**).

◆ Select photos, choose Copy ($\boxed{\text{Cmd}}\boxed{\text{C}}$) from the Edit menu, click the desired destination album, and choose Paste ($\boxed{\text{Cmd}}\boxed{\text{V}}$) from the Edit menu.

◆ $\boxed{\text{Control}}$ -click one or more selected photos, choose Copy from the contextual menu that appears, switch to the desired album, $\boxed{\text{Control}}$ -click a blank spot in the display pane, and choose Paste from the contextual menu. It's the same idea as the previous method.

✔ Tip

■ You can add a photo to a source only once. To put a photo in a source twice, you must duplicate it—see "Duplicating Photos" in Chapter 4, "Editing Photos."

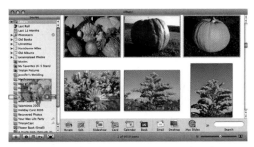

Figure 3.31 To add photos to a source, select them and drag them onto the desired source in the Source pane. Note how the destination source gets a thick black border and how the pointer changes from a plain arrow to one with a + badge. iPhoto also tells you, via a number in a red circle, how many images you're dragging.

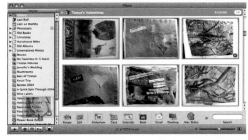

Figure 3.32 To create an album and add photos to it in one fell swoop, select the images and drag them to the Source pane, but not onto any specific album.

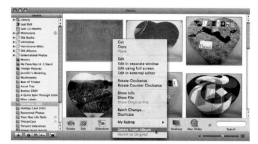

Figure 3.33 Control-click a photo and choose Delete from Album to remove the picture from that album.

Removing Photos from Sources

As you work with a source, you may decide that you don't want some of the images in the source. Luckily, they're easy to remove.

Ways to remove photos from sources:

◆ Making sure you're in the desired source, select the photos you want to remove and press Delete.

◆ Select the photos you want to remove, and choose Delete from Album from the Photos menu (Cmd Delete) or, for albums only, Cut (Cmd X) from the Edit menu.

◆ For albums only, drag the photos you want to remove to the Trash album.

◆ For albums only, Control-click one or more selected photos, and then choose Cut or Delete from Album from the contextual menu (**Figure 3.33**).

◆ To remove a photo from a smart album you must either redefine the smart album or change the photo's information such that the photo no longer matches the smart album's criteria.

✔ Tips

■ Removing a photo from an album, book, card, calendar, or saved slideshow doesn't delete it from your Library.

■ iPhoto doesn't ask for confirmation when you remove photos from a source; if you make a mistake, either choose Undo Delete Photo from Album from the Edit menu (Cmd Z) or add them again.

■ Dragging a photo to the Trash album from another album merely removes the photo from that album; it does not delete it from your Library, nor does it copy the photo to the Trash album.

Sorting Photos

iPhoto can perform five sorts, or you can move images around manually, which is useful for arranging photos in albums you can use for books, calendars, and slideshows.

To sort photos automatically:

1. When in any album, choose the desired sort method from the View menu's Sort Photos hierarchical menu (**Figure 3.34**).

2. From the Sort Photos hierarchical menu, choose either Ascending or Descending to control the direction of the sort (ascending sorts go from oldest to newest, A to Z, 1 to 9, whereas descending sorts go from newest to oldest, Z to A, 9 to 1).

To sort photos manually:

◆ Drag one or more photos to the desired location in the album, as marked by a black line (**Figure 3.35**).

◆ To make iPhoto forget your manual changes, switch to an automatic sort and then choose Reset Manual Sort.

✔ Tips

■ Albums maintain individual sort settings.

■ iPhoto remembers how you've sorted photos manually even if you switch to another sort order and back to Manually.

■ You can't sort photos manually in the Library, Last Roll, Last 12 Months, or smart albums, and By Film Roll is available only when you're in the Library album.

■ iPhoto 6 has replaced the Place Most Recent Photos at the Top checkbox from previous versions with the Ascending and Descending menu items.

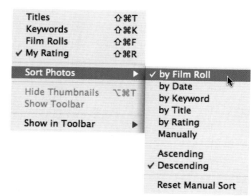

Figure 3.34 To sort photos, choose the desired method from the Sort Photos menu.

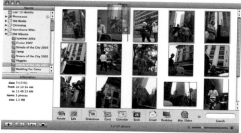

Figure 3.35 To sort photos manually, drag one or more photos to the desired location, as indicated by a thick black line between photos.

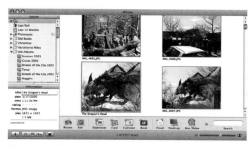

Figure 3.36 To assign a title to a photo, select it and enter the name in the Title field in the Information pane.

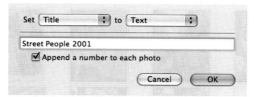

Figure 3.37 Batch Change enables you to set the titles of multiple selected photos all at once, appending numbers if you so desire.

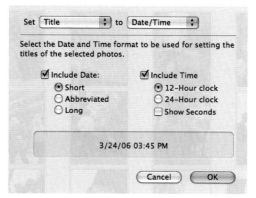

Figure 3.38 When changing the title of a photo to Date/Time, set the format in the dialog before clicking the OK button.

Assigning Titles to Photos

Digital cameras assign sequential numeric names to photos, but iPhoto lets you add your own descriptive titles. Smart albums can look for text in titles, and iPhoto can use the titles when you design books or publish to the Web.

To assign a custom title to a photo:

◆ Make sure the Information pane is showing, and then select a photo and enter a title for it in the Title field (**Figure 3.36**).

To assign titles to multiple photos:

1. Select a number of photos, and choose Batch Change (Cmd Shift B) from either the Photos menu or by Control-clicking the photos.

2. In the dialog that appears, choose Title from the Set pop-up menu, and then choose Empty, Text, Roll Info, Filename, or Date/Time from the To pop-up menu (**Figure 3.37**).

3. If you chose Text or Date/Time, select the desired options in the dialog (**Figures 3.37** and **3.38**).

   iPhoto changes the titles appropriately.

✔ Tips

■ Titles stick to their photos no matter what mode you're in. So, if you assign a title to a photo in an album, that same title shows up in the Library, and when you're designing a book.

■ Keep titles short so they're easy to read in the display and Information panes and so they fit when used in Web pages.

■ Wouldn't it be nice if you could edit titles directly in the display pane? Choose Provide iPhoto Feedback from the iPhoto menu and enter your suggestion in Apple's feedback Web page.

Assigning Comments to Photos

It's often helpful to describe a photo briefly so you remember the original scene better. That's one good use for iPhoto's comments, and iPhoto also uses comments as descriptive text in some of the book designs.

To assign a comment to a photo:

◆ Make sure the Information pane is showing, and then select a photo and type your comment in the Comments field (**Figure 3.39**).

To assign comments to multiple photos at once:

1. Select a number of photos, and choose Batch Change ([Cmd][Shift][B]) from either the Photos menu or by [Control]-clicking the photos.

2. In the dialog that appears, choose Comments from the Set pop-up menu, and then enter the comment to attach to each photo (**Figure 3.40**).

3. If you want to append your text to each comment, instead of replacing what's there, select Append to Existing Comments and click OK.

   iPhoto changes the comments.

✔ Tips

■ Like titles, comments stick to their photos no matter which mode you're in.

■ You can use iPhoto's spelling tools in the Comments field. For more details, see "Checking Spelling as You Type" in Chapter 7, "Cards, Books, and Calendars."

■ Resize the Comments field by dragging the size handle at the top of the Information pane and the thin line at the right edge of the Source pane.

Drag to make the Information pane taller and wider to show large comments. / Comments field. / Information button.

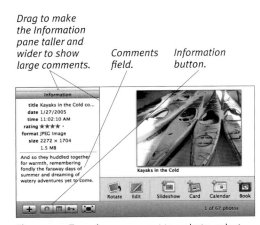

Figure 3.39 To assign a comment to a photo, select the photo and enter the comment in the Comments field in the Information pane.

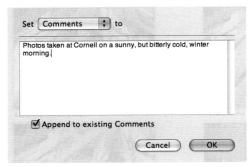

Figure 3.40 Use the Batch Change command to change or append comments for a number of photos at once.

✔ More Tips

■ Expanding the Information pane is the only way to see more of the Comments field. iPhoto doesn't provide a scroll bar, but you can drag or use the arrow keys to scroll through too-long comments.

■ The Comments field can hold an essentially unlimited amount of text. If you need long comments, create them in another application and paste them into iPhoto.

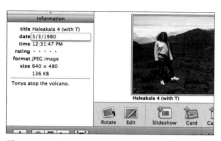

Figure 3.41 To change a photo's date, edit the Date field in the Information pane.

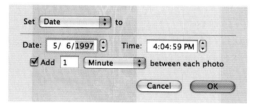

Figure 3.42 Use the Batch Change command to modify the dates of multiple photos at once, adding a set amount of time between each photo if you wish.

✔ More Tips

- If iPhoto is set to arrange photos by date, changing a photo's date causes it to re-sort according to the new date. Keep that in mind if a photo isn't where you expect it to be after changing its date.

- In the Batch Change dialog, you can type numbers into the date and time fields, use the arrow keys to move the values up and down, or click the little up/down arrow controls to increase or decrease the selected number.

- When using Batch Change to modify a number of photos with a time increment, note that iPhoto changes them in the order (left to right, top to bottom) that they're currently arranged.

- It's a good idea to use the time increment to ensure that you know how photos will sort by date later; if they're all set to exactly the same date and time, iPhoto may sort them unpredictably.

Editing Photo Dates

It's not uncommon for digital cameras to forget the date, which can result in a set of photos being imported as though they had been taken in 1980, for instance. Plus, some older digital cameras didn't store the date with the photo, so if you import photos taken with such a camera, the date will be set to when you imported, not when the picture was taken. You can edit photo dates in iPhoto to correct this annoyance.

To edit a photo's date:

◆ Make sure the Information pane is showing, and then select a photo and edit its date in the Date field (**Figure 3.41**).

To edit multiple photo dates at once:

1. Select a number of photos, and choose Batch Change (Cmd Shift B) from either the Photos menu or by Control-clicking the photos.

2. In the dialog that appears, choose Date from the Set pop-up menu, and then use the controls to set the date to attach to each photo (**Figure 3.42**).

3. If you want to add a set amount of time by which to increment each photo's date, select the checkbox, enter a number, choose Seconds, Minutes, Hours, or Days from the pop-up menu, and click OK. iPhoto changes the dates appropriately.

✔ Tips

- You can change photo times too, using the Time field in the Information pane.

- Although iPhoto recognizes a large number of date formats, it ignores improperly formatted dates when you're typing them manually, so to avoid confusion, it's easiest to edit the date using the same date format iPhoto uses.

Assigning Ratings

Just as with iTunes, where you can rate your favorite songs on a scale of 1 to 5 stars, you can rate your photos, which is a great way to identify your favorites easily.

Ways to assign ratings:

◆ Select one or more photos, and from the hierarchical My Rating menu in the Photos menu, choose the desired rating. Note the Cmd 0 through Cmd 5 keyboard shortcuts—if you're ever going to use keyboard shortcuts, now is the time.

◆ Select one or more photos, Control-click one of the selected photos, and choose the desired rating from the hierarchical My Rating menu (**Figure 3.43**).

◆ With a photo selected, click the appropriate star button in the Information pane.

◆ With the slideshow controls turned on, click the star buttons to assign ratings while the slideshow runs.

After you choose a rating, iPhoto applies it to the selected photos, displaying it below each photo if you have My Rating (Cmd Shift R) turned on in the View menu.

✔ Tips

■ The keyboard shortcuts for rating photos are available at all times, even when you're playing a slideshow!

■ You can change the rating for a photo at any time; it's by no means set in stone.

■ iPhoto considers 5 stars better than 1 star, although there's nothing stopping you from assuming the reverse.

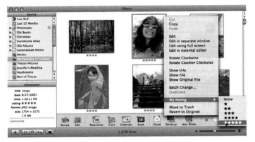

Figure 3.43 To assign a rating to a photo, Control-click the photo and choose the desired rating from the My Rating menu (or use the keyboard shortcuts, which are a lot faster in this situation). Here you can see my star ratings underneath the photos.

Consider Using Only High Ratings

Don't assume you must rate all your photos. My feeling is that there's relatively little point in rating anything with 1 or 2 stars, since those ratings basically mean, "I like this photo only enough to keep it." I consider 3 stars an average rating, so I usually don't use that either, reserving my rating effort for the 4- and 5-star photos that are my favorites.

Remember too that you can create smart albums that match photos whose ratings are lower than a set number, so you could easily find all the photos that didn't have 4 or 5 stars.

ASSIGNING RATINGS

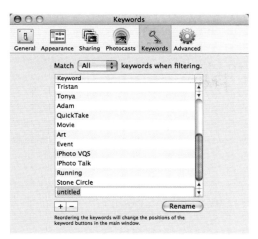

Figure 3.44 Add, remove, and rename keywords in the Keywords pane of iPhoto's Preferences window.

Keywords vs. Albums

Use keywords for categories of pictures that recur throughout your photo collection. In contrast, use albums for unique categories that appear only once in your collection. Keywords work well for identifying pictures of your family, landscapes, or recurring events; an album would be better for a specific trip's photos.

Working with the Checkmark Keyword

iPhoto provides a special checkmark keyword that, when applied to a photo, appears on top of the image itself, rather than under it, like all other keywords. Plus, the checkmark appears whether or not keywords are set to be visible. Use the checkmark keyword as a temporary marker. For instance, when my grandparents ask for prints of certain photos that I'm showing them, I mark those photos with the checkmark keyword so I can easily find them when I order the prints.

Managing Keywords

Along with titles, comments, and ratings, you can assign keywords to your photos. First, you must learn how to create, rename, and delete keywords. Before performing these tasks, open iPhoto's Preferences window by choosing Preferences (Cmd,) from the iPhoto menu, and then click the Keywords tab.

To create a keyword:

1. Click the + button.

iPhoto creates a new untitled keyword (**Figure 3.44**).

2. Name the new keyword.

To rename a keyword:

1. Either double-click a keyword or select one and click the Rename button.

2. Enter the new name.

To delete a keyword:

◆ Select a keyword and click the – button. iPhoto deletes the keyword immediately.

✔ Tips

■ The Match pop-up menu lets you switch between finding just photos that contain *all* the selected keywords or photos that contain *any* of the selected keywords.

■ You can create an unlimited (or at least very large) number of keywords.

■ You can rearrange keywords (throughout iPhoto) by dragging them in the list.

■ Photos inherit keyword changes, so if a photo has the "Nature" keyword and you rename the keyword to "Landscape," the photo updates to match.

■ If you delete a keyword, iPhoto removes it from all photos to which it was assigned.

Assigning and Removing Keywords

Once you've customized your list of key-words, you can assign keywords to individual images. For this task, click the Key button under the Source pane to make sure the Keywords pane is showing.

To assign keywords to photos:

◆ Drag one or more photos to a keyword in the Keywords pane (**Figure 3.45**).

◆ Select one or more photos, choose Get Info (Cmd I) from the Photos menu, and in the Keywords tab, select the checkbox(es) next to the desired keyword(s) (**Figure 3.46**).

To remove keywords from photos:

◆ Holding down Option, drag one or more photos to a keyword in the Keywords pane.

◆ Select one or more photos, choose Get Info (Cmd I) from the Photos menu, and in the Keywords tab, deselect the checkbox(es) next to the desired keyword(s) (**Figure 3.46**).

✔ Tips

■ When dragging photos to the Keywords pane, you can add or remove only a single keyword at a time. It's faster to work in the Keywords pane of the Photo Info window if you need to add or remove multiple keywords at once.

■ Be careful when selecting photos and keywords to avoid assigning the wrong keywords to the wrong photos. You can always choose Undo (Cmd Z) from the Edit menu if you make a mistake.

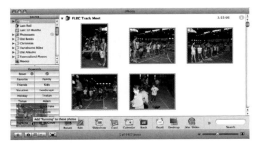

Figure 3.45 You can assign a keyword by dragging photos to a keyword in the Keywords pane.

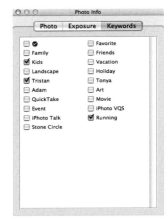

Figure 3.46 You can also add and remove keywords from selected photos in the Keywords pane of the Photo Info window.

Keyword Assistant

If you like using the keyboard more than the mouse, Ken Ferry's free Keyword Assistant plug-in enables you to type keywords, with auto-completion, auto-matically assigning the keyword to the selected photos. It's a slick little utility, and if you spend a lot of time keyword-ing your photos, I strongly encourage you to give it a try. Download a copy from `http://homepage.mac.com/kenferry/software.html`.

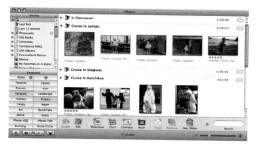

Figure 3.47 Here I've searched for all the photos in my Library that have both the "Tristan" keyword and the "Vacation" keyword. Note that there are 45 photos showing.

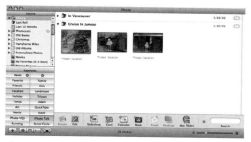

Figure 3.48 Now I've narrowed the search by Option-clicking the "iPhoto Talk" keyword, which removes photos from the display pane that have the "iPhoto Talk" keyword. Note that there are now only 30 photos showing (most of which are in the closed film roll).

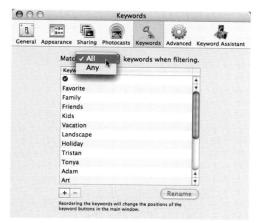

Figure 3.49 Choose either All or Any from the Match pop-up menu to control how keyword searches work.

Searching with the Keyword Pane

Keywords make it easy to find just those photos associated with certain keywords. When you search for photos, iPhoto doesn't merely select matching photos—it displays only those you want to see. These tasks take place in the Keywords pane; open it by clicking the key button under the Source pane.

To search for photos via keyword:

◆ Click one or more keywords.

iPhoto displays all those photos that have all the selected keywords (**Figure 3.47**).

To narrow a search:

◆ (Option)-click one or more keywords.

iPhoto removes from the display pane those photos with the (Option)-clicked keyword (**Figure 3.48**).

Ways to show all photos:

◆ Click the Reset button in the Keywords pane.

◆ Switch to the Calendar pane.

◆ Switch to any other album.

✔ Tips

■ Searches take place in the current album, unless you first select multiple albums.

■ The setting for the Match pop-up menu in the Keywords preference pane controls whether clicking multiple keywords finds photos that have *all* the selected keywords or *any* of the selected keywords (**Figure 3.49**). Choosing Any from the Match menu results in more photos being found, but the results you get from choosing All will likely be more what you want, since they are similar to the way you search in Google, for instance.

Searching with the Search Field

For quick searches, use the Search field that's always showing in organize mode. What's especially neat about the Search field is that it finds matches in filenames, titles, comments, keywords, and film roll names. It tends not to be as granular as a keyword search (searching for "Jen" finds not only pictures of my sister, but also pictures she sent me, and pictures of a high school friend named Jennifer).

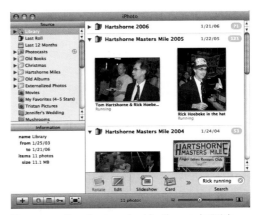

Figure 3.50 Here I've searched for the words "Rick running" and iPhoto has displayed all those photos that have either of those words associated with them.

To search for photos using the Search field:

◆ Type one or more words into the Search field.

iPhoto displays all those photos that in some way are associated with all the words you typed (**Figure 3.50**).

Ways to show all photos:

◆ Click the X button in the Search field.

◆ Switch to any other album.

✔ Tips

■ Searches take place in the current album, unless you first select multiple albums.

■ Searches are not case-sensitive.

■ As you type more words, your search becomes ever more narrow.

■ iPhoto is happy to search for word fragments, so when I search for "Julia", iPhoto also finds pictures of my friend Julian.

■ There's a bug that could cause confusion. If you perform a search, and then add to the search phrase a word that appears in a film roll title, the photos in that film roll disappear, which shouldn't happen.

Drag to
expand the
Calendar
pane.

Click to
jump to
the current
date.

Click to
move back
in time.

Click to
move ahead
in time.

Click to
toggle
between
month and
year views.

Click to
clear the
selection.

Selected
months.

Black shows
that photos
were taken
these
months.

Gray indi-
cates that
no photos
were taken
these
months.

Click to
hide and
show the
Calendar
pane.

Click to
select year.

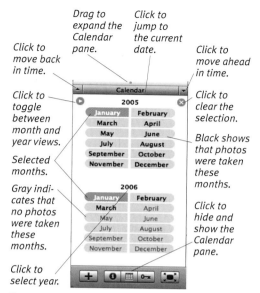

Figure 3.51 Here, in year view, I've searched for photos taken in either January 2005 or January 2006.

Drag to
expand the
Calendar
pane.

Click to
jump to
the current
date.

Click to
move back
in time.

Click to
move ahead
in time.

Click to
toggle
between
month and
year views.

Click to
clear the
selection.

Click to
select entire
month.

Black shows
that photos
were taken
these days.

Gray indi-
cates that
no photos
were taken
these days.

Selected
days.

Click to
hide and
show the
Calendar
pane.

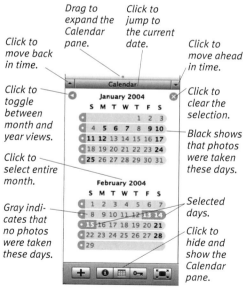

Figure 3.52 Here, in month view, I've searched for photos taken over Valentine's Day weekend in 2004.

Searching with the Calendar Pane

The Calendar pane makes it easy to display just photos within certain date ranges. The tasks explained below take place in the Calendar pane; open it by clicking the Calendar button under the Source pane.

To change the Calendar pane's view:

◆ To switch to year view, click the view triangle so it points right (**Figure 3.51**).

◆ To switch to month view, click the view triangle so it points left (**Figure 3.52**).

◆ To see more dates, drag up the handle at the top of the Calendar pane.

◆ To display earlier or later months or years, click the up or down triangle.

◆ To jump to the current month, click the word Calendar at the top of the pane.

◆ To clear the results of a search, click the X button or switch to any other album.

To search for photos using the Calendar pane:

◆ Select the days or months corresponding to the time period in which you want to find photos. You can (Shift)-click or (Cmd)-click to select multiple contiguous or noncontiguous dates.

◆ Click a month or year heading to select all the days or months within.

✔ Tips

■ Searches take place in the current album.

■ Pay attention to whether a month or day is black or gray. Black dates contain photos; gray dates do not.

Viewing Photo Information

iPhoto presents information about photos in two places: the Information pane and the Photo Info window.

To view info in the Information pane:

◆ If the Information pane is hidden, click the Information button underneath the Source pane once to display the Information pane (**Figure 3.53**).

To view information in the Photo Info window:

1. Select a photo and choose Get Info from the Photos menu ([Cmd][I]).

   iPhoto displays the Photo Info window's Photo Tab (**Figure 3.54**).

2. Click the Exposure tab to see exposure information (**Figure 3.55**).

3. Click the Keywords tab to see and assign keywords associated with the photo.

✔ Tips

- When the Photo Info window is showing, you can click another photo to see its information immediately.

- You can change photo titles, dates, and comments in the Information pane, but you can change only keywords in the Photo Info window.

- The Photo Info window picks up its information from the EXIF (Exchangeable Image File) data stored by most digital cameras. EXIF is an industry standard that's designed to help interoperability among cameras, printers, and other imaging devices. In theory, EXIF support could help a printer produce a better rendition of an original image, although the theory appears to fall short of reality.

Information pane, with Title, Date, Time, Rating, Format, Size, and Comments fields.

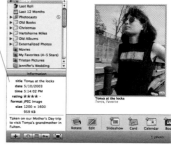

Figure 3.53 iPhoto's Information pane displays some basic information about selected photos.

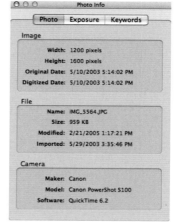

Figure 3.54 The Photo Info window's Photo tab provides detailed information that was recorded about the image by the camera.

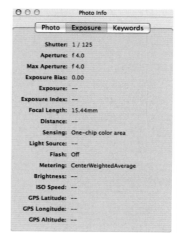

Figure 3.55 The Exposure tab of the Photo Info window displays information about the camera's settings at the time it took the image.

Editing
Photos

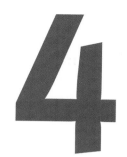

If you're anything like me, not all your photos come out perfect. In fact, lots of them are probably pretty bad, and those you can delete after import. No harm, no foul, and you didn't pay for developing.

What about those pictures that are okay, but not great? Most of the time they merely require a little work. Perhaps you need to crop out extraneous background that distracts the eye from the subject of the photo, or maybe you want to remove the red glow from your cute baby's eyes (it's the fault of the camera flash, not a sign of a demon child). iPhoto can help with those tasks.

I'm not suggesting that you whip out an image-editing application, clip your cousin's ex-husband out of the family reunion photo, and use filters that sound like alien death rays (Gaussian blur?) to make it appear as though he was never there. If you can do that, great, and iPhoto will even let you use any other image-editing application. But I can't do that, and I doubt most people can. For us, iPhoto provides the basic set of tools we need.

The main thing to remember is that there's no shame in editing photos to improve them. All the best photographers do it, and now you can do it too, thanks to iPhoto.

Super Secret
Advanced Editing Mode

Just before this book went to press, Macworld published details about some secret advanced editing options available in iPhoto for the Red-eye and Retouch tools. The options enable you to change the size of the Retouch tool's brush, lighten the area underneath the Retouch tool's brush, and to select red eyes more accurately with the Red-eye tool. Switching into super secret advanced editing mode requires video game-like dexterity; read the full instructions at: www.macworld.com/weblogs/macosxhints/2006/05/ip6edit/

Entering Edit Mode

Since you can edit a photo in the display pane, in full screen mode, in a separate window, or in another application, it make sense that you can enter edit mode in several ways.

To choose how to edit photos:

1. From the iPhoto application menu, choose Preferences (Cmd,).

   iPhoto opens the Preferences window. Click the General tab (**Figure 4.1**).

2. From the Edit Photo pop-up menu, choose how you want iPhoto to edit photos by default.

3. To use another program, choose In Application, and select a program in the Open dialog (**Figure 4.2**).

4. Close the Preferences window.

Ways to enter edit mode:

◆ Double-click a photo in organize or slideshow mode, or double-click a photo *twice* when making a book, calendar, or card.

   iPhoto switches to edit mode and displays the photo according to the setting in the Preferences window.

◆ In organize mode, select one or more photos and click the Full Screen button under the display pane to edit the photos in full screen mode.

◆ Option-double-click a photo in any mode to open the photo in either the display pane or a separate window, whichever is *not* the default in iPhoto's preferences.

◆ Control-click a photo in organize mode, and choose one of the editing commands from the contextual menu that appears (**Figure 4.3**). Book mode offers a slightly different contextual menu.

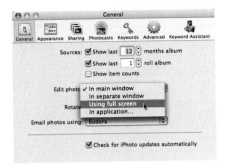

Figure 4.1 In the Preferences window, choose how you want iPhoto to react when you double-click a photo.

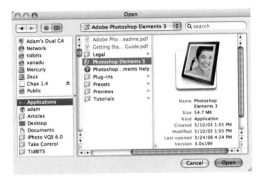

Figure 4.2 To use another program, choose In Application, and then find your desired program in the Open dialog.

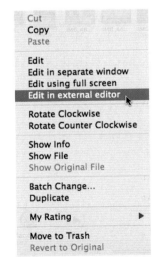

Figure 4.3 Control-click a photo in organize mode and choose one of the editing commands from the contextual menu. This is a particularly good way to edit in an external application on an occasional basis.

✔ Tip

- Hide or show the Thumbnail list at the top of the window by choosing Hide/Show Thumbnail (Cmd Option T) from the View menu.

Edit Tools Overview (Display Pane)

Here's a quick look at the tools available when you edit an image in the display pane (**Figure 4.4**).

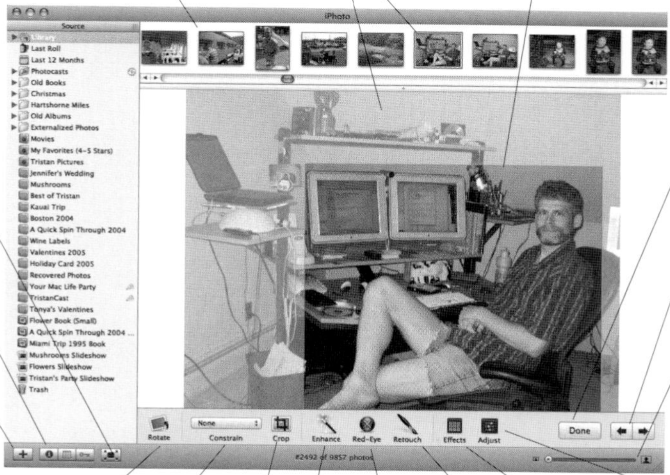

Images around the photo being edited appear in the Thumbnail list. Click one to edit it.

The selected image appears in the display pane for editing.

Selection rectangle. Drag in the image area to select. Parts of the image outside the selected area appear fogged out.

Click Done to save your changes to the photo (and return to the previous mode).

Use the previous and next buttons to navigate to the previous or next photo in the current album.

Click to switch to full screen mode.

Click to hide or show the Information pane (currently hidden).

Click to add an album.

Size slider. Adjust this slider to zoom in and out of the picture in the display pane.

Figure 4.4

Click to rotate the image counterclockwise. Option-click to rotate clockwise.

To constrain a selection to a specific aspect ratio, choose the desired ratio in the Constrain pop-up menu, and then select a portion of the image.

Click the Enhance button to fix photos automatically.

Click the Adjust button to open the Adjust panel.

Click the Effects button to open the Effects panel.

To crop a photo, select a portion of the image, and then click the Crop button.

To eliminate red-eye in a picture of a person or pet, click the Red-Eye button and then click the subject's eyes.

Use the Retouch tool to scrub out unwanted blemishes.

Edit Tools Overview (Full Screen)

When you edit a photo in full screen mode, the editing tools and thumbnails are the same, but they automatically appear and disappear at the bottom and top of the screen when you move your pointert to those locations, and there are several other buttons that provide necessary features (**Figure 4.5**).

✔ Tips

- The Information panel stands in for the Information pane in the main window.

- The Navigation panel appears when you zoom in, since there are no scroll bars.

Click the Info button to open the Information panel.

Click the Compare button to compare this image with the next one to the right.

Effects panel. Click an effect to apply it to the image.

Images around the photo being edited appear in the Thumbnail list. Click one to edit it.

The selected image takes over the entire screen for editing.

Adjust panel. Use the controls in here to modify the image.

Information panel. Use it to view information, and change titles, date, and time.

Navigation panel. Drag the selection rectangle to scroll around in the image.

Use the previous and next buttons to navigate to the previous or next photo in the current album.

Close button. Click to leave full screen mode.

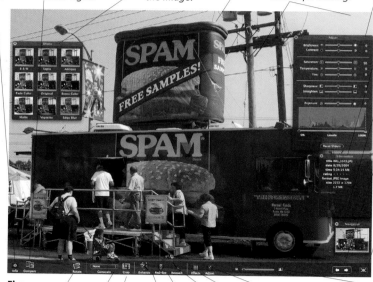

Figure 4.5

Click to rotate the current image counter-clockwise. Option-click to rotate clockwise.

To constrain a selection to a specific aspect ratio, choose the desired ratio in the Constrain pop-up menu, and then select a portion of the image.

To crop a photo, select a portion of the image and click the Crop button.

Click the Enhance button to fix photos automatically.

Use the Retouch tool to scrub out unwanted blemishes.

To eliminate red-eye in a picture of a person or pet, click the Red-Eye button and then click the subject's eyes.

Size slider. Adjust this slider to zoom in and out of the picture. Automatically opens the Navigation panel.

Click the Adjust button to open the Adjust panel.

Click the Effects button to open the Effects panel.

✔ Tips

- The image-editing window doesn't remember its size, so you may need to resize or zoom the window each time.

- Editing in windows can be a good way to compare multiple images, or even multiple copies of the same image.

- Hide or show the Thumbnail list by choosing Hide/Show Thumbnail ([Cmd][Option][T]) from the View menu.

- Use the Window menu to switch to windows you can't see.

Edit Tools Overview (Separate Window)

When you edit a photo in a separate window, the tools are the same as in edit mode, except for the Size menu that lets you resize the image; it replaces the size slider (**Figure 4.6**).

Images around the photo being edited appear in the Thumbnail list. Click one to edit it.

The selected image appears in the display pane for editing.

Selection rectangle. Drag a rectangle over the image to create a selection. Parts of the image outside the selected area appear fogged out.

Click the close button to close the window when you're done editing. Equivalent to the Done button.

Click the zoom button to zoom the window to the largest possible size.

Click to rotate the current image counter-clockwise. Option-click to rotate clockwise.

Click the Adjust button to open the Adjust panel.

Use the previous and next buttons to navigate to the previous or next photo in the current album.

Resize handle. Drag to resize both the window and the photo.

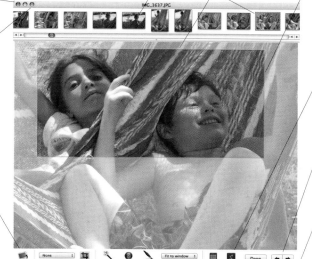

Figure 4.6

To constrain a selection to a specific aspect ratio, choose the desired ratio in the Constrain pop-up menu, and then select a portion of the image.

To crop a photo, select a portion of the image and click the Crop button.

Click Done to save your changes to the photo (and return to the previous mode).

Click the Effects button to open the Effects panel.

Use the Retouch tool to scrub out unwanted blemishes.

Click the Enhance button to fix photos automatically.

To eliminate red-eye in a picture of a person or pet, click the Red-Eye button and then click the subject's eyes.

Choose the size of the photo from the Size pop-up menu.

Editing RAW Files

Some digital cameras offer the option of shooting in RAW format, in which the image isn't compressed at all. RAW is considered a "digital negative" format that isn't to be modified, which has some implications when you want to edit a RAW photo in iPhoto.

Useful facts about working with RAW:

◆ The first time you edit a RAW file in iPhoto, a small RAW badge appears in the lower right corner of the display pane. On subsequent edits, the RAW badge doesn't appear.

◆ On that initial edit, iPhoto converts the RAW file to JPEG, leaving the RAW file in the Originals folder in your iPhoto Library folder and storing the JPEG version in the Modified folder. All changes are made to the JPEG version.

◆ JPEG is an inherently lossy compression format, which means that some detail is lost. iPhoto 6 now offers you the option to save edited RAW files in TIFF format, which uses lossless compression to preserve all the original detail in the RAW file. Change this setting in the Advanced pane of iPhoto's Preferences window by selecting Save Edited RAW files as 16 Bit TIFFs (**Figure 4.7**).

◆ If you prefer to edit RAW files in an external editor like Adobe Photoshop, you can select Use RAW Files with External Editor in the Advanced pane of iPhoto's Preferences window (**Figure 4.7**). That setting overrides iPhoto's normal preferences for how you edit photos.

◆ If you select an edited RAW photo (really the JPEG or TIFF version) and choose Revert to Original from the Photos menu, iPhoto reverts all the way back to the RAW file.

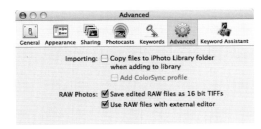

Figure 4.7 Set your RAW preferences in the Advanced pane of the iPhoto Preferences window.

Lossy vs. Lossless Compression

There are two basic ways of compressing a file so it takes up less space on disk: lossy and lossless.

With lossy compression, some data is deleted from the file, usually in ways that aren't particularly noticeable but that always reduce the overall quality. Files compressed with lossy compression methods are usually much smaller than their originals. Lossy compression methods work well with pictures and sound where data that most people can't see or hear can be eliminated.

In contrast, lossless compression methods preserve all the data in the original file perfectly when compressing it. That's best for retaining quality, but means that the files aren't nearly as small.

The basic difference then, is the trade-off between size and quality. For higher quality, choose file formats like TIFF that use lossless methods of compression; for smaller files, stick with file formats like JPEG that use lossy compression.

EDITING RAW FILES

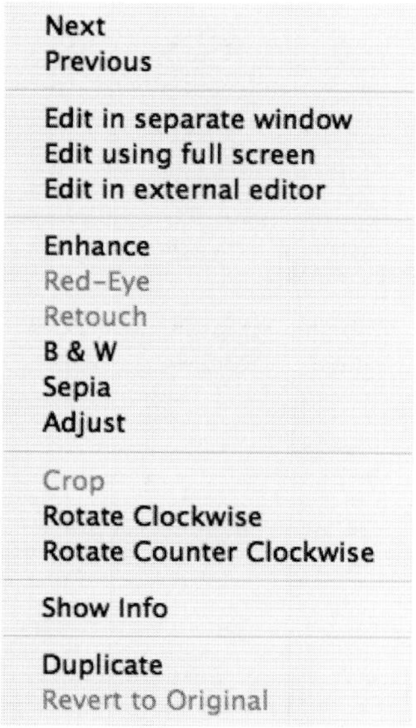

Next
Previous

Edit in separate window
Edit using full screen
Edit in external editor

Enhance
Red-Eye
Retouch
B & W
Sepia
Adjust

Crop
Rotate Clockwise
Rotate Counter Clockwise

Show Info

Duplicate
Revert to Original

Figure 4.8 Control-click a photo in the display pane in edit mode or in full screen mode to display iPhoto's contextual menu shortcuts.

Next
Previous

Enhance
Red-Eye
Retouch
B & W
Sepia
Adjust

Crop
Rotate Clockwise
Rotate Counter Clockwise

Revert to Original

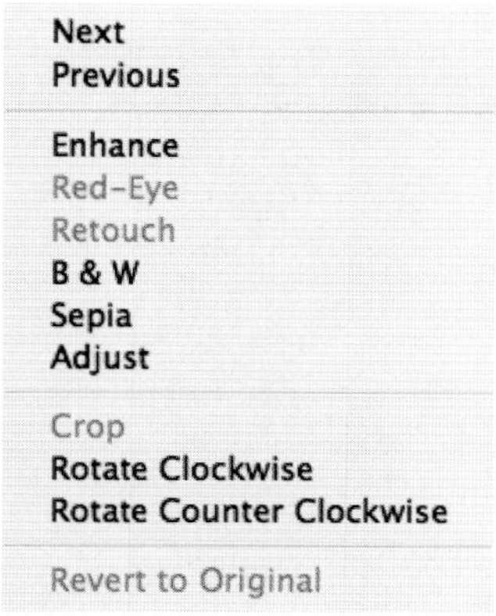

Figure 4.9 Control-click a photo when editing in a separate window to display a slightly different set of contextual menu shortcuts.

Contextual Menu Shortcuts

You can Control-click (or, if you have a two-button mouse, right-click) a photo in edit mode to bring up a contextual menu that lets you perform a number of actions without going to the display pane's editing tools or the separate window's toolbar (**Figure 4.8** and **Figure 4.9**).

Contextual menu shortcuts:

◆ Use Next and Previous to move to the next and previous photos in the album.

◆ The Edit commands are useful for opening the current photo in full screen mode or a separate window, and for opening the photo in an external editor without changing iPhoto's preferences.

◆ The Enhance, Red-Eye, Retouch, B & W, Sepia, Adjust, and Crop commands work just like their equivalent buttons.

◆ The Rotate, Show Info, Duplicate, and Revert to Original commands are exactly the same as those in the Photos menu, so you can use whichever feels most comfortable.

✔ Tips

■ The Edit commands aren't available in the contextual menu in full screen mode.

■ Oddly the B & W and Sepia commands, though they no longer exist as separate buttons outside the Effects panel, remain in the contextual menu.

■ Equally oddly, there's no Effects menu item for opening the Effects panel.

Zooming Photos

It can be helpful to zoom in and out while editing, particularly when using the Retouch tool or clicking eyes for red-eye reduction.

To zoom in the display pane:

◆ With an image showing in the display pane in edit mode, drag the size slider to the right to zoom in (**Figure 4.10**). To zoom out, drag the slider to the left (**Figure 4.11**).

To zoom in full screen mode:

◆ Drag the size slider to the right to zoom in and to the left to zoom out. As soon as you zoom in, the Navigation panel appears to help you scroll around in the photo (**Figure 4.12**).

To zoom in the image-editing window:

◆ With the Size menu set to Fit to Window, drag the resize handle to resize the window and the photo. The window resizes proportionally. This approach limits zooming to the maximum and minimum window sizes.

◆ Choose the desired zoom level from the Size menu.

✔ Tips

■ If you select a portion of the photo *before* zooming, iPhoto zooms to the selected portion of the picture.

■ If your mouse or trackball has a scroll wheel, you can use it to scroll vertically within a zoomed photo, even in full screen mode. Press (Shift) while moving the scroll wheel to scroll horizontally.

■ Unfortunately, the old shortcut of scrolling around in the image by (Cmd)-dragging is still missing in iPhoto 6.

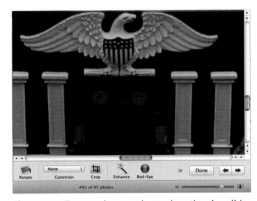

Figure 4.10 To zoom in on a photo, drag the size slider to the right. Here I've zoomed in most of the way.

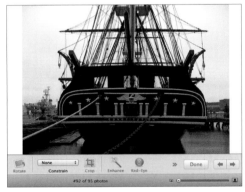

Figure 4.11 To zoom back out, drag the slider to the left. Here I've zoomed back out to the size that matches the display pane's size.

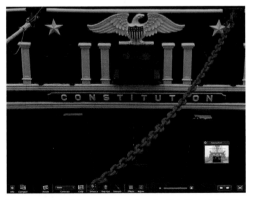

Figure 4.12 In full screen mode, use the size slider to zoom in and out, and navigate around with the tiny Navigation panel that appears (lower right).

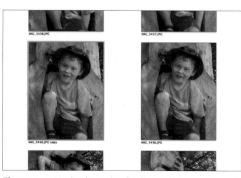

Figure 4.13 Notice how the duplicated photo appears next to its original and how it has "copy" appended to its title.

Duplicating Photos

iPhoto lets you duplicate photos, which can be useful in a variety of situations.

Reasons to duplicate a photo:

◆ If you want a photo to appear twice in a book (as you might if you want it to be the cover image and to show up inside as well), you must duplicate that photo.

◆ If you want to crop a photo in different ways, or if you want to print the same photo in color and black-and-white, you must duplicate the photo first.

Ways to duplicate photos:

◆ In any mode, select photos and from the Photos menu, choose Duplicate (Cmd D).

◆ Control-click a photo and choose Duplicate from the contextual menu.

iPhoto switches to import mode, duplicates the photo, appends "copy" to the title of the duplicate, and switches back to organize mode (**Figure 4.13**).

✔ Tips

■ The duplicate image shows up next to the original in the Library, and iPhoto does not create a new film roll.

■ The Last Roll album does not show the duplicated photo.

■ If a specific source other than the Library is selected when you duplicate a photo, the duplicate is added to that source too. However the photo won't be duplicated in any other sources that contain it.

■ There's no need to duplicate photos to open multiple copies in separate editing windows; you can do that by using the contextual menu.

■ iPhoto duplicates everything about the original, including keywords and ratings.

Rotating Photos

If you've turned your camera to switch from landscape view (horizontal) to portrait view (vertical), you may need to rotate the image in iPhoto to view it right side up.

Ways to rotate photos:

◆ In organize or edit mode, to rotate one or more photos clockwise, select them and click the Rotate button (**Figure 4.14** and **Figure 4.15**). To rotate the selected photos counter-clockwise, hold down Option and click the Rotate button.

◆ In organize or edit mode, select one or more photos, Control-click one, and choose the desired rotation direction from the contextual menu that appears.

◆ In organize, edit, or slideshow mode (but not book mode), select one or more photos and choose either Rotate Clockwise (Cmd R) or Rotate Counter Clockwise (Cmd Option R) from the Photos menu.

✔ Tips

■ You can change the direction used by the Rotate buttons in iPhoto's Preferences window; Option-clicking always reverses the default direction (**Figure 4.16**). How you set it is purely personal preference based on how you tend to rotated your camera for portrait-orientation pictures.

■ It may be easiest to rotate photos in batches in organize mode. Shrink the thumbnail size so you can see a number of photos at once, Cmd-click the ones that need rotating clockwise, and click Rotate. Repeat with any images that need counter-clockwise rotation, holding down Option when you click Rotate.

■ Some cameras automatically rotate the image, eliminating the need for Rotate.

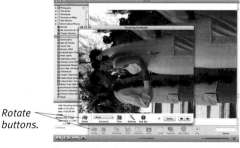

Rotate buttons.

Figure 4.14 Here I'm showing a "before" photo in the display pane and in its own window just so you can see both Rotate buttons.

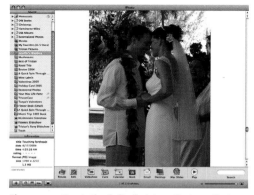

Figure 4.15 Here's the "after" picture that resulted from clicking the Rotate button.

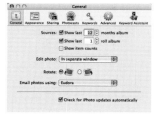

Figure 4.16 In the Preferences window, select which direction you want iPhoto to rotate photos by default.

Rotation Facts

◆ iPhoto 6 creates copies of rotated photos in the Modified folder rather than rotating just the thumbnail, as some previous versions did.

◆ If you rotate a GIF image, iPhoto converts the image to a JPEG, which may be undesirable.

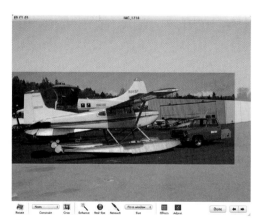

Figure 4.17 To select a portion of a photo, drag to create a selection rectangle. Move it by dragging it; resize it by dragging an edge. Here I've created a selection rectangle with no specific proportion to focus on the seaplane and the odd truck.

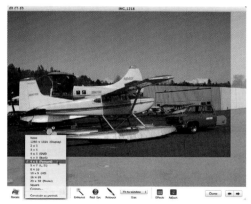

Figure 4.18 To constrain an image to specific proportions, choose an aspect ratio from the Constrain pop-up menu (here I've chosen 4 x 6, which will make a good print while not detracting from the subject of the picture). You can move and resize the selection rectangle while maintaining the selected aspect ratio.

Selecting Portions of Photos

iPhoto's next tool—the cropping tool—requires that you select a portion of the picture first.

To select part of a photo:

◆ In edit mode, drag to create a selection rectangle in the image. iPhoto fogs the photo outside your selection rectangle to help you focus on what you have selected (**Figure 4.17**).

◆ To move your selection rectangle around, drag it (your pointer should be a hand). You may need to move a selection rectangle to align it to the edges of a picture, since it's hard to start selecting right at the edge.

◆ To resize a selection rectangle, drag the rectangle's edge.

◆ To constrain the selection rectangle to specific proportions, choose an aspect ratio from the Constrain pop-up menu. If you haven't created a selection rectangle, it will be constrained when you do; if you have one already, iPhoto resizes it (**Figure 4.18**). To remove a constraint, choose None from the Constrain menu.

◆ To constrain the selection rectangle to custom proportions, edit the image in its own window, and enter the desired aspect ratio before you start selecting.

◆ To deselect everything and start over, click in the fogged area.

SELECTING PORTIONS OF PHOTOS

Specific Aspect Ratios

If you want to order prints of a photo, you first should crop it to the appropriate aspect ratio (**Figure 4.19**). See the opposite page to learn about cropping photos and see "Understanding Aspect Ratios" in Appendix A, "Deep Background," for more details about aspect ratios.

Uses for specific aspect ratios:

◆ Use 1280 x 1024 (Display) before you crop the image for use as a Desktop picture. These numbers are specific to your monitor's resolution.

◆ Use 4 x 3 (DVD) and 16 x 9 (HD) for a landscape image for a DVD slideshow created with iDVD.

◆ Use Square when you want a square selection; I've found it helpful for making images for use on the Web.

◆ Use a custom ratio if some external use, such as a Web page, calls for a specific aspect ratio (**Figure 4.20**).

✔ Tips

■ iPhoto assumes you want to crop in the same orientation as the photo, but you can change that. See the sidebar to the right for details.

■ iPhoto has some duplicate aspect ratios, presumably for people who don't realize that aspect ratios are ratios between numbers and multiplying those numbers by some value doesn't change the ratio.

■ Don't bother cropping for books, cards, and calendars; it's better to use the zoom and pan feature instead because the zoom and pan feature doesn't modify the original image the way cropping does.

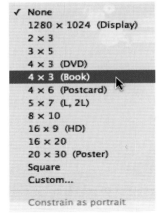

Figure 4.19 Before cropping, choose the aspect ratio that matches your intended use.

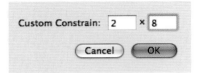

Figure 4.20 For an unusual custom aspect ratio, choose Custom and enter the desired aspect ratio in the Custom Constrain fields in the dialog that appears.

Switching between Portrait and Landscape Orientation

You may often find yourself wanting to switch between the constrained portrait (vertical) and landscape (horizontal) aspect ratios as you crop different photos, and you may also find yourself cursing a specific aspect ratio as you try to select a person's eyes to reduce red-eye. iPhoto has two hidden features to assuage your annoyance.

◆ Press (Option) while dragging to switch between portrait and landscape. This trick has the same effect as toggling the Constrain As menu item.

◆ Press (Shift) while dragging to switch temporarily to None so you can more easily select eyes for red-eye reduction.

SPECIFIC ASPECT RATIOS

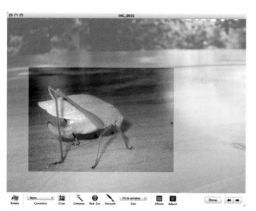

Figure 4.21 To crop an image, select the desired portion and then click the Crop button. Here I've cropped out all the irrelevant background around the insect.

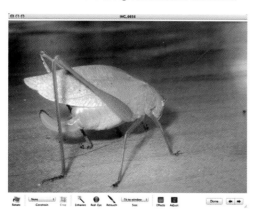

Figure 4.22 As you can see, cropping this image improves it immensely.

Adjust Shooting Style

When taking pictures, you usually want to fill the frame with the scene, but if you plan to order prints of all your photos, you might want to include a little extra space on the edges to allow for cropping to a print aspect ratio. See Appendix B, "Taking Better Photos," for more tips!

Cropping Photos

If you are planning to print a photo or display it on your Desktop, you should crop it using an appropriate aspect ratio. (See "Understanding Aspect Ratios" in Appendix A, "Deep Background," for details.) Even if you don't plan to print a photo, cropping extraneous detail can improve an image.

To crop a photo:

1. Select the desired portion of the image, using a constrain setting if you plan to use the image for display or printing.

2. Click the Crop button in the edit pane or the image-editing window's toolbar, or (Control)-click and choose Crop from the contextual menu.

   iPhoto deletes the fogged area of the picture, leaving just what you had selected (**Figure 4.21** and **Figure 4.22**).

✔ Tips

- Pressing and releasing (Control) no longer toggles between the "before" and "after" views when you're cropping in iPhoto.

- If your selection rectangle is very close to one of the standard aspect ratios, it's best to use the standard aspect ratio in case you want to print the image later.

- When you crop a photo, you remove pixels from it. So if you crop a 1600 x 1200 pixel photo (1,920,000 pixels) down to 1200 x 900 (1,080,000 pixels), you've removed almost half the image. Thus, if you print the original and the cropped version at the same size, the original will be of a much higher quality. Heavy cropping is one reason why iPhoto shows a low-resolution warning icon when you're creating books or prints. For details, see "Understanding Resolution" in Appendix A, "Deep Background."

Enhancing Photos

Traditional photo processors learned long ago that fiddling with brightness and contrast and messing with the colors could turn a plebeian picture into a luminescent photo. iPhoto aims to help you do the same for your photos with its one-click Enhance tool.

To enhance a photo:

1. In edit mode, click the Enhance button.

   iPhoto adjusts several aspects of your photo, including color levels, color saturation, and brightness and contrast.

2. Press and release Control to toggle between the "before" (**Figure 4.23**) and "after" (**Figure 4.24**) views of your photo.

3. If you like what Enhance has done to your photo, continue working. If not, choose Undo Enhance Photo (Cmd Z) from the Edit menu.

✔ Tips

■ Don't assume Enhance will always improve your photo. It's worth trying, but only you can decide if its results are better or worse than the original.

■ If the photo is way too dark or way too bright, Enhance isn't likely to work as well as using the Adjust tools manually (**Figure 4.25**).

■ Enhance seems to key off the main color in the image when tweaking color saturation, which can lead to unwanted effects.

■ The order in which you perform edits can make a difference. For instance, if you plan to crop a photo, try Enhance before you crop, and if you don't like the results, undo the enhance, crop, and try Enhance again to see if you get different results.

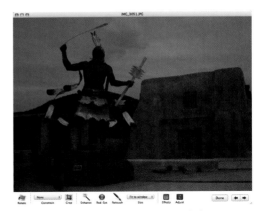

Figure 4.23 The original photo. It's too dark.

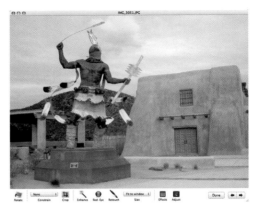

Figure 4.24 The photo after clicking Enhance. It's better, but now too light and somewhat blown out.

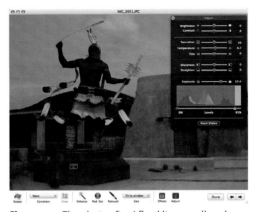

Figure 4.25 The photo after I fixed it manually using the Adjust controls, lightening the exposure, lowering the white point, and increasing the temperature.

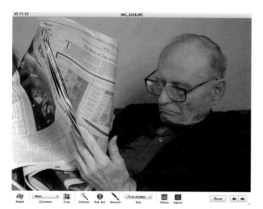

Figure 4.26 To convert a photo to black-and-white, switch to edit mode and click the B & W button. Here I'm converting a picture of my grandfather reading the newspaper to avoid a few distracting color elements from the cover photo and his shirt.

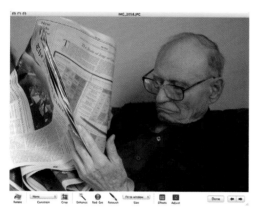

Figure 4.27 I like it a bit better in black-and-white; sepia also works well for this photo, since it gives it a more old-time feel.

Making Photos Black-and-White or Sepia

Although digital cameras take photos in color by default, some photos are improved by conversion to black-and-white. That's often true of portraits of people, since switching to black-and-white smooths out skin coloration and blemishes. Some landscapes also benefit tremendously from conversion to black-and-white, since eliminating color helps the viewer focus on the composition and lighting. Think Ansel Adams.

To make a photo black-and-white or sepia:

◆ In one of the editing modes, (Control)-click the photo and choose B & W or Sepia from the contextual menu.

◆ Click the Effects button to open the Effects panel, then click the B & W or Sepia button in the Effects panel (for more details about the Effects panel, see page 78).

✔ Tips

■ To decide whether you like the color or black-and-white/sepia version of a photo better, press and release (Control) a few times to toggle instantly between the "before" (**Figure 4.26**) and "after" (**Figure 4.27**) views of your photo. If you don't like the change, choose Undo Convert to B &W/Sepia ((Cmd)(Z)) from the Edit menu.

■ The Effects panel shows small previews comparing black-and-white and sepia versions of the photo as well.

■ Another way to compare color and black-and-white/sepia versions of the same photo is to open it twice in separate editing windows (this works best if you have multiple monitors attached to your Mac).

Reducing Red-Eye

Perhaps the most annoying thing that can go wrong in a photograph is *red-eye,* a demonic red glow to subjects' eyes that plagues flash photography. iPhoto provides a solution to red-eye, though its results aren't always ideal.

To reduce red-eye in a photo (I):

1. Draw a selection rectangle around the eyes (**Figure 4.28**).

2. Click the Red-Eye button.

    If all goes well, iPhoto converts the red shades in the clicked areas to dark gray.

To reduce red-eye in a photo (II):

1. Click the Red-Eye button.

    iPhoto switches to the red-eye reduction crosshair pointer, and displays a small pop-up with instructions.

2. Click in the center of the subject's eyes.

    If all goes well, iPhoto converts the red shades in the clicked areas to dark gray.

3. When you're done, click the Red-Eye button or the X button in the pop-up.

✔ Tips

- Sometimes one method works better than the other; if necessary, try both.

- It can be easier to click the subject's eyes accurately if you zoom in first.

- Press and release (Control) to toggle between the "before" and "after" views.

- The Red-Eye tool works poorly if the subject isn't facing the camera directly.

- iPhoto's technique makes people look as though they have black eyes, and it won't work on green-eye in dogs. You can achieve better results in other image-editing programs. Also consider converting the photo to black-and-white.

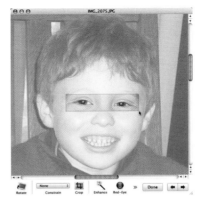

Figure 4.28 To reduce the effect of red-eye in a photo, draw a rectangle around the eyes and click the Red-Eye button.

What Is Red-Eye?

Red-eye is a phenomenon that occurs in photographs when light from the camera's flash reflects off the blood vessels in the retina of the subject's eyes. It's worse when the flash is close to the lens, with young children, with blue or gray eyes (which reflect more light than darker eyes), and in dim settings.

You can reduce the likelihood of red-eye occurring in the first place:

- Try to cause the subject's pupils to contract by increasing the room light, asking the person to look at a bright light right before taking the picture, or using a red-eye reduction feature in your camera (which pulses the flash before taking the picture).

- Have the subject look slightly away from the camera lens rather than directly toward it.

- If your camera supports an external flash unit, use it to increase the distance between the flash and the camera lens.

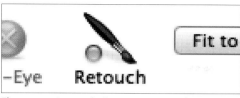

Figure 4.29 A green ball appears next to the Retouch wand when it's active. That's useful to know, because you must click the Retouch button again to turn it off and be able to make selection rectangles again.

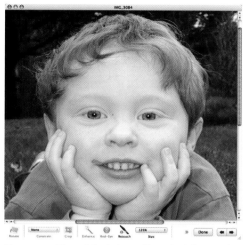

Figure 4.30 The original photo. Note the jelly smudge on the left side of Tristan's lips.

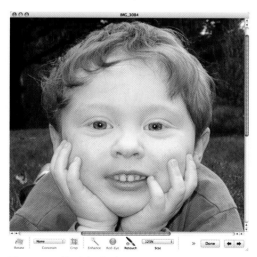

Figure 4.31 Much better!

Retouching Photos

Cindy Crawford's famous mole notwithstanding, many otherwise great photos are marred by small blemishes. Perhaps it's a smear of jelly on your toddler's face, or someone's chapped lips. Either way, iPhoto's Retouch tool can help.

To retouch a photo:

1. Click the Retouch button.

    iPhoto puts a green ball next to the Retouch wand to indicate that it's active (**Figure 4.29**).

2. Click and scrub over the blemish you want to remove, using short strokes.

    iPhoto blurs the area under the Retouch tool's pointer, blending it with the surrounding colors and textures.

3. Press and release Control to toggle between the "before" (**Figure 4.30**) and "after" (**Figure 4.31**) views of your photo.

4. When you're done, click the Retouch button again.

✔ Tips

■ For additional accuracy, zoom in first.

■ Retouch is not a panacea. It can fix small blemishes but will make large ones look like dust bunnies. It works best on skin.

■ Avoid the Retouch tool on sharp color edges, such as between Tristan's hands and his blue shirt. When the Retouch tool hits edges, it smears the sharp lines. Luckily, you can always undo mistakes.

■ Retouch can be good for taking the flash shine off eyes or other reflective surfaces, and it's worth a try if the Red-Eye tool fails.

RETOUCHING PHOTOS

Using the Effects Panel

Although the B & W and Sepia commands still exist in the contextual menu, their buttons have been replaced in iPhoto 6 by the Effects panel, which provides single-click access to a variety of different effects.

To use the Effects panel:

1. Click the Effects button.

   iPhoto opens the translucent Effects panel (**Figure 4.32**; opposite page).

2. Click a button in the Effects panel to apply the associated effect to the current photo.

✔ Tips

- For all the buttons other than B & W, Sepia, and Original, clicking the button multiple times applies the effect again and again. I recommend you do this because you can achieve some really interesting results with multiple applications of an effect.

- You can combine effects simply by clicking multiple buttons. For instance, make a photo look old by clicking Antique and Vignette a few times.

- Click the Original button to revert to the original look of the photo; this is a fast way to undo a number of changes in the Effects panel.

- Edge Blur, combined with cropping, can be a good way to focus attention on the subject of the photo.

Effect Descriptions

Since the Effects panel does such a good job of showing what the result of clicking its buttons will be, refer to **Figure 4.32** on the opposite page for examples.

- **B & W:** Makes the photo black-and-white. There's no point in clicking it more than once.

- **Sepia:** Makes the photo sepia-toned, exactly as the Sepia command in the contextual menu does. There's no point in clicking it more than once.

- **Antique:** Desaturates the color in the photo and gives it a sepia tint for that old-time look. Click it multiple times to reduce the color saturation and replace more of the color with sepia.

- **Fade Color:** Fades the color in the photo, exactly like moving to the Saturation slider in the Adjust panel to the left. Click it repeatedly to remove all color.

- **Original:** Returns the photo to its original look with a single click.

- **Boost Color:** Increases the color saturation in the photo, exactly like moving to the Saturation slider in the Adjust panel to the right. Click it multiple times to make the photo's color truly shocking.

- **Matte:** Applies a white oval mask around the photo. Click it multiple times to increase the size of the mask, obscuring more of the picture.

- **Vignette:** Exactly like Matte, except its mask is black, instead of white.

- **Edge Blur:** Exactly like Matte, except its mask consists of blurred pixels in the photo, instead of plain white.

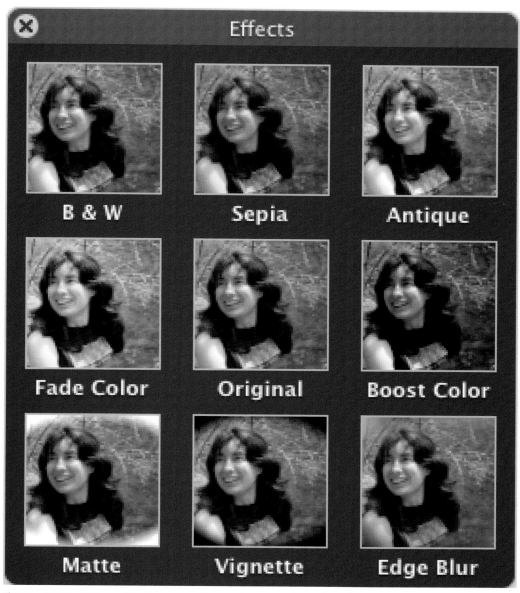

Figure 4.32 iPhoto 6's new Effect's panel enables you to apply a wide variety of effects to your photos.

Using the Adjust Panel

The Adjust panel enables you to modify photos in all sorts of useful ways. Although using the Adjust panel can be a fair amount of effort, it's usually worth the results.

To use the Adjust panel:

1. Click the Adjust button, or (Control)-click the image and choose Adjust from the contextual menu.

   iPhoto opens the translucent Adjust panel (**Figure 4.33**).

2. Drag the various sliders until the photo looks the way you want (see the following pages in this chapter for details).

✔ Tips

- There is no "right" way to adjust a given photo other than what looks good to you!

- Click the icons at either end of a slider to nudge the slider in one-point increments.

- Pressing (Control) to toggle between the "before" and "after" views shows you the view before you started working with the Adjust panel, not in between the use of each individual slider, so it doesn't help discern the effect of a given slider.

- It's difficult to center a slider, so if you decide you don't like the effect of one, use Undo immediately rather than trying to reset it to the middle manually.

- Click Reset Sliders to reset all the sliders to the middle.

- Click the X button in the upper left of the Adjust panel to close it, but note that there's no need to do so unless you want to avoid the screen clutter.

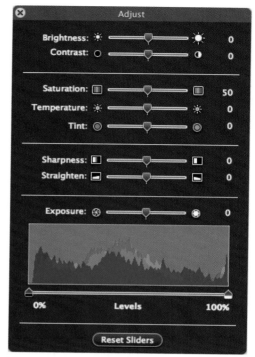

Figure 4.33 Use the sliders in the Adjust panel to modify the brightness and contrast, color levels, sharpness, exposure, and more.

Color Reproduction

I can't be certain of how the colors in the example photos in the rest of this chapter will reproduce onto paper, so if my comments about what a photo looks like and how I adjusted it seem off, rest assured that I'm describing what I see on my screen! For more details, see "Understanding Color Management" in Appendix A, "Deep Background."

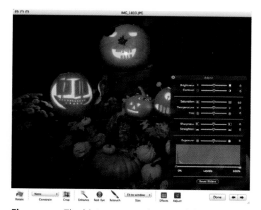

Figure 4.34 The histogram tends toward the left in dark photos like this one of Halloween pumpkins.

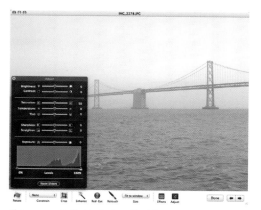

Figure 4.35 In light photos, the histogram moves to the right, as in this bridge picture.

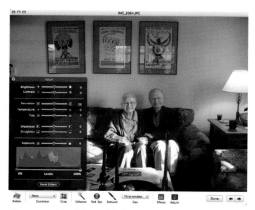

Figure 4.36 In this well-balanced photo, the histogram is fairly balanced, neither too far right nor left.

Understanding the Levels Histogram

Since all the sliders (except the oddly placed Straighten) affect the Levels histogram, it's helpful to understand what it's telling you.

A histogram is a bar chart with each horizontal bar representing a brightness value (0 equals black, and 100 equals white) and the height of each bar representing the proportionate distribution of pixels with that brightness value. iPhoto's Levels histogram contains three separate graphs, one each for red, blue, and green. I like to think of them as mountain ranges.

So, if a picture has a lot of blue in it, the blue mountain range will probably be large, and will likely be on the right side (since it's the brightest color). The red and green mountain ranges may also be large, but will likely be further to the left, since they're being used combinatorially to provide the exact shade of blue that you see.

The histogram for a too-dark photo will be pushed over to the left (**Figure 4.34**) and one that's too light will be pushed to the right (**Figure 4.35**). In general, a good photo has a balanced histogram, with roughly equal areas shown on either side of the midpoint (**Figure 4.36**). Balancing the histogram is a suggestion, not a rule, but keep it in mind when you're editing.

Every photo's histogram looks different, and every change you make to the contents of the image will change the histogram in some way, since it's merely another way of representing the content of the photo.

As we look at each of the Adjust controls, I'll explain what each does to the histogram so you can use them effectively to create balanced, attractive photos.

Adjusting Brightness

If a photo is too dark or too light for your intended purpose, you may be able to improve it by using the Brightness slider (although the Exposure slider works better).

To adjust the brightness of a photo:

◆ In the Adjust panel, drag the Brightness slider to the left to make a photo darker or the right to make it lighter.

What the Brightness slider does:

In **Figure 4.37**, you can see a photo of trees reflected in an ice-covered pond. It was a gray day, and the photo came out quite light. In **Figure 4.38**, I've reduced the brightness significantly, which brings out the reflections of the tree branches.

Note how the mountain ranges in the histogram have slid to the left; the Brightness slider essentially slides the mountain ranges to the left and right within the histogram without changing their size or shape. That's because the histogram is a measure of brightness; the slider just changes which pixels appear in which brightness positions.

✔ Tips

■ Remember that different levels of brightness look different on different monitors, in printouts, and in prints you order.

■ The Exposure slider provides a similar effect; however, it changes brightness without massively overexposing or underexposing the image. The advantage of the Exposure slider is that it doesn't change the black and white points of the photo, as does the rather crude Brightness slider. (In fact, brightness controls in most programs are quite blunt instruments; iPhoto isn't unusual in this respect.) See "Adjusting Exposure," later in this chapter, for a better approach.

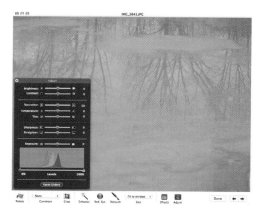

Figure 4.37 This photo is simply too bright, and although the subject matter is interesting, without help it won't be a particularly good picture.

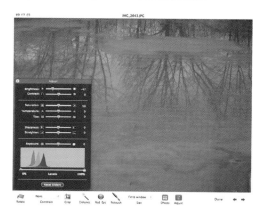

Figure 4.38 With the brightness reduced, the reflected trees show up much better, rescuing an otherwise hopeless photo.

What Else Would I Do?

This photo, because it's not terribly realistic (so people don't have expectations of how it should look), would also benefit from an increase in contrast and saturation, as well as a bump up in sharpness to bring out the details of the reflections and snow. And honestly, I'd even consider (on a duplicate) changing its colors radically with the Temperature and Tint sliders.

ADJUSTING BRIGHTNESS

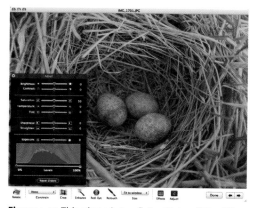

Figure 4.39 This photo is too flat, with too little difference between the dark and light areas of the nest.

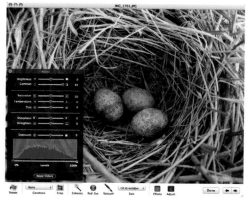

Figure 4.40 By increasing the contrast, I made the individual twigs in the nest stand out, giving the picture more depth and detail.

What Else Would I Do?

Since this photo has a lot of detail in it, I'd definitely increase the sharpness to define the edges of the twigs further, and I'd probably warm up the temperature a bit (see "Adjusting Temperature," later in this chapter). Lastly, I'd decrease the exposure just slightly to darken it up a touch.

Adjusting Contrast

The contrast of a photo is the difference between the darkest and lightest areas of a photo. With too much contrast, you end up with overly dark and bright areas; with too little contrast, your photo appears flat.

To adjust the contrast of a photo:

◆ In the Adjust panel, drag the Contrast slider to the left to decrease the contrast or the right to increase the contrast.

What the Contrast slider does:

In **Figure 4.39**, the photo of eggs in a nest was quite flat, with little difference between the light and dark areas of the scene. In **Figure 4.40**, I've increased the contrast significantly to give the photo more depth and vibrancy. Note that most photos are unlikely to need significant contrast adjustments; usually a little nudge will be all you need.

Note how the mountain ranges in the histogram have been flattened and spread out by the increase in contrast. If I had reduced contrast, the mountain ranges would have been squished in and up instead. Put another way, increasing contrast distributes the pixels in the photo over a greater range of brightness values, whereas reducing the contrast increases the number of pixels within a small range.

✔ Tip

■ Like the Brightness slider, though to a lesser extent, the Contrast slider is an unsophisticated tool. You're better off using the black and white point sliders in the Levels histogram to set which colors should be considered pure black and pure white, which has essentially the same effect as using the Contrast slider. For details, see "Adjusting Black and White Points," later in this chapter.

Adjusting Saturation

The saturation of a photo is a measure of how intense the colors are. Highly saturated colors are said to be deep, vivid, or rich, whereas desaturated colors (think pastels) are often thought of as being dull, weak, or washed out.

To adjust the saturation of a photo:

◆ In the Adjust panel, drag the Saturation slider to the left to make the colors weaker or the right to make them more intense.

What the Saturation slider does:

This example is a bit subtle, but in essence, **Figure 4.41**, taken of coastal wetlands and salt flats while landing at the San Francisco International Airport, was fairly light and washed out. By increasing the color saturation, as in **Figure 4.42**, I've made a fairly dull photo far more vivid and arresting. Most photos are unlikely to need significant saturation adjustments.

When you increase saturation, the mountain ranges move to the left (the picture gets a little darker) and they tend to separate, since each color has more independent brightness values (the reds are redder, the greens are greener, and the blues are bluer).

If you decrease saturation, the mountain ranges move to the right (the picture gets lighter) and overlap more. Decreasing the saturation entirely causes the mountain ranges to overlap entirely, giving you a monochrome image.

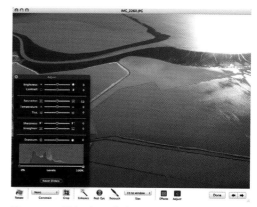

Figure 4.41 This photo feels washed out thanks to the bright light and shooting through a plane window.

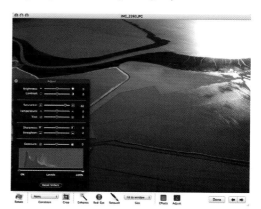

Figure 4.42 Bumping up the saturation brings up the colors significantly, making it look much more vivid (and the way I remember it looking in real life).

What Else Would I Do?

Although increasing the saturation is the main way I'd improve this photo, I would also lower the exposure slightly and move the black point up a bit to compensate for the bright sun reflecting off the water.

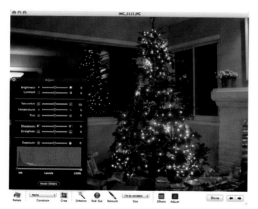

Figure 4.43 The strong incandescent light in this photo resulted in an overly yellow cast.

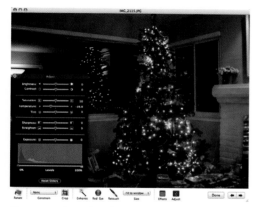

Figure 4.44 Lowering the temperature compensated for the extra yellow, bringing the photo back down to a more neutral color.

What Else Would I Do?

Since there is a lot of detail in the Christmas tree, I'd also increase the sharpness to bring out the edges of the needles, lights, and ornaments.

Adjusting Temperature

The temperature of a photo refers to your perception of which wavelengths of light illuminate the scene in a photo. That's a roundabout way of saying that the Temperature slider lets you adjust the colors of a photo from cool (bluish) to warm (yellowish).

To adjust the temperature of a photo:

◆ In the Adjust panel, drag the Temperature slider to the left to make the colors cooler and bluer or the right to make them warmer and more yellow.

What the Temperature slider does:

Figure 4.43 is a picture of a Christmas tree taken indoors with incandescent light, which resulted in too-warm tones. By decreasing the temperature a bit in **Figure 4.44**, I've compensated for the overly yellow cast.

When you decrease the temperature, as I've done here, the green mountain range stays put, the blue mountain range moves to the right to increase the amount of blue in the photo, and the red mountain range moves to the left to decrease the amount of red. If you increase temperature, the red mountain range move to the right to increase the yellow and the blue mountain range moves to the left to decrease the amount of blue.

✔ Tip

■ Daylight is considered neutral, so it's most likely you'll need to adjust the temperature of artificially lit photos. Indoor lighting may give a yellow cast to your photos, whereas flash lighting may provide a bluish cast.

Adjusting Tint

Whereas the Temperature slider helps you adjust the blue and yellow colors in a photo, the Tint slider modifies the magenta and green colors in a photo.

To adjust the tint of a photo:

◆ In the Adjust panel, drag the Tint slider to the left to add magenta to the photo or to the right to add green.

What the Tint slider does:

Check out **Figure 4.45**, a picture of my aunt and uncle at my sister's wedding in Hawaii. For whatever reason, their skin tones ended up a bit too pink. By moving the Tint slider slightly to the right in **Figure 4.46**, I've added just a touch of green, which gives them more normal skin tones.

As you would expect, moving the Tint slider toward the right moves the green mountain to the right as well, and slides both the red and blue mountain ranges to the left, increasing the amount of green and decreasing the amount of magenta (since magenta is composed of both red and blue). Moving the Tint slider to the left has the opposite effect. Also, note that the mountain ranges also change in size and shape somewhat.

✔ Tip

■ To adjust tint and temperature quickly, (Cmd)-click on a portion of the photo you think should be a light gray (a shadow on a white shirt, or the white of an eye), but which is not overexposed. This shortcut is difficult to control and is best used as a starting point from which you'll tweak the Tint and Temperature sliders more carefully by hand.

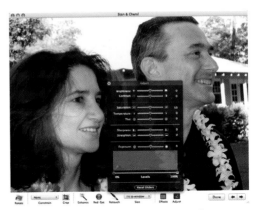

Figure 4.45 The skin tones in this picture of my aunt and uncle were a little too pink.

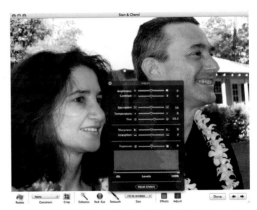

Figure 4.46 Tweaking the Tint slider slightly toward the green side gave them more normal skin tones.

What Else Would I Do?

Overall, this picture doesn't need much more help, though I might bump up the sharpness a bit to increase the definition of fine details in the photo.

ADJUSTING TINT

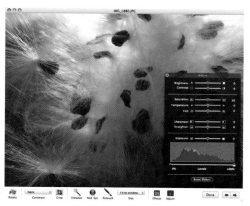

Figure 4.47 The fine detail in the fluff suffers a bit from too much blur.

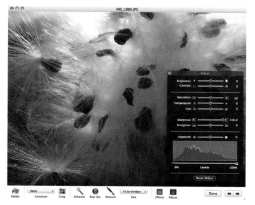

Figure 4.48 Radically increasing the sharpness brought out the fine edge detail in the fluff.

What Else Would I Do?

A small increase in contrast also helped improve this photo slightly, though no other adjustments made useful changes.

Adjusting Sharpness

Many photos are slightly blurry due to motion of the subject or the camera. You can use the Sharpen slider to increase the sharpness—the contrast between adjacent pixels—and thus sharpen the perceived focus of the photo (sharpening the actual focus can be done only with the camera lens, and it's too late for that).

To adjust the sharpness of a photo:

◆ In the Adjust panel, drag the Sharpness slider to the right to increase the sharpness of the image or to the left to make the photo fuzzier.

What the Sharpness slider does:

The photo in **Figure 4.47** is a picture of the fluff from a milkweed pod. I had good light and managed to hold the camera still, but there was still a little more blur than I would have liked. So I increased the sharpness quite a lot in **Figure 4.48**, and you can see that the result is more sharply defined edges on the milkweed fluff. I find that many photos are similarly improved by increased sharpness.

It's a little hard to predict exactly what changes to the sharpness will do to the histogram's mountain ranges, but in general, increasing the sharpness tends to "erode" them away, making them shorter and wider, whereas decreasing the sharpness makes them taller and narrower.

✔ Tip

■ Be careful when increasing the sharpness on photos that contain a lot of mostly solid colors, since the increased contrast between adjacent pixels will make those previously solid colors appear blotchy.

Straightening Photos

Most of the time, we're pretty good at keeping the horizon level in photos, but every now and then we mess up, as in the picture of a glacier in **Figure 4.49**. Since iPhoto can straighten images with the Straighten slider in the Adjust panel, it was easy to rotate the angle by 1.7 degrees to make it straight, as you can see in **Figure 4.50**.

To adjust the angle of a photo:

◆ In the Adjust panel, drag the Straighten slider to the left to rotate the image clockwise or to the right to rotate the image counter-clockwise, using the yellow grid lines as a reference for true vertical and horizontal.

✔ Tips

■ The Straighten slider actually zooms in on your photo and crops it slightly to keep the edges straight. The white bands on the top and bottom of the photo in **Figure 4.50** are an indication that the cropping has taken place, since the photo is now slightly smaller.

■ You can use the Straighten slider to tweak the angles of photos up to 10 degrees in either direction.

■ If 10 degrees isn't enough (and remember that the greater the angle, the more iPhoto is cropping), save your changes, edit the photo again, and use the Straighten slider one more time.

■ I haven't the foggiest idea why Apple chose to include the Straighten slider in the Adjust panel, since it's completely different from all the other controls and doesn't affect the histogram at all. They probably couldn't think of anywhere else to put it.

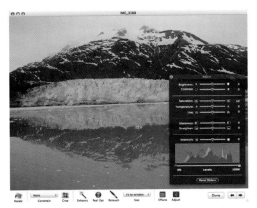

Figure 4.49 I'm going to blame my inability to take a straight photo of a glacier on the rocking boat.

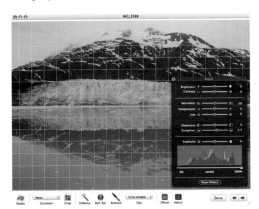

Figure 4.50 Luckily, iPhoto's Straighten slider lets me eliminate the need for the lame excuse.

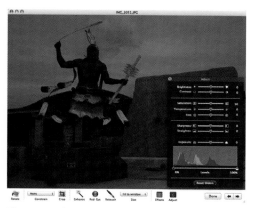

Figure 4.51 This photo is underexposed, although not terribly so.

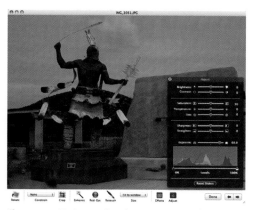

Figure 4.52 By increasing the exposure so the scene appears, I rescued the photo from instant deletion.

What Else Would I Do?

I might increase the saturation and the temperature of this photo slightly, to bump up the terra cotta color of the adobe walls.

Adjusting Exposure

Exposure is the most fundamental aspect of photography, since it refers to the amount of light that strikes the camera's sensor. Most cameras control exposure automatically and do a good job, but they can be fooled, producing an underexposed (too dark) or overexposed (too light) image. If that happens, you'll want to use iPhoto's Exposure and Levels (discussed on the next page) sliders.

To adjust the exposure of a photo:

◆ In the Adjust panel, drag the Exposure slider to the left to make it seem as though less light hit the camera sensor or to the right to make it seem as though more light hit the camera sensor.

What the Exposure slider does:

The photo of this statue in Santa Fe in **Figure 4.51** is somewhat underexposed, since I took it at dusk. By increasing the exposure in **Figure 4.52**, I've lightened the photo without giving the photo a whitish cast, as would have happened with the Brightness slider.

Increasing exposure squishes the mountain ranges and slides them to the right (and decreasing exposure makes them taller and moves them left), but keeps the end points that define the blackest black and whitest white the same. In contrast, the Brightness slider simply slides the mountain ranges left or right, changing the black and white points and losing pixels that fall off either end of the histogram.

✔ Tip

■ The Exposure slider is roughly equivalent to the gamma slider in Photoshop's Levels histogram.

ADJUSTING EXPOSURE

Adjusting Black and White Points

The Levels slider under the histogram gives you two independent controls for adjusting the black and white points, which define the pixels that should be considered pure black and those that should be considered pure white.

To adjust the black and white points of a photo:

◆ In the Adjust panel, drag the left Levels slider to the right to set the black point.

◆ Drag the right Levels slider to the left to set the white point.

What the Levels sliders do:

If, when you look at a photo's histogram, you see a blank space between the end of the mountain ranges and the black or white points (**Figure 4.53**), it's often safe to move those sliders toward the middle of the histogram, which is conceptually the same as grabbing the edges of the mountain ranges and pulling them out to the edges of the histogram. In **Figure 4.54**, I've moved the black point to the right to deepen the shadows; it's redefining what was a dark gray as total black. In **Figure 4.55**, I've moved the white point to the left to set a new value for what should be considered white, thus making the water glow a bit.

✔ Tip

■ It's best to use the Exposure and Levels sliders in favor of the Brightness and Contrast sliders. Exposure can increase and decrease brightness without blowing out the image, as would happen with the Brightness slider. And the Levels sliders let you set the black point and the white point independently, which is impossible to do with the Contrast slider.

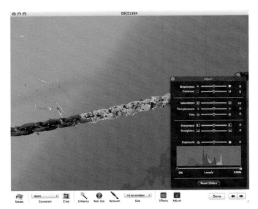

Figure 4.53 All the pixels in this image are huddled together in the middle of the histogram.

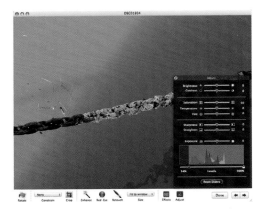

Figure 4.54 By redefining the black point, I give the picture a little more depth and darkness.

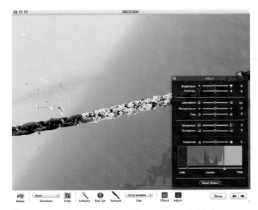

Figure 4.55 Then, resetting the white point brings up the luminosity a bit.

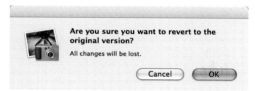

Figure 4.56 To revert to the original version of an image after making a number of edits, select it and choose Revert to Original from the Photos menu. iPhoto warns you that you'll lose all your changes.

Recovering Originals

It turns out that Revert to Original isn't doing anything complicated. When you edit a photo, iPhoto makes a copy of the original in a folder named for the photo's film roll, stored in the Modified folder. As long as this happens, you can recover the original image no matter what edits you make to it.

In fact, this is why Revert to Original works even if you edit a photo in another program—iPhoto starts tracking the original as soon as you double-click the photo. However, don't drag a photo from iPhoto to the Dock icon of another program to edit it; if you do so, iPhoto can't track the changes.

You can locate an original image in the Finder by Control-clicking it and choosing Show File (to find the original if unedited, or the modified version if it has been edited) or Show Original File (to find the original file if the photo has been edited).

Undoing Changes

We all make mistakes, and that's certain to happen on occasion when you're working with your photos too. With digital photos, though, your changes aren't irrevocable.

Ways to undo changes to a photo:

◆ After you've performed an action, to undo just that action, choose Undo from the Edit menu (Cmd Z). Keep choosing Undo to undo earlier actions.

◆ To remove all changes from a photo, select it and choose Revert to Original from the Photos menu, or Control-click the image and choose Revert to Original from the contextual menu.

If you are in edit mode and have made at least one change, iPhoto removes all changes from the photo that were made that session. In any other situation, iPhoto warns that you'll lose all changes to the photo, and swaps in the original image (**Figure 4.56**).

◆ To revert to the original look of a photo while working in the Effects panel, click its Original button.

✔ Tips

■ You can undo changes made in edit mode *only* until you save the changes to that photo.

■ To see what the photo would look like if you were to undo a change, press Control. You must still choose Undo if desired.

■ iPhoto modifies the Undo command in the Edit menu to reflect your last action.

■ Anything you can undo via the Undo command, you can redo via the Redo command in the Edit menu.

UNDOING CHANGES

Editing in Another Program

iPhoto's minimal editing tools are sufficient for most tasks, but for more involved changes to photos, iPhoto lets you turn to another image-editing program.

To set a default external editor:

1. From the iPhoto application menu, choose Preferences (Cmd,) to open the Preferences window. If necessary, click the General tab.

2. From the Edit Photos pop-up menu, choose In Application (**Figure 4.57**).

3. In the Open dialog that appears, choose the desired program.

4. Close the Preferences window.

To edit in an external editor (I):

1. Double-click one or more selected photos. iPhoto launches your selected editing program and opens the photos in it.

2. Make your desired changes, and when you're done, save and close the photos.

To edit in an external editor (II):

1. Select an external editor, but don't set iPhoto to open photos in it by default.

2. Control-click one or more photos and choose Edit in External Editor from the contextual menu (**Figure 4.58**).

✔ Tips

- Revert to Original works on photos edited in another program as long as you open them from within iPhoto (don't drag to the other application to open).

- Click the Full Screen button or Option-double-click to avoid opening a photo in an external editor when that's the default.

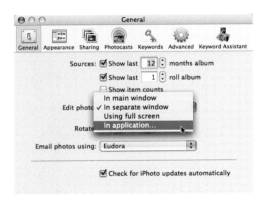

Figure 4.57 To configure iPhoto to use another program for editing photos, choose In Application from the Edit Photos pop-up menu in the General pane of iPhoto's Preferences window.

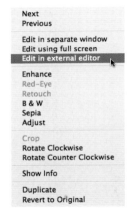

Figure 4.58 To edit a photo in an external editor without switching iPhoto's preferences, Control-click the image and choose Edit in External Editor from the contextual menu.

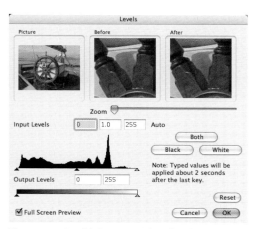

Figure 4.59 GraphicConverter's interface is more technical than iPhoto's, but as with the Levels dialog, it can offer more feedback and control.

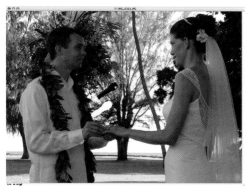

Figure 4.60 GraphicConverter enables you to edit out problematic parts of photos, like this microphone.

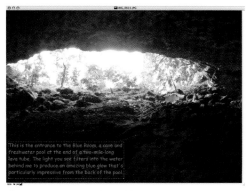

Figure 4.61 You can also add text to photos in GraphicConverter, which is impossible in iPhoto.

Try GraphicConverter

You can use any image-editing program with iPhoto. However, a good one to start with is Lemke Software's GraphicConverter, which costs only $30 shareware, or may already be on your Macintosh for free, since Apple bundles it with many Macs. If you don't have it, you can download a copy from www.lemkesoft.com/en/graphcon.htm.

Reasons you might want GraphicConverter:

◆ Apart from the Red-Eye and Retouch tools, iPhoto restricts you to working only on the entire photo. GraphicConverter provides similar tools for sharpening, adjusting levels, and changing brightness and contrast, but you can apply those to selections, and those selections don't have to be rectangular as they are with iPhoto.

◆ Although GraphicConverter's interface is significantly more technical than iPhoto's, it also offers additional flexibility and control in some places (**Figure 4.59**).

◆ You can not only apply changes to selections, but also delete them and paste or paint in new pixels in place of them, as I'm about to do here to eliminate the microphone sticking out of my brother-in-law's side (**Figure 4.60**).

◆ If you wish to add text to a photo, you can do so quite easily (**Figure 4.61**).

◆ iPhoto supports a relatively small number of file formats for importing and exporting photos, whereas GraphicConverter can import about 190 file formats and export about 79. If you need a photo in an unusual format, you need GraphicConverter.

Try Photoshop Elements

What if you want more power than GraphicConverter offers? Look to the $90 Adobe Photoshop Elements, the baby brother of industry heavyweight Photoshop. Learn more about it at www.adobe.com/ products/photoshopelmac/.

Reasons you might want Photoshop Elements:

◆ Some of Photoshop Elements' tools, like Red-Eye, are more capable than iPhoto's.

◆ Photoshop Elements enables you to select and edit portions of a photo in easier and more powerful ways than is possible in GraphicConverter.

◆ Photoshop Elements offers a helpful set of "recipes," or canned procedures that walk you through fixing photos in common ways. The recipes are useful in their own right and help you learn how to use many tools in Photoshop Elements (**Figure 4.62**).

◆ Whereas editing in the other programs I've mentioned involves changing the actual image, Photoshop Elements lets you create a "layer" (like a sheet of clear plastic over the image) and overlay changes on the layer over the original.

◆ You can use the filters and effects in Photoshop Elements to turn normal photos into amazing images that look like they were painted, embossed, photo-copied, or drawn with charcoal.

◆ You can buy other books that teach you more about Photoshop Elements; I recommend you check out Scott Kelby's *The Photoshop Elements 3 Book for Digital Photographers*. Books about Photoshop also contain many useful techniques that may work in Photoshop Elements.

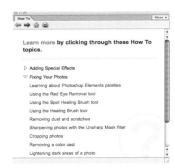

Figure 4.62 Start with the recipes in Photoshop Elements to learn how some of its tools work.

Dealing with Layers

Layers in Photoshop Elements are wonderful, since they let you work on a photo without changing the base image. However, you can't save layers in a JPEG file (likely the original format of your photo), and if you save a photo as a Photoshop file, iPhoto won't see the edited photo. So, when you're sure you're done editing, choose Flatten Image from the Layers menu in Photoshop Elements, and then save the photo with its original name and location. That way, when you return to iPhoto, it will see your changes to the photo, though you lose access to the separate layers for future editing.

If you want to retain layers for multiple editing sessions, follow these steps:

1. Drag a photo from iPhoto to the Photoshop Elements icon in the Dock.

2. Add a layer, but don't make any other changes, so you retain a clean original.

3. Save the photo as a Photoshop file on your Desktop. Close the file.

4. Drag the photo from your Desktop back into iPhoto to re-import it. Delete the copy on your Desktop.

5. From then on, use iPhoto to edit the photo *only* in Photoshop Elements.

SHOWING
PHOTOS ONSCREEN

5

Although there are those for whom a photo isn't real unless it appears on a piece of paper (and iPhoto can satisfy those people too), one of iPhoto's coolest features is its capability to present photos on screen in a wide variety of ways, ranging from slideshows on your Mac and Web-based presentations that anyone can view to customized screen savers and QuickTime movies.

Gone are the days of the carousel projector and a darkened room; now a slideshow involves high-resolution photographs slipping on and off a computer screen, complete with elegant transitions between pictures. But that's only the beginning with iPhoto 6. Your slideshows can take advantage of the Ken Burns Effect, which zooms and pans around photos, turning them from still images to scenes in a movie.

iPhoto's various onscreen presentation tools are not only the best way to display your photographs to friends and relatives, but also the best way for you to experience your own photos, whether through a constantly changing Desktop picture or a slideshow-based screen saver that kicks in whenever your Mac is idle.

Read on for instructions and advice on how to present your photos on screen!

Types of Slideshows

Like iPhoto 5, iPhoto 6 offers two types of slideshows, which I call "basic" slideshows and "saved" slideshows.

About basic slideshows:

Basic slideshows are akin to the slideshow feature in earlier versions of iPhoto. They're simple to use and offer a basic set of options that apply equally to all slides.

Use basic slideshows when you want to show someone a set of photos quickly, without any fuss or bother. Basic slideshows can also be useful for reviewing just-taken photos and culling the lousy shots.

Lastly, you can use *only* basic slideshows when viewing images from a shared iPhoto Library over the network.

About saved slideshows:

Saved slideshows appear in the Source pane like albums, books, cards, and calendars, and any changes you make to them are saved for the future. You can organize saved slideshows in folders, duplicate them to experiment with different approaches, and export them to QuickTime movies.

Use saved slideshows when you want to put some effort into making a slideshow as visually impressive as possible. You can add and remove individual photos from the slideshow, apply temporary effects to photos during the slideshow, change the time each slide appears on screen, adjust the Ken Burns Effect for each slide, set the transition between any two slides, and more.

What's particularly neat about saved slideshows is that they're created with default settings, so you can customize them as much or as little as you like.

Book Slideshows

New in iPhoto 6 are "book slideshows." which are almost identical to basic slideshows. When in book mode, you can click the Play button at the right end of the toolbar to display the standard Slideshow dialog; clicking Play in it displays each page in the book in a slideshow format. The only difference between a book slideshow and a basic slideshow (other than showing a book page instead of a single photo at a time) is that a number of the options in the Slideshow dialog aren't available for book slideshows because they don't make sense in the context of a book page. In particular, you cannot scale photos; turn on the Ken Burns Effect; or show titles, ratings, or controls.

Slideshow Tools Overview

When you select a saved slideshow in the Source pane, iPhoto displays a new set of tools for customizing your slideshow (**Figure 5.1**).

Thumbnails of the photos in the slideshow, in order. Click one to display it. Command- or Shift-click to select multiple photos.

The current photo on which you're working.

Source pane. Create and work with saved slideshows here.

Saved slideshow in the Source pane.

Click to open a panel that lets you adjust the slide duration, transition, and transition speed.

Click to open the default slideshow settings dialog.

Click to create a saved slideshow from the selected photos.

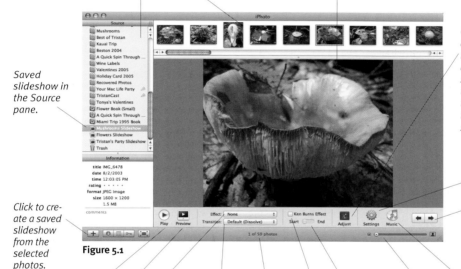

Figure 5.1

Click to move back and forward through slides.

Click to open the music settings dialog.

Click to play the saved slideshow.

Click to preview a few frames of the slideshow in the display pane; click again to stop the preview.

Choose an effect (black-and-white or sepia) to apply to the currently selected photo(s).

Choose a transition to assign to the currently selected photo(s).

Toggle between the starting point (Start) and the finishing point (End) for manual overrides of the Ken Burns Effect.

Use the size slider to set the start and end magnifications for the Ken Burns Effect.

The number of photos in the slideshow (50).

Select to override the default Ken Burns Effect settings for the selected photo(s).

Setting Up Basic Slideshows

A basic slideshow is the easiest way to display your photos while at your computer. For playing music during your slideshow, iPhoto integrates with Apple's iTunes music software.

To configure a basic slideshow:

1. In organize mode, select one or more photos or albums, and click the triangular Play button at the right end of the toolbar (the bottom right of **Figure 5.2**).

   iPhoto opens the Slideshow dialog. Click the Settings tab (**Figure 5.2**).

2. Set the transition type, direction (by clicking the appropriate arrow in the round direction controller), and speed.

3. Enter the length of time you want each photo to remain on the screen, and select any desired additional display options.

4. If you want music to play during your slideshow, see "Assigning Music to Slideshows," on the next page.

5. Click Save Settings or click Play.

✔ Tips

■ Save Settings records your settings for future uses of basic slideshows.

■ I recommend use of the Ken Burns Effect; it significantly improves most slideshows.

■ Scale Photos to Fill Screen causes a slideshow to display only the center of portrait-orientation photos but eliminates black bands on the sides.

■ Show Slideshow Controls and Show My Ratings aren't necessary, since you can display the slideshow controls, which include the rating, just by moving the pointer during the slideshow.

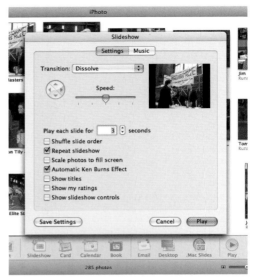

Figure 5.2 Configure how your slideshow appears using the Settings pane of the Slideshow dialog.

Arranging Basic Slideshows

Basic slideshows start with the image in the upper-left position of the selection or the album. So if you want to display the pictures in the reverse order, choose either Ascending or Descending (whichever isn't currently selected) from the Sort Photos submenu of the View menu. Of course, whatever sort is in effect applies, so you can change the order by changing to a different sort too.

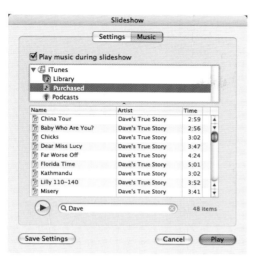

Figure 5.3 Pick either an entire playlist or a song to play during your slideshow.

Assigning Music to Slideshows

Unless you plan to narrate your slideshow, playing carefully selected songs from your iTunes Library during the slideshow can enhance the presentation.

To select music:

1. For saved slideshows, click the Music button to open the Music Settings dialog; for basic slideshows, click the Music tab in the Slideshow dialog.

2. Select Play Music During Slideshow.

3. Either select a playlist from the list above the songs or a song from the song list (**Figure 5.3**).

✔ Tips

- You cannot select multiple songs at once. Until Apple addresses this limitation, the only way to play multiple songs is to select an entire playlist (select the playlist and *don't* select any songs in it).

- To search for a song, enter the first few characters in its name or the artist's name in the Search field. iPhoto narrows the list as you type. Click the X button to clear the Search field and expand the list.

- To sort the list of songs, click the header of the Song, Artist, or Time column; sorting by time makes it easier to match the music to your slideshow's length.

- Click the triangular Play button to play the selected song; click it again to stop. You can also double-click a song to play it.

- If iPhoto doesn't pick up the sort order of a playlist from iTunes correctly, quit iTunes.

More Slideshow Music

iPhoto can play any MP3 or AAC file you have in iTunes, along with AIFF and WAV files. You can create MP3 and AAC files from your audio CD collection in iTunes, or you can download (legally!) MP3 files from the Internet; search with Google (www.google.com).

Depending on your Mac and your music skills, you may be able to use Apple's GarageBand software to create instrumental tracks for playing during slideshows. GarageBand comes with new Macs and is included in the iLife '06 suite along with iPhoto.

99

Creating and Deleting Saved Slideshows

Basic slideshow are easy, but for more control over your slideshow's presentation, create a saved slideshow instead. Saved slideshows are also ideal if you plan to show the same slideshow on multiple occasions.

To create a saved slideshow (I):

◆ Select one or more photos or albums, and click the Slideshow button underneath the display pane.

iPhoto creates a new saved slideshow in the Source pane and displays the slideshow tools under the display pane (**Figure 5.4**).

To create a saved slideshow (II):

1. Select one or more photos or albums, and click the + button underneath the Source pane.

2. In the dialog that appears, choose Slideshow from the New pop-up menu and enter a name for the slideshow in the Name field (**Figure 5.5**).

iPhoto creates a new saved slideshow in the Source pane and displays the slideshow tools under the display pane.

To delete a saved slideshow:

◆ Select the saved slideshow in the Source pane, press [Delete], and click Delete when iPhoto asks if you're sure. Or just press [Cmd][Delete] to avoid the warning dialog.

◆ Either select the slideshow and choose Delete Slideshow from the Photos menu or [Control]-click it and choose Delete Slideshow from the contextual menu.

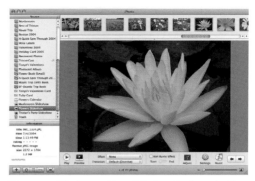

Figure 5.4 iPhoto provides slideshow tools under the display pane only when you select a saved slideshow in the Source pane.

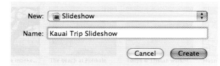

Figure 5.5 When creating a saved slideshow via the + button, iPhoto gives you a chance to change the automatic name it creates based on the currently selected album.

✔ Tips

■ iPhoto automatically names your slideshow after the currently selected album.

■ iPhoto won't let you create a saved slideshow if you select a book, card, calendar, or another saved slideshow instead of an album or individual photos.

■ You can also create a slideshow by duplicating an existing one, which can be helpful if you want to experiment with different settings without losing any work. With the slideshow selected, choose Duplicate from the Photos menu or [Control]-click it and choose Duplicate from the contextual menu.

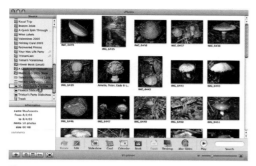

Figure 5.6 Drag photos to a saved slideshow in the Source pane to add them to the slideshow.

Manipulating Slideshow Photos

Whereas basic slideshows merely present the selected photos in the current sort order, saved slideshows give you more control. Use these instructions to add, remove, and rearrange photos in saved slideshows.

To add photos to a slideshow:

◆ Select one or more photos or albums, and drag them to the saved slideshow in the Source pane (**Figure 5.6**).

To remove photos from a slideshow:

◆ Select one or more photos in the scrolling list of photos above the display pane, and press Delete.

To rearrange photos in a slideshow:

◆ Before you create the slideshow, drag the photos into the order you want in an album. iPhoto retains that manual sort order in the saved slideshow.

◆ After you've created a slideshow, drag photos around in the scrolling photo list above the display pane.

✔ Tips

■ Pay attention to the sort order of the album from which you create a slideshow. There's no shame in deleting a saved slideshow and recreating it after sorting the source album properly.

■ In particular, if you're sorting by date in any way, note that you'll probably want to choose Ascending from the View menu's Sort Photos submenu to ensure that your slideshow moves forward in time, rather than backward.

Selecting Default Settings

Although you can change the settings for each slide in a saved slideshow, you can save effort by ensuring that your defaults are set the way you want to start. Click the Settings button to bring up the settings dialog, which looks much like the Slideshow dialog used for basic slideshows (**Figure 5.7**).

To adjust default settings:

1. Set the length of time you want each slide to play in the Play Each Slide For field.

2. Choose a default transition, and set the transition speed and direction, if available, by clicking the appropriate arrow in the round direction controller. iPhoto offers numerous transitions (**Figure 5.8**).

3. Select the desired checkboxes for additional display options.

4. Decide whether you want to repeat the selected music during the slideshow or if you want iPhoto to adjust the length of the slideshow to fit the music.

5. Choose the screen format (Current Display, 4:3 for iDVD and TV, or 16:9 Widescreen) from the Slideshow Format pop-up menu.

6. Click OK when you're done.

✔ Tips

■ Select Scale Photos to Fill Screen to display only the center of portrait-orientation photos and eliminate the black bands on the sides.

■ Checking the Show Slideshow Controls and Show My Ratings checkboxes isn't necessary, since you can display the slideshow controls, which include the rating, just by moving the pointer during the slideshow.

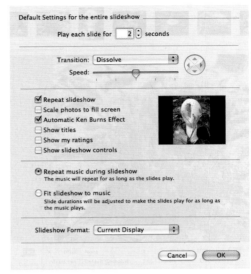

Figure 5.7 Click the Settings button for a saved slideshow to set defaults.

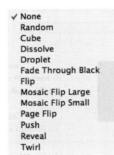

Figure 5.8 iPhoto provides a wide variety of transitions, but I recommend using relatively few per slideshow to avoid visual over-stimulation.

Music for Saved Slideshows

To select music for playing during saved slideshows, follow the instructions given a few pages earlier in "Assigning Music to Slideshows."

Since a saved slideshow is likely to be longer and more carefully arranged than a basic slideshow, you may wish to put the effort into creating a playlist in iTunes for it.

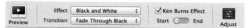

Figure 5.9 Use the controls in slideshow mode to customize the way each photo displays in the slideshow.

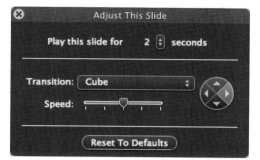

Figure 5.10 Use the Adjust This Slide window's controls to override default settings for slide duration and transition type, direction, and speed.

Duration Locked?

If you find yourself unable to change the amount of time a slide will stay on screen, the reason is likely that you selected Fit Slideshow to Music in the Settings dialog. Since iPhoto has to calculate the length of time to display each photo when that checkbox is selected, it prevents you from changing the slide durations.

Customizing Slides

The last few pages have helped you get ready; now it's time to customize each slide. Remember that each of these actions is optional!

To customize slides:

1. Select the first slide in the scrolling list above the display pane.

2. Choose an effect to apply to the photo from the Effect pop-up menu. See "Editing Slide Photos" on the next page for more information.

3. To override the default transition, choose a different transition from the Transition pop-up menu (**Figure 5.9**).

4. To override the default slide duration, click the Adjust button, and click the up or down triangle buttons to increase or decrease the slide duration. You can also override the default transition type, direction, and speed here (**Figure 5.10**).

5. If you're using the Ken Burns Effect, use the Start/End switch along with the size slider to control the effect. See "Configuring the Ken Burns Effect," later in this chapter.

6. To see how your changes look, click the Preview button to preview the current and next slides in the display pane.

7. Select the next photo by pressing ⇥ (the right arrow key), clicking the right arrow button, or clicking the photo in the scrolling list. Then repeat steps 2–7 until you've customized each slide as desired.

✔ Tip

- You can access all the slideshow tools by [Control]-clicking anywhere in the display pane and choosing the desired command from the contextual menu.

Editing Slide Photos

You will most likely have edited your photos before you create a slideshow, but if not, you can do so while customizing your slides. Some edits must be permanent; others don't have to be.

To edit slide photos permanently:

1. Double-click the photo that's showing in the display pane to switch to edit mode.

2. Make whatever changes you wish, and when you're done, click the Done button to return to your slideshow.

To edit slide photos temporarily:

You can make several types of temporary edits that iPhoto applies to the photo only in the saved slideshow. These changes do not affect the original photo in any way.

◆ Choose either Black and White or Sepia from the Effect pop-up menu to render the photo either black-and-white or sepia.

◆ If you aren't using the Ken Burns Effect (it's off in the settings dialog and for the current slide), you can use the size slider to zoom in on the photo.

◆ If you zoom in on a slide, you can drag the photo to set what portion of the zoomed photo appears.

✔ Tips

■ If the photo is rotated incorrectly, fix it without entering edit mode by choosing Rotate Clockwise (Cmd R) or Rotate Counter Clockwise (Cmd Option R) from the Photos menu.

■ Use temporary edits when possible unless you want the changes to apply everywhere that photo is used (books, prints, and so on).

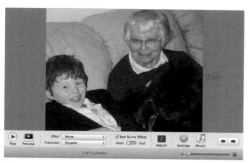

Figure 5.11 For my starting point on this slide, I've zoomed slightly so you can see both Tristan and my grandmother Helen in the frame.

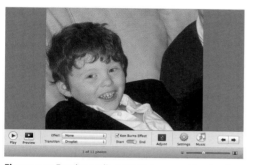

Figure 5.12 For the ending point, I zoomed in about a third of the way and panned so the frame focuses on Tristan's face.

Manual Configuration Necessary for Exported QuickTime Movies

The Automatic Ken Burns Effect generally works very well, but note that it is random, which means that it won't necessarily be the same on any two playings of the same slideshow. As a result, if you're particular about the final slideshow, and particularly if you're saving the slideshow as a QuickTime movie, you should set the Ken Burns Effect manually for each slide. Otherwise, you simply won't know how it will work on any given playing of the slideshow.

Configuring the Ken Burns Effect

In most cases, Apple's setting for Automatic Ken Burns Effect will provide a completely acceptable result. However, if you wish to zoom further, change the zoom direction, or even turn on the Ken Burns Effect only for a particular slide, you can do so.

To configure the Ken Burns Effect:

1. In a saved slideshow, select the Ken Burns Effect checkbox.

2. Click the Start end of the toggle switch.

3. Using the size slider, zoom to the size at which you want the photo to appear first (**Figure 5.11**).

4. Drag the photo in the display pane so the starting view is showing.

5. Click the End side of the toggle switch.

6. Using the size slider, zoom to the size at which you want the photo to fade out.

7. Drag the photo in the display pane so the appropriate part is showing (**Figure 5.12**).

8. Click the Preview button to see if your settings work as desired.

9. Select the next photo and repeat steps 1–9.

✔ Tips

- Increase the slide duration to slow down the Ken Burns Effect, and decrease the slide duration to speed up the Ken Burns Effect.

- Think carefully about whether it makes more sense to zoom in on the photo or to zoom out of the photo, given each particular picture.

Controlling Slideshows

Configuring slideshows is easy, but controlling them while they run is even easier. Just move the pointer during a slideshow to show the hidden slideshow controls.

To run a saved slideshow:

1. Select the slideshow in the Source pane.

2. Click the Play button.

To control a slideshow:

◆ To pause and restart the slideshow, click the Play/Pause button in the slideshow controls or press [Spacebar].

◆ To move back and forth between slides, whether or not the slideshow is paused, click the left or right arrow button in the slideshow controls or press either [←] (the left arrow key) or [→] (the right arrow key).

◆ Press [↑] (the up arrow key) to speed up the slide display time by one second per slide per keypress; press [↓] (the down arrow key) to slow it down by one second per slide per keypress.

◆ To stop the slideshow, press any alphanumeric key or click the mouse.

✔ Tips

■ The slideshow controls are a great help, but note that keyboard shortcuts for rotating, rating, and deleting photos also work during a slideshow, whether or not slideshow controls are showing.

■ If no photos are selected for a basic slideshow, iPhoto shows all the photos in the current album.

Slideshow Advice

Although setting up and playing slideshows is easy, you can produce better results by keeping these tips in mind:

◆ To avoid black edges (primarily with portrait-orientation photos) on monitors that don't use a 4 x 3 aspect ratio (such as most of Apple's flat-panel displays), either zoom in on photos or set the Scale Photos to Fill Screen option.

◆ Avoid using images smaller than your screen (in pixels), since they will look jaggy when iPhoto scales them to fit.

◆ If you really want to show small images, consider pasting them onto a larger background in a graphics program to increase their size and avoid iPhoto's scaling.

◆ Remember that Macs can drive TVs via an S-video cable (you may have to buy it or an adapter separately). If you have a huge television handy, why not use that for a slideshow?

◆ Another way of running a slideshow on a TV is to copy selected photos to your digital camera's memory card via a card reader and then display them via the camera, using its TV cable. Make sure to name the photos as your camera does and put them in the same location as the camera does to fool your camera into displaying them.

◆ If you're playing the same slideshow continuously (at a party, for instance), select a large iTunes playlist to avoid repeating music.

◆ If you have two monitors, slideshows appear on the one containing the iPhoto window.

CONTROLLING SLIDESHOWS

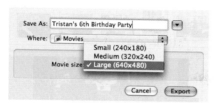

Figure 5.13 In the Export dialog, name your movie, choose a destination folder, and choose how large you want the movie to be.

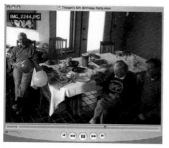

Figure 5.14 To view your movie, double-click it in the Finder to open it in QuickTime Player.

Exporting Photos to QuickTime

There's another quick and dirty way to create a QuickTime movie, though the results lack the Ken Burns Effect and any transitions you've set.

1. Select the photos you wish to export, and choose Export from the File menu ([Cmd][Shift][E]).

2. In the Export Photos dialog, click the QuickTime tab.

3. Enter the maximum width and height for the images, a slide duration, and select a background color.

4. To include the music associated with basic slideshows, select Add Currently Selected Music to Movie.

5. Click Export, name your movie in the Save dialog, choose a destination for it, and click OK to build the movie.

Exporting Slideshows to QuickTime Movies

iPhoto slideshows are great if people can gather at your computer, but iPhoto's QuickTime movie export is the easiest way—much easier than iMovie or iDVD—to create a slideshow you can post on a Web page or send to others in email or on CD.

To export a slideshow to a QuickTime movie:

1. Select the saved slideshow you wish to export.

2. Choose Export from the File menu ([Cmd][Shift][E]).
   iPhoto displays the Export dialog.

3. Name your movie in the Save As field, choose a destination from the Where pop-up menu, and choose how large you want the movie to be from the Movie Size pop-up menu (**Figure 5.13**).

4. Click Export to build the movie.

5. Switch to the Finder, locate your movie, and double-click it to see the results in QuickTime Player (**Figure 5.14**).

✔ Tips

- QuickTime movies created in this fashion include the Ken Burns Effect, along with your transitions and slide timing settings.

- If you select Show Titles in the slideshow settings dialog, titles will appear in the QuickTime movie as well; that's not true of ratings or slideshow controls.

- If your movies stop unexpectedly, try changing the transition, slide timing, or Ken Burns Effect for the affected slide.

- If you're posting on the Web, QuickTime Pro (see next page) will help you shrink your movie to a more palatable size.

Distributing QuickTime Movies

QuickTime movies can be an excellent way to distribute slideshows.

Ways to distribute QuickTime movies:

◆ Copy the full-size movie to a CD-R.

◆ Send the movie via email, but be sensitive about the size of movies. For movies larger than 5 MB, try YouSendIt.com at `www.yousendit.com`.

◆ If you have FTP or Web space available with your Internet account, upload the movie (perhaps using iWeb) and send people the link. If you're a .Mac member, you can upload the movie to your iDisk's Public folder for others to download.

◆ If you're a .Mac member, copy the movie to your iDisk's Movies folder and use the HomePage Web publishing tool to make a movie page. Unfortunately, this method results in a rather small viewing size.

◆ If you're a .Mac member, you can also copy the movie to your iDisk's Sites folder and send people the link in this form:
`http://homepage.mac.com/membername/moviename.mov`.

With this method, the movie plays at the size you chose in iPhoto, and the movie is hidden from the world (but not secured!).

✔ Tips

■ Using QuickTime 7 Pro (a $29.99 upgrade from the free QuickTime Player; visit `www.apple.com/quicktime/buy/`), you can play movies at full-screen size.

■ QuickTime Pro also lets you make some changes to your movies; see *QuickTime 6 for Macintosh & Windows: Visual QuickStart Guide* for details, or use iMovie instead.

Movies on the Web

To make QuickTime movies smaller for posting on the Web, use these steps. If you don't have or wish to buy QuickTime Pro, stick with the smallest size when exporting from iPhoto.

1. Open your movie in QuickTime Player Pro (you need the Pro version).

2. Choose Export from the File menu.

3. From the Use pop-up menu, choose the settings that best match the Internet connection speed your viewers will be using. You may want to try several of the settings to compare the trade-offs in size and quality.

4. Give your movie a short name that has no spaces (such names are easier to represent in URLs), select a location, and then click Save.

QuickTime for Windows

One of the nice things about QuickTime is that it's available for both the Mac and Windows. Some Windows users don't have QuickTime installed, however, so you may need to tell them how to get it. Send them to `www.apple.com/quicktime/download/` for a free copy.

Audio tab.   Photos tab.

Photo Settings panel.

Preview pane.

Timeline.
Drag clips
here.

Play buttons.

Hide / Show
Photo Settings
button.

Media
button.

Editing
button.

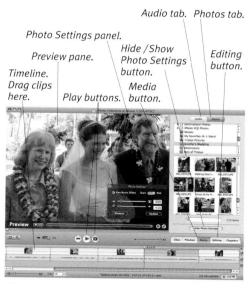

Figure 5.15 Use iMovie to produce and distribute slideshows that are significantly more complex than is possible in iPhoto alone.

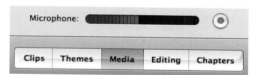

Figure 5.16 To record audio, click the Audio tab, click the round button to the right of the Microphone feedback, and speak. Click that button again to stop.

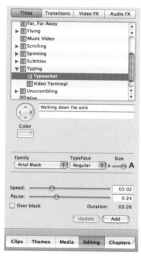

Figure 5.17 To add titles, click the Titles tab and use the controls to type and format your title.

Creating an iMovie Slideshow

What if you want to add captions or narration to a slideshow? Turn to Apple's iMovie video editor. These instructions are an overview; refer to iMovie's help or Jeff Carlson's *iMovie HD 6 & iDVD 6 for Mac OS X: Visual QuickStart Guide* for more details.

To create an iMovie slideshow:

1. In iMovie HD, click the Media button at the bottom of the screen, click the Photos tab at the top, select an album, and then drag the desired photos into the timeline in the order you want (**Figure 5.15**).

2. To record audio, select the first photo, click the Audio tab next to the Photos tab, click the red button next to Microphone, and record your narration, clicking the button again to stop recording (**Figure 5.16**). Repeat for each photo's voice-over.

3. In the timeline, drag the endpoints of each photo to match the length of the associated voice-over clips.

4. For each photo, click Show Photo Settings and adjust the Ken Burns Effect zoom and position (just as you do in iPhoto) for the start and end, clicking the Update button when you're done.

5. Click the Editing button at the bottom of the screen, click the Titles tab at the top, select a title style, and then type your text in the available fields (**Figure 5.17**). Adjust the time the title will display to match the photo clip length, and click the Add button. Repeat for each photo.

6. View your slideshow by positioning the timeline slider all the way to the left and clicking the Play or Play Full Screen buttons.

CREATING AN iMOVIE SLIDESHOW

109

Creating a DVD Slideshow with iDVD

iPhoto can send a set of photos to iDVD 5 to create a DVD slideshow that can be viewed on any TV with a DVD player. You must have a Macintosh with a SuperDrive to burn such a slideshow to disc.

To create a DVD slideshow with iDVD:

1. Select one or more albums or slideshows ([Shift]- or [Cmd]-click to select multiple items), and choose Send to iDVD from the Share menu.

   iPhoto works for a bit, launches iDVD, and shows the iDVD main screen with pre-built iDVD slideshows.

2. Click the Themes button, choose a theme, and customize it with text and images (**Figure 5.18**).

3. To add audio, photos, or video to the main title screen, click the Media button, choose Audio, Photos, or Movies, and drag items to drop zones.

4. Double-click a slideshow icon to switch to a screen where you can add, delete, and rearrange photos (only for the album-based slideshows), plus set a slide transition, select music, and set other options for the slideshow (**Figure 5.19**).

5. As you work, use the Preview button to verify that your slideshows play as you desire. A small player window simulates a DVD remote control.

6. When you're ready, click the Burn button to start burning your DVD.

✔ Tip

■ For even easier creation of DVD slideshows, launch iDVD, click Magic iDVD, and drag albums and music into the Photos area (**Figure 5.20**).

Drop photos in the drop zones.   *Burn button.*   *Theme pane. Click to choose a theme.*

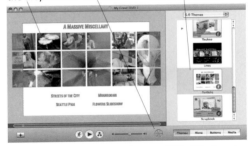

Figure 5.18 Select a theme for your DVD slideshow in the Themes pane; switch to the Media pane to drop photos or movies into the drop zones.

Photo list. Drag to rearrange; press Delete to remove.   *Media pane. Click to switch between audio, photos, and movies.*

Click to preview.   *Click to return to the main screen.*   *Drag photos to the photo list to add them.*

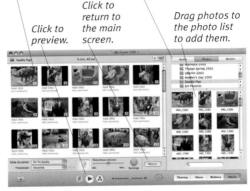

Figure 5.19 Customize your slideshow in iDVD using the Media pane.

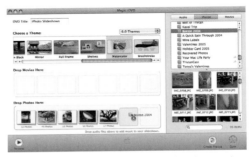

Figure 5.20 Drag photo albums from the Photos tab into iDVD's Magic iDVD screen to create slideshows of them. Switch to the Audio tab and drag songs or playlists onto the same spots to add music to your slideshows.

Making Good DVD Slideshows

It's fairly easy to work with iPhoto and iDVD, but you must still expend some effort when creating a DVD-based slideshow if you want good results. Keep in mind that TV quality will always be lower than the computer screen quality.

◆ Use iDVD's Preview heavily, and run through all your slideshows from start to end before burning.

◆ Landscape photos work better than portrait photos, which have large black borders.

◆ Make sure Always Scale Slides to TV Safe Area is set in iDVD's Slideshow preferences tab (choose Preferences from the iDVD menu and click the Slideshow tab).

◆ Resist the temptation to put as many photos in each slideshow as possible; instead, whittle down the slideshow to the most relevant photos. Very similar photos are boring when seen one after another.

◆ You can choose the duration between slides, but it's generally best to fit the slideshow length to the audio length. But don't pick so much music that individual slides appear for too long.

◆ Be forewarned; it can be hard to find good music for slideshows. Think about the subject and the mood of the photos, and then browse through your iTunes collection to see what songs might fit. It's easier to browse quickly in iTunes than in iDVD.

◆ Click the Motion button (the walking person) to turn off the theme's motion while you work.

iDVD Slideshow Tips

Look to other sources for full instructions on how to use iDVD, such as Jeff Carlson's *iMovie HD 6 & iDVD 6 for Mac OS X: Visual QuickStart Guide* or Jim Heid's *The Macintosh iLife '06,* also from Peachpit Press. That said, these tips should help you use iDVD more effectively.

Tips for using iDVD:

◆ iPhoto sends saved slideshows to iDVD as QuickTime movies, which you can't edit inside iDVD. Remember to choose the 4:3 format for your slideshow!

◆ The 99-photo per slideshow limitation in previous versions of iDVD is now gone.

◆ Save your iDVD project with a good name; it's the disc name in the Finder.

◆ Turn on Show TV Safe Area in the View menu to verify that everything you're doing will fit on a TV screen.

◆ iDVD also lets you choose multiple songs without selecting an entire playlist.

◆ If you select Always Add Original Photos to DVD-ROM Contents in iDVD's Slideshow preferences tab, iDVD also makes the photos available as files on the DVD for use with computers. These are stored as normal files and not in an iPhoto Library folder.

◆ Quit all unnecessary applications when burning; if anything interrupts the burn process, it can ruin your DVD-R disc.

◆ DVD-R discs hold 4.7 GB, so you probably won't be able to fill one with slideshows. To use all the space, add video.

Setting the Desktop Picture

In Mac OS X, you can display a picture on your Desktop, and with iPhoto, putting one (or more, in rotation) of your photos on your Desktop is a matter of just clicking a button.

To set the Desktop picture:

1. Select one or more photos, and click the Desktop button or choose Desktop from the Share menu (**Figure 5.21**).

   If you selected only one photo, iPhoto immediately changes the picture on your Desktop (**Figure 5.22**).

   If you selected multiple photos, iPhoto opens the Desktop & Screen Saver preference pane (**Figure 5.23**).

2. If you selected multiple photos, choose how you want the images to appear on the Desktop.

✔ Tips

■ You can also display the photos in an iPhoto album on your Desktop by selecting the album in the folder list in the Desktop & Screen Saver preference pane's Desktop tab. (Note that rotation among photos doesn't work within albums.)

■ If the picture is in landscape orientation, iPhoto scales the photo to make it fit.

■ If the photo is in portrait orientation, iPhoto takes a landscape chunk out of the middle to display on the Desktop. Stick with photos in landscape orientation, or crop them appropriately first.

■ iPhoto can put a picture on only one monitor. To put a picture on the second monitor, open the Desktop & Screen Saver preference pane and select the iPhoto Selection folder to rotate through the same photos on the second monitor.

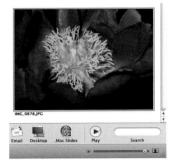

Figure 5.21 Click the Desktop button to set the selected photo as your Desktop picture.

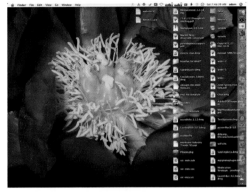

Figure 5.22 With a single click, you can put the photo you have selected in iPhoto on your Desktop.

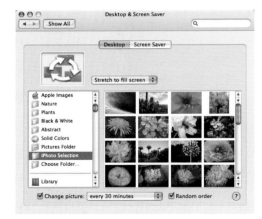

Figure 5.23 In the Desktop pane of your Desktop & Screen Saver preferences, configure how you want your Desktop pictures to appear, and how often they should rotate.

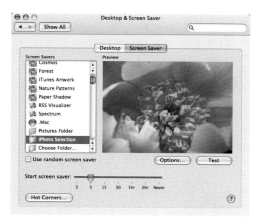

Figure 5.24 When you click the Desktop button in iPhoto, the Desktop & Screen Saver preference pane opens automatically.

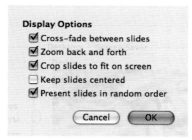

Figure 5.25 Configure how the screen saver displays your photos in the Display Options dialog. Play with these settings to see how they interact with the photos you're using—I've found varying results with different types and sizes of photos.

Try Image Puzzle Too!

If you really like screen savers, check out Gereon Frahling's $9.99 shareware Image Puzzle screen saver, which uses the pictures in your iPhoto Library to build a photo-mosaic, using another photo in your library as the template. It's very cool. Find it at: www.image-puzzle.com.

Creating a Screen Saver

The Desktop button in iPhoto does double duty, not just putting one or more photos on your Desktop, but also setting them as your screen saver.

To create a screen saver:

1. With more than one or no photos selected (in the latter case, iPhoto uses the current album), click the Desktop button or choose Desktop from the Share menu.

   iPhoto opens the Desktop & Screen Saver preference pane (**Figure 5.24**).

2. If necessary, click the Screen Saver tab.

3. Adjust the Start Screen Saver slider to set how long the screen saver should wait for activity before kicking in. If you want to set a hot corner, click the Hot Corners button and pick a hot corner in the dialog that appears.

4. To configure options for how the screen saver slideshow looks, click Options and then select the desired checkboxes in the Display Options dialog (**Figure 5.25**). Click OK when you're done.

   iPhoto sets Mac OS X's screen saver to use the selected photos or album. The next time your screen saver kicks in, you'll see it displaying those photos.

✔ Tip

- You can also display the photos in an iPhoto album as your screen saver by selecting the album in the folder list in the Desktop & Screen Saver preference pane's Screen Saver tab.

Setting Up a .Mac Account

Before you can use Apple's HomePage Web publishing tool or .Mac Slides tool, you need a .Mac account. It's easy to set up but does cost $99 per year. Luckily, Apple offers a 60-day free trial so you can see if iWeb and .Mac Slides, along with .Mac's other features, are worth the cost to you.

To set up a trial .Mac account:

1. Choose System Preferences from the Apple menu to open the System Preferences window, and then click the .Mac icon to display the .Mac preference pane (**Figure 5.26**).

2. Make sure you're connected to the Internet and click the Learn More button.

   Your default Web browser launches and takes you to the .Mac home page. Click the link for a free trial.

3. Enter your information in the fields provided (**Figure 5.27**). When you're done, click Continue.

   Your browser displays a summary page (**Figure 5.28**), offers you the chance to send an iCard announcing the fact that you have an optional new email address (yourusername@mac.com), and takes you to the .Mac home page.

4. Return to the .Mac preference pane, and enter your new .Mac member name and password.

5. Close the System Preferences window.

✔ Tip

■ Since many people have registered .Mac accounts, you may need to choose a more awkward username than would be ideal. Try combining your first name and last name and, if all else fails, add a number.

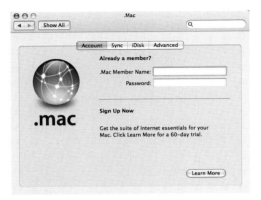

Figure 5.26 To start setting up a .Mac account, click the Learn More button in the .Mac preference pane, which takes you to the .Mac home page in your Web browser.

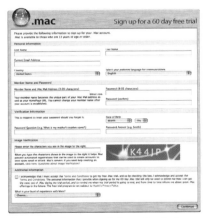

Figure 5.27 Enter your information in the .Mac signup page, and click Continue.

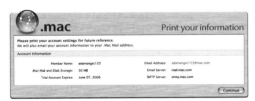

Figure 5.28 A confirmation page appears; copy the username and password from that page to the .Mac preference pane and you're done.

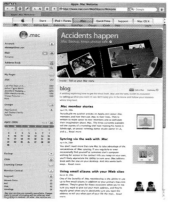

Figure 5.29
Explore the
.Mac Web page
to learn about
all that .Mac
offers.

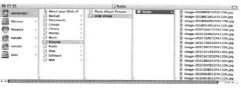

Figure 5.30 Your iDisk stores any pictures you upload to HomePage or .Mac Slides.

Whither HomePage?

Until the release of iLife '06, you created Web albums (and other types of pages) on .Mac using the online HomePage tool, which integrated with iPhoto for easy uploading of photos. HomePage still exists on the .Mac Web site, but doesn't integrate with iPhoto 6 in any way. HomePage was easy to use only through iPhoto (it was always clumsy to use via a Web browser), so I highly recommend that you use iWeb instead now.

You can link to your existing HomePage albums in iWeb, or you can export the same photos to iWeb and publish them again, deleting the HomePage albums and related photos when you're done, to avoid wasting your iDisk space on duplicate pictures. Or you can just leave the existing HomePage albums alone and create all new albums in iWeb. It's up to you.

Some Major .Mac Features

.Mac provides many features, some of which integrate with iPhoto. Explore the .Mac page at www.mac.com to configure and use each tool, to download the free software like Backup, and to access various special offers (**Figure 5.29**). For full, up-to-date, information about .Mac, I strongly recommend Joe Kissell's *Take Control of .Mac* at www.takecontrolbooks.com/dot-mac.html.

iWeb

Apple's new iWeb program, part of iLife '06, integrates with .Mac to make uploading photo slideshows (and other Web pages) easy (see the next page for details).

iDisk

Apple provides 1 GB of disk space for each .Mac user, accessed like any other disk. To mount your iDisk, choose My iDisk from the hierarchical iDisk menu in the Finder's Go menu (Cmd Shift I). Predefined folders store backups, documents, pictures, movies, public files to share, Web pages, music, and software you can download.

When you publish photos using .Mac Slides, the files are uploaded to your Pictures folder (**Figure 5.30**). Web albums you publish via iWeb live in the Web folder.

Mail

.Mac provides you with another address— yourusername@mac.com. You can either retrieve mail from it directly (via your email program or a webmail client) and/or have it forward messages to another account.

Groups

.Mac Groups enable you to share photos, messages, calendar events, announcements, links, and even iDisk space with friends.

Publishing Photo Pages with iWeb

iPhoto's integration with iWeb is similar to its integration with iDVD: it just hands off selected photos. You can create two types of pages when starting from within iPhoto: photo pages and blog pages.

To publish a photo page:

1. Select an album or the individual photos you wish to publish.

2. From the Share menu's Send to iWeb submenu, choose Photo Page.

   iPhoto launches iWeb, creates a new page, and asks you to select a template (**Figure 5.31**).

3. Select a template and click Choose.

   iWeb imports the photos and presents you with a page that simulates your eventual photo Web page (**Figure 5.32**).

4. Edit the various text blocks for the page name, description, and photo titles as desired (click a block twice to edit it).

5. From the File menu choose either Publish to .Mac or Publish to Folder.

   If you choose Publish to .Mac, iPhoto uploads your pictures to your iDisk, and, when it's done, shows a dialog that tells you the URL for your page and offers to let you visit the page or announce it.

   If you choose Publish to Folder, iWeb asks for a location and saves the HTML and image files to the folder, which you can then upload manually to any Web server.

✔ Tips

■ For more details about iWeb, see Steven Sande's *Take Control of iWeb* at `www.takecontrolbooks.com/iweb.html`.

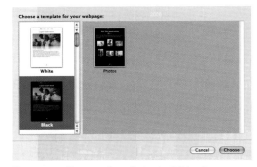

Figure 5.31 After sending photos to iWeb, choose a template for your photo page.

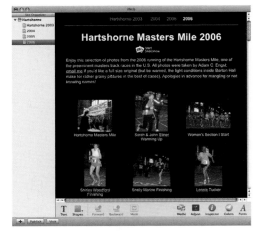

Figure 5.32 In iWeb, edit the text blocks that name and describe your page.

✔ More Tips

■ Web-based slideshows are cooler when uploaded to .Mac than when displayed on another Web site. iWeb's built-in page counter also works only on .Mac.

■ It's best to give your photos titles in iPhoto, rather than in iWeb, in case you wish to use the photos for any other purpose where titles would be helpful.

■ Arrange your photos as desired (left to right, top to bottom) in iPhoto before you send them to iWeb.

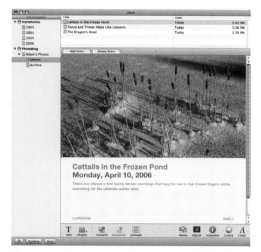

Figure 5.33 When you send a photo to an iWeb blog, iWeb creates a new entry for the photo page.

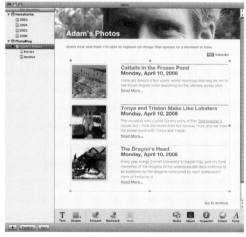

Figure 5.34 iWeb automatically updates the main page for your blog once you've entered details for a specific blog entry.

Publishing Blog Photos with iWeb

Whereas a photo page looks much as you'd expect a Web photo album to look, a photo blog features a single photo per chronological entry.

To publish a photo to an iWeb blog:

1. Select a photo, and from the Share menu's Send to iWeb submenu, choose Blog.

   iPhoto launches iWeb and creates a new blog entry (**Figure 5.33**).

2. Edit the various text blocks for the blog post title and description as desired (click a block twice to edit it).

   iWeb automatically updates the main page for your blog as well (**Figure 5.34**).

3. From the File menu choose either Publish to .Mac or Publish to Folder.

   If you choose Publish to .Mac, iPhoto uploads your pictures to your iDisk, and, when it's done, shows a dialog that tells you the URL for your page and offers to let you visit the page or announce it.

   If you choose Publish to Folder, iWeb asks for a location and saves the HTML and image files to the folder, which you can then upload manually to any Web server.

✔ Tips

- For more details about iWeb, see Steven Sande's *Take Control of iWeb* at www.takecontrolbooks.com/iweb.html.

- You can drag photos from iPhoto into various spots in iWeb, either into a page for free-placement of the photo, or into one of iWeb's image placeholders.

- Double-click a photo in iWeb to resize it within its placeholder.

Publishing .Mac Slides

Using the .Mac Slides Publisher feature of
.Mac along with iPhoto, .Mac members can
easily upload a set of photos that anyone
with a Mac running Mac OS X 10.2 or later
can use as a screen saver.

To publish photos as .Mac Slides:

1. Select the photos you want to publish,
   and click the .Mac Slides button or
   choose .Mac Slides from the Share menu.

   iPhoto displays a confirmation dialog
   (**Figure 5.35**).

2. Click the Publish button.

   iPhoto compresses and shrinks the size of
   the photos to reduce transfer time
   and uploads the photos to your iDisk
   (**Figure 5.36**).

   When it's done, a confirmation dialog
   appears (**Figure 5.37**).

3. Click the Announce Slideshow button.

   In your default email program, iPhoto
   creates a message with instructions you
   can send to the people who might want
   to subscribe to your .Mac Slides.

✔ Tips

- You can move the .Mac Slides upload
  progress dialog out of the way and keep
  working while iPhoto uploads in the
  background.

- You can find the .Mac Slides in your iDisk
  in Pictures/Slide Shows/Public.

- It appears that you can select as many
  photos to upload as .Mac Slides as you
  want, subject to the amount of free disk
  space available on your iDisk.

- You can store only one set of .Mac Slides
  at a time—every time you click the .Mac
  Slides button, the selected photos replace
  the previous set.

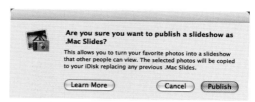

Figure 5.35 iPhoto checks to make sure you realize
that publishing photos as .Mac Slides replaces the
previous set of .Mac Slides.

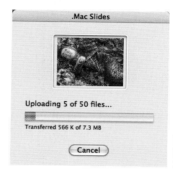

Figure 5.36
iPhoto provides
a visual prog-
ress dialog as
it uploads your
photos as .Mac
Slides.

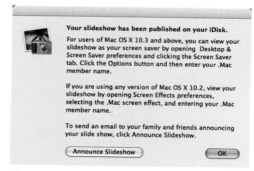

Figure 5.37 Once iPhoto finishes uploading your .Mac
Slides photos to your iDisk, it lets you announce the
slideshow via email to your friends and relatives.

Make a .Mac Slides Album

If you want to add to your set of .Mac
Slides rather than overwriting the previous set, create a .Mac Slides album, add
photos to it whenever you wish, and after
each addition, publish the entire album.

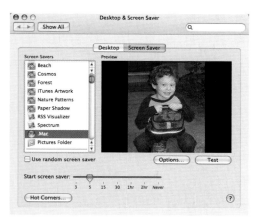

Figure 5.38 Configure the .Mac screen saver in the Screen Saver pane of the Desktop & Screen Saver preferences.

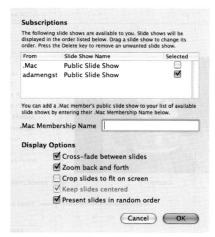

Figure 5.39 In the Subscriptions dialog, enter the .Mac membership name of the person whose slides you want to view and set screen saver options.

Using the Screen Saver

The screen saver comes on automatically after the idle time you set in the Screen Saver pane of the Desktop & Screen Saver preferences has passed. You can also invoke it manually by putting the pointer in a pre-defined "hot corner."

Subscribing to .Mac Slides

Although only .Mac members can upload .Mac Slides, anyone using Mac OS X 10.2 Jaguar or later can subscribe to them and have them shown as a screen saver.

The instructions below are for Mac OS X 10.3 Panther; in Jaguar, use the controls in the Screen Effects preference pane.

To subscribe to .Mac Slides:

1. From the Apple menu, choose System Preferences, click the Desktop & Screen Saver icon, and then click the Screen Saver tab (**Figure 5.38**).

2. Click .Mac in the Screen Savers list.

3. Click the Options button to display the Subscriptions dialog.

4. In the .Mac Membership Name field, enter the member name of the .Mac member whose slides you want to view and click OK.

   iPhoto adds the .Mac member name to the available subscriptions and closes the dialog.

5. Click Options again to make sure the checkbox for your newly entered .Mac member name is selected, and select the other screen saver options from the checkboxes at the bottom of the dialog (**Figure 5.39**).

6. Click OK and close System Preferences.

✔ Tips

- Mac OS X downloads the .Mac Slides in the background when you connect to the Internet.

- Because .Mac Slides are compressed and reduced in size, they're not as crisp as local pictures used for slideshows.

Exporting to Web Pages

Although iWeb can create Web pages you can upload to your own server, iPhoto has a built-in way of doing this as well that's simple and effective, even if its results aren't as visually interesting.

To export photos to Web pages:

1. Select an album or the individual photos you wish to publish via the Web.

2. Choose Export from the File menu ([Cmd][Shift][E]).
   iPhoto shows the Export Photos dialog.

3. If it's not selected, click the Web Page tab (**Figure 5.40**).

4. Enter the title for your Web page.

5. Enter the desired number of columns and rows of photo thumbnails.

6. If desired, select a background color or image.

7. Select the maximum width and height for the thumbnails and the full-size images.

8. Select the Show Title and Show Comment checkboxes as desired.

9. Click Export, navigate to the desired destination folder (it's best to create a new folder inside your user directory's Sites folder), and click OK.
   iPhoto exports the photos and builds the appropriate HTML files, naming everything for the enclosing folder.

10. Switch to the Finder, open the folder in which you saved your Web page, and double-click the HTML file to open it in your Web browser (**Figure 5.41**).

11. If necessary, upload the folder to your Web site using an FTP program like Interarchy (www.interarchy.com).

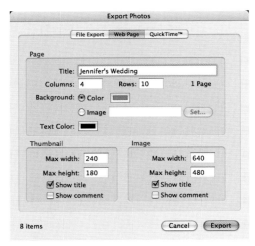

Figure 5.40 Use the options in the Web Page tab of the Export Photos dialog to set how your photos will appear on the Web page.

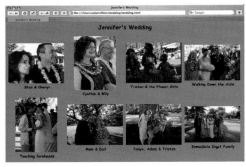

Figure 5.41 To see how your Web page turned out, switch to the Finder, open your destination folder, and double-click the HTML file inside it. To view an image at full size, click its thumbnail.

Managing Plug-ins

To manage plug-ins, select iPhoto in the Finder, choose Get Info ([Cmd][I]) from the File menu, and use the checkboxes and buttons in the Plug-ins pane to enable, disable, install, and uninstall the plug-ins.

For a listing of plug-ins, check out the iPhoto Plugins News blog at http://wheezersociety.blogs.com/iphoto_plugins/.

Other Web Export Tools

There are many other tools for generating Web-based photo albums. I can't list them all, but this collection will get you started. For more utilities, search for "iPhoto" on VersionTracker (www.versiontracker.com). Beware of old and potentially incompatible plug-ins!

◆ FlickrExport by Frasier Speirs; free. iPhoto export plug-in for uploading to the Flickr photo-sharing site. connectedflow.com/flickrexport/

◆ BetterHTMLExport from Geeks R Us; $20. iPhoto export plug-in for making Web pages. www.geeksrus.com/software/betterhtmlexport/

◆ ShutterBug by XtraLean Software; $49.95. Drag photos in from iPhoto; full-featured; neat Web slideshow. www.xtralean.com/SBOverview.html

◆ iPhotoToGallery by Zachary Wily; free. iPhoto export plug-in for uploading to Gallery-driven Web sites. www.zwily.com/iphoto/

◆ PictureSync by Holocore; $14. Imports from iPhoto and uploads to many Web services. www.holocore.com/?PictureSync

◆ webPhoto by Alex Johnson; free. Provides a live Web interface for browsing your entire iPhoto Library. www.ionize.org/webPhoto/

◆ iPhotoWebShare by bitpatterns; free. Easy to use preference pane that serves iPhoto albums directly. www.bitpatterns.com/iPhotoWebShare/

◆ myPhoto by Michael Mulligan; free. Serves iPhoto albums directly with no exporting. http://agent0068.dyndns.org/~mike/projects/myPhoto/

Web Page Export Tips

iPhoto's Web page export isn't particularly flexible, although it's fine for basic Web pages. There are workarounds for some of its limitations, though not for others.

Web page export tips:

◆ iPhoto doesn't let you add a line of descriptive text to your thumbnail page, as iWeb photo pages do by default. If you know a little HTML, you can easily add text to that page using a text editor.

◆ If you select a background image instead of a color, iPhoto tiles the image under the thumbnails. That can work well if the image is large and light colored, but avoid using small, dark background images—they make for a cluttered presentation.

◆ Assuming you have a permanent Internet connection (like DSL or a cable modem) and an IP address that never changes, you can make your pages available on your Mac by turning on Personal Web Sharing in the Sharing preference pane.
If you have a permanent Internet connection but not a static IP address, you can learn more about how to work around this limitation with dynamic DNS. See www.technopagan.org/dynamic/ for more information. Also consider using iPhotoWebShare, webPhoto or myPhoto (see "Other Web Export Tools" to the left) to serve your photos directly.

◆ If you feel as though you're wasting a huge amount of time fussing with Web pages exported from iPhoto, I encourage you to check out Apple's .Mac service (www.mac.com). iWeb's integration with .Mac works very nicely.

Copying Photos to an iPod

Forget about carrying dog-eared photos in your wallet—now you can copy photos to your iPod (assuming yours has a color screen) and display them in their full glory. Though the photos come from iPhoto, you use iTunes to copy them to your iPod.

To copy photos to an iPod:

1. In iTunes, open the Preferences window (Cmd ,) and click the iPod tab.

2. Click the Photos tab to display the photo-copying preferences (**Figure 5.42**).

3. Select either the Copy All Photos and Albums radio button or the Copy Selected Albums Only button.

4. If you selected Copy Selected Albums Only, select specific albums in the scrolling list.

5. Click OK to save your preferences and start the synchronization process.

✔ Tips

■ To save space, iTunes shrinks the photos for display on the iPod's tiny screen.

■ If you have a lot of space on your iPod, or you want to use the iPod to transfer photos to another Mac, select the Include Full Resolution Photos checkbox.

■ If you have a smaller iPod (or a lot of photos), it's best to copy individual albums rather than everything. Smart albums are especially useful in this regard.

■ iTunes shows you how many photos are in each album, which can give you a rough approximation of which albums will fit on your iPod.

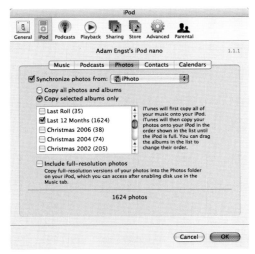

Figure 5.42 Choose which photos will be copied to your iPod in the Photos screen of the iPod tab in the iTunes Preferences window.

Viewing Photos on an iPod

It's easy to view the photos once you've copied them to your iPod.

1. At the top level of the iPod interface, use the clickwheel to select Photos, then press the center button.

2. Select an album and press the center button to see tiny thumbnails of the photos in that album.

3. Either use the clickwheel to select a particular photo or just press the center button to display the selected photo at the largest possible size.

4. Use the Forward and Back buttons to navigate through the photos, or press the Play button to switch into automatic slideshow mode, in which the iPod cycles through the photos automatically.

Printing Photos

6

Digital photography has brought with it an increased interest in viewing photos on the computer screen, which accounts for iPhoto's slideshow features. But even still, there's no denying the power of being able to send prints of your kids to their grandparents. Just as the computer didn't give us a paperless office, digital photography won't eliminate the desire for prints. People like paper.

iPhoto provides two ways you can apply your photos to paper: printing directly from iPhoto to your own printer and ordering prints in standard sizes from Apple.

Printing on your own printer provides instant gratification and feedback, since you can see exactly what the print looks like, make any corrections to account for the difference between the screen and paper, and print again. iPhoto can print photos in a variety of sizes and layouts. However, printing on your own printer isn't cheap (on a per-print basis), and unless you have a good printer, the quality might not be optimal.

For good quality—thanks to a true photographic process—and reasonable per-print costs, look into ordering prints from Apple. You have to wait a few days before your prints arrive, but ordering prints is also a great way to get sizes that most standard printers won't give you (20" x 30", anyone?).

Gutenprint/Gimp-Print Drivers

What your printer can do is determined by its *driver,* system-level software provided by Apple or the manufacturer. There's also Gutenprint (formerly called Gimp-Print), an open source set of drivers for over 700 printers, which offers support for printer options that the manufacturers may not support in Mac OS X. For instance, if you want to print on roll paper or other unusual paper sizes, you may need to use Gutenprint. It's built into Mac OS X, though it may be worth downloading and installing the latest version so you have all the current printer drivers. Learn more and download a copy from: `http://gimp-print.sourceforge.net/MacOSX.php3`.

Printing Photos

Many people prefer to print their photos on inexpensive color inkjet printers rather than waiting for online orders.

To print photos:

1. Select one or more photos to print.

2. Choose Print from the File menu (Cmd P).
   iPhoto displays the Print dialog (**Figure 6.1**).

3. From the Presets pop-up menu, choose appropriate settings (the contents are printer-specific). If you don't like the presets, you can access all available settings by clicking the Advanced button.

4. From the Style menu, choose the desired style: Contact Sheet, Full Page, Greeting Card, N-Up, Sampler, or Standard Prints.

5. Set the options for the style you selected.

6. Enter the number of copies to print.

7. Click the Print button.
   iPhoto sends your photos to the printer.

✔ Tips

- In book mode, choosing Print from the File menu lets you print book pages that mix photos and text on a single page.

- If you see a yellow warning icon in the Print dialog, see "Dealing with Warning Icons" in Chapter 9, "Troubleshooting."

- If necessary, iPhoto shrinks images proportionally to fit, thus increasing the border size.

- Save changes made in the Advanced dialog for repeated use by choosing Save As from the Presets menu while you're viewing the Advanced settings.

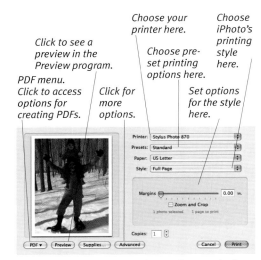

Choose your printer here.

Choose iPhoto's printing style here.

Click to see a preview in the Preview program.

Choose pre-set printing options here.

PDF menu. Click to access options for creating PDFs.

Click for more options.

Set options for the style here.

Figure 6.1 To print selected photos, choose Print from the File menu to display the Print dialog, select your desired options, and click the Print button.

Adding a Printer

If you've never printed from Mac OS X before, follow these steps to add a printer (make sure it's connected and turned on first).

1. In the Print dialog, choose Edit Printer List from the Printer pop-up menu to display the Printer Browser window in the Printer Setup Utility.

2. Select the printer to add and click the Add button.

3. Quit the Printer Setup Utility.

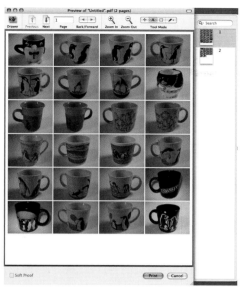

Figure 6.2 To check a printout in Preview (shown above), click Preview in the Print dialog.

Test, Test, Test!

A few things can affect how a photo looks when it comes out of your printer.

◆ Printer capabilities, both what they can do physically and what their drivers allow in the Page Setup and Print dialogs, vary by brand and model.

◆ Inkjet printers print very differently on different types of paper, and it's important to match the print settings to the type of paper you're using.

◆ iPhoto's print styles (covered next) offer a variety of options.

It may take several tries to determine the best combination of options. You may be able to try some in economy mode on cheap paper, but in the end, you may have to expend some ink on a few sheets of expensive photo paper. To reduce the waste and cost, keep good notes for subsequent printing sessions.

Previewing Prints

Ink and paper for color inkjet printers are expensive, particularly glossy photo paper. If you're unsure about what's going to print, it's best to preview the output before committing it to expensive paper. Another reason to preview your printout is that the picture in the Print dialog shows you only the first page of photos to print.

To preview prints:

1. Select one or more photos to preview.

2. Choose Print from the File menu ($\boxed{\text{Cmd}}\boxed{\text{P}}$).

3. Pick a style and set desired options.

4. Click the Preview button.

   iPhoto "prints" the selected photos to a temporary PDF document called "Untitled" and opens it in Apple's Preview application (**Figure 6.2**).

5. Click the thumbnails on the right side to see multiple pages, and when you're done, close the window or, if you like what you see, click the Print button.

✔ Tips

■ Uncheck the Soft Proof checkbox in Preview (at the lower left) to see the photos in color.

■ You can save the temporary document in the Preview application if you want a PDF version.

■ Previewing in this fashion won't help you determine if your photos will fit within the margins of your printer. Also, any printer-specific changes you make (such as forcing black ink on a color printer) won't be reflected in the preview. See if your printer has an economy or draft mode you can use to test printer-specific features on a single page of photos.

Printing Contact Sheets

The first printing style iPhoto offers is the Contact Sheet style, which prints multiple images per sheet of paper (**Figure 6.3**).

Uses for contact sheets:

◆ Contact sheets are traditionally used to look at a number of photos at once, which is handy for comparing different versions of the same picture, or for letting relatives who don't have a computer pick which photos they'd like you to order for them as prints.

◆ You can buy special paper for stickers or decals, so printing a contact sheet could be an easy way to make custom stickers. You don't have enough control in iPhoto to print on perforated or peel-off sticker stock, so you must cut out the stickers.

✔ Tips

■ Select Save Paper to print portrait photos in landscape orientation, thus enabling more photos to fit on a page.

■ If you select only one photo and print a contact sheet, iPhoto replicates the photo as many times as possible on the page.

■ See "Printing N-Up Photos" in this chapter for slightly different options.

■ The maximum number of photos to print across the page is 8; that gives you 13 rows for a total of 104 pictures.

■ For more white space between photos and a layout that doesn't print all the photos in landscape orientation (only when printing multiple photos), deselect the Save Paper checkbox.

■ If you see a yellow warning icon on a photo in the Print dialog, try increasing the number of photos per page to print the photos at a smaller size.

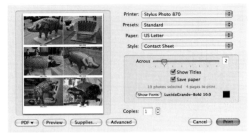

Figure 6.3 iPhoto's Contact Sheet style prints multiple images per sheet of paper. Titles are optional.

Titles, Finally!

New in iPhoto 6 is the capability to add each photo's title underneath the image, which is key for making contact sheets useful (otherwise it can be difficult to match a photo on a contact sheet to the original in iPhoto).

To include titles on your contact sheets, select the Show Titles checkbox. You can also change the font and color of the titles using the controls in the Fonts palette; click Show Fonts to display it.

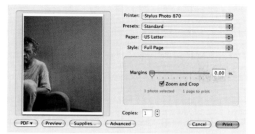

Figure 6.4 iPhoto's Full Page style prints a single photo at the largest size that will fit on a piece of paper.

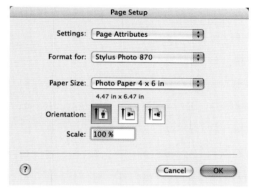

Figure 6.5 To print on 4" x 6" paper, you must first select the appropriate paper size either from the Paper menu in the Print dialog or in the Page Setup dialog.

Printing Full-Page Photos

iPhoto's second printing style prints each selected photo at the largest size that will fit on a piece of paper (**Figure 6.4**).

Uses for full-page prints:

◆ Anything you want to print as large as possible but don't mind if it doesn't match standard aspect ratios.

◆ Prints on unusually sized perforated paper or roll paper; make sure to choose the proper paper size from the Paper pop-up menu before printing.

✔ Tips

■ Select the Zoom and Crop checkbox to have iPhoto zoom into and crop your photo appropriately so it matches the aspect ratio of the printable area. Otherwise, if a photo's aspect ratio does not match that of your paper, iPhoto shrinks the photo proportionally to make it fit, which increases the white borders.

■ Don't assume iPhoto can print to your printer's minimum margins. Test a few full-page prints in economy mode first to learn what will come out.

■ Don't bother entering your printer's minimum margins to get the smallest possible margins; any number (including 0.00) lower than the printer's minimum margins results in a printout that uses as much of the paper as possible.

■ If you see a yellow warning icon in the Print dialog, try increasing your margins.

■ The Paper menu in iPhoto's Print dialog matches the Paper Size pop-up menu in the Page Setup dialog, which is how you had to set paper size in previous versions of iPhoto (**Figure 6.5**).

Printing Greeting Cards

iPhoto's third printing style offers two options for printing folded greeting cards (**Figure 6.6**). For better results, check out iPhoto 6's new capability to create and print cards (see Chapter 7, "Cards, Books, and Calendars").

Uses for greeting cards:

◆ Print your own holiday cards rather than buying pre-printed ones.

◆ Make custom birthday cards for friends and family.

◆ Print invitations to a party.

✔ Tips

■ You can choose between single-fold and double-fold greeting cards. Single-fold greeting cards print the photo on half the paper; double-fold greeting cards print the photo on one-quarter of the paper.

■ Cropping a photo to an aspect ratio of 8 x 5 increases the size of the photo for a single-fold greeting card. However, cropping to 5.5 x 4.25 for a double-fold greeting card doesn't make a noticeable difference because it's so close to the original aspect ratio of 4 x 3.

■ There's no way to prevent photos from printing right at the folded edges, which looks particularly amateurish with double-fold cards. Easy Card (see sidebar) does a better job.

■ iPhoto doesn't let you enter text inside the greeting cards or print a photo on the inside of the card. Consider one of the alternatives mentioned in the sidebar to work around this problem.

■ You can buy special photo paper for greeting cards that's pre-scored for easier and more attractive folding.

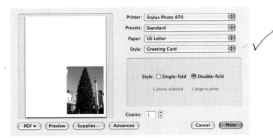

Figure 6.6 iPhoto's Greeting Card style lets you choose between single-fold and double-fold greeting cards. Unfortunately, it doesn't let you enter text.

Greeting Card Alternatives

So you want more control over your greeting cards? Here are some options:

◆ Use iPhoto 6's new capability to create cards, which you can order directly from Apple. You can also print them on your own printer, though you must manually flip paper over to print on the inside. See Chapter 7, "Cards, Books, and Calendars."

◆ Buy a copy of Script Software's $30 Easy Card, which does a great job of creating and printing greeting cards and custom envelopes. You can even drop photos into it from iPhoto. Download a copy of Easy Card from www.scriptsoftware.com/ecc/.

◆ Buy a copy of Nova Development's $49.95 Print Explosion Deluxe or $49.95 Greeting Card Factory, which are designed to create greeting cards, along with a wide variety of other printed materials. Find them at www.novadevelopment.com.

◆ Write your message inside the card by hand! (Perhaps that's obvious.)

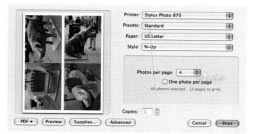

Figure 6.7 iPhoto's N-Up style lets you pick how many photos will appear on the page from the Photos Per Page pop-up menu.

Printing N-Up Photos

iPhoto's fourth printing style looks and works much like the Contact Sheet style covered previously, but lets you pick exactly how many photos you want to appear on the page: 2, 4, 6, 9, or 16 (**Figure 6.7**).

Uses for N-Up prints:

◆ Full-page layouts of photos with even margins.

◆ Anything for which you might use the Contact Sheet style.

✔ Tips

■ If you select only one photo when using the N-Up style, iPhoto replicates the photo in as many spots on the page as are available. That's handy for wallet photos.

■ To print multiple copies of the same image on each page, select the One Photo Per Page checkbox.

■ If you see a yellow warning icon on a photo in the Print dialog, try increasing the number of photos per page to print the photos at a smaller size.

N-Up vs. Contact Sheet

The N-Up and Contact Sheet styles differ in three important ways:

◆ The Contact Sheet style now supports printing titles underneath photos, which isn't true of the N-Up style.

◆ With the N-Up style, you pick how many photos will appear on the page, whereas with Contact Sheet you pick how many columns of photos will print on the page.

◆ The N-Up style does a better job of spacing photos out so they fill the entire page. The Contact Sheet style can leave a large bottom margin.

Whether you use N-Up or Contact Sheet depends on precisely what you're trying to achieve, since their printing styles are very similar.

Printing Sampler Sheets

iPhoto's fifth printing style provides two templates that mix photos of different sizes. The first template places three photos on a page (**Figure 6.8**); the second arranges six photos on a page.

Uses for sampler sheets:

◆ Print collections of photos for relatives, instead of printing individual prints.

◆ Print your most recent photos for an informal, gallery-style display.

✔ Tips

■ Unless you plan to cut the printed photos out, make sure all the photos you print with a Sampler layout are of the same orientation. If you mix landscape (horizontal) and portrait (vertical) photos, iPhoto can't orient them all correctly.

■ If you want your printed page to be in portrait orientation, use landscape photos with Template 1 (**Figure 6.9**) or portrait photos with Template 2. If you want your printed page to be in landscape orientation, use portrait photos with Template 1 or landscape photos with Template 2 (**Figure 6.10**).

■ Pay close attention to iPhoto's preview to make sure you know exactly what will print before clicking the Print button!

■ To control their page location, arrange the photos manually in an album first.

■ If you select only one photo, iPhoto uses that photo in all the spots on the page.

■ With careful trimming, you can fit a sampler sheet into an 8" x 10" frame.

■ For different layouts, either print pages from a book layout or see "Printing Custom Layouts," later in this chapter.

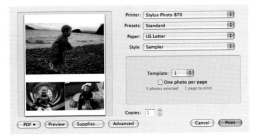

Figure 6.8 Template 1 of iPhoto's Sampler style prints three photos on a page.

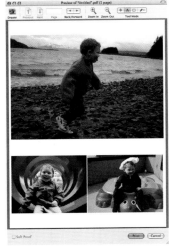

Figure 6.9 Here's the preview of landscape photos printed with Sampler Template 1, which results in a page in portrait orientation.

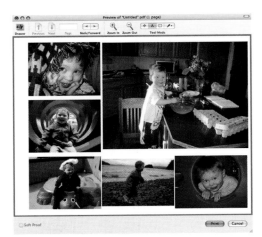

Figure 6.10 Here's the preview of landscape photos printed with Sampler Template 2, which results in a page in landscape orientation.

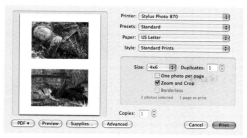

Figure 6.11 iPhoto's Standard Prints style enables you to print photos at traditional sizes so they fit in standard frames and photo albums.

Printing Standard Prints

iPhoto's sixth and final printing style prints photos in five standard sizes: 2" x 3", 3" x 5", 4" x 6", 5" x 7", and 8" x 10" (**Figure 6.11**).

Uses for standard prints:

◆ Print photos for inclusion in traditional photo albums.

◆ Frame your pictures using standard frame sizes.

✔ Tips

■ Either crop photos to the right aspect ratio before printing or select the Zoom and Crop checkbox; otherwise iPhoto shrinks the images proportionally to fit, increasing the white borders.

■ If you are printing more than one 2" x 3", 3" x 5", 4" x 6", or 5" x 7" photo, deselect the One Photo Per Page checkbox to print two per page, thus saving paper.

■ If you want multiple copies of each photo, click the Duplicate arrows to increase or decrease the number of copies to print.

■ To print on paper of unusual sizes, you must select the desired paper size from the Paper pop-up menu. You may see the better results by using the Full Page style instead; my printer doesn't completely fill 4" x 6" paper when I use iPhoto's 4" x 6" option in Standard Prints.

■ If you see a yellow warning icon on an 8" x 10" print, see if you get the warning icon in the Full Page style as well. If not, the warning is probably spurious; otherwise pick a smaller print size.

Printing Borderless

The Borderless checkbox in **Figure 6.11** above isn't available for me because my printer doesn't support borderless printing. If yours does, you can select it to print on special paper that matches with the standard print sizes.

Printing Custom Layouts

Despite the availability of the Sampler style, many people want more flexibility when printing custom layouts. iPhoto won't help you beyond what you can do with book layouts, but several third-party utilities will.

Portraits & Prints

The $30 Portraits & Prints, from Econ Technologies, provides a number of layouts, some of which merely try to fit many same-size photos onto a page, others of which provide a mix of sizes (**Figure 6.12**). With the $50 Portraits & Prints Pro, you can design your own custom layouts with photos, simple graphics (boxes and lines), and even text.

To bring photos in from iPhoto, just drag them from iPhoto to the Portraits & Prints window, then pick a template and choose which photo goes in which slot. Especially nice is the way Portraits & Prints lets you slide a photo around in its slot if the aspect ratios between the slot and the photo don't match. No need for cropping! Download a demo from www.econtechnologies.com.

photoprinto

SmileOnMyMac's $29.95 photoprinto provides a number of templates and lets you create your own (**Figure 6.13**). You can add frames to photos, jazz up your pictures with soft edges and other effects, and quite a bit more. In some ways, photoprinto is actually more comparable to iPhoto's book mode, since it lets you create photos albums, with multiple pages, each with a different layout.

You can import photos automatically from iPhoto albums, from folders on your hard disk, or by dragging them in from iPhoto or the Finder. Download a demo copy from www.smileonmymac.com/photoprinto/.

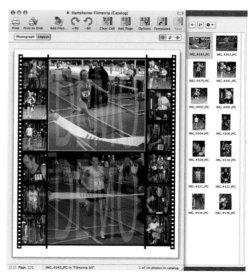

Figure 6.12 Portraits & Prints offers numerous layouts, complete with interesting frames and captions.

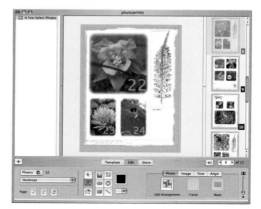

Figure 6.13 SmileOnMyMac's photoprinto offers a number of interesting templates into which you can place your photos.

Remember Book Layouts

Keep in mind that the cheapest and easiest way to put a number of photos on the same page is by printing a page from a book layout. See Chapter 7, "Cards, Books, and Calendars," for details.

Paper Types

Computer superstores sell a vast number of different types of inkjet papers. What should you buy? You're almost certain to get good results with paper made by the manufacturer of your printer. Papers from other manufacturers will likely work well too, but aren't as guaranteed. The basic paper types include:

◆ Plain paper. Use it only for drafts or text; photos will look awful.

◆ Matte paper. These papers are heavier than plain paper and have a smooth, but not glossy, finish. Matte paper can be very good for photos.

◆ Glossy photo paper and film. These papers, which come in a bewildering variety of types and weights, are heavier yet and have a glossy surface that looks like standard photo paper. Glossy film is actually polyethylene, not paper. Use glossy paper for your best prints.

◆ Specialty papers. You can buy papers that look like watercolor paper, have a metallic sheen, are of archival quality, or are translucent. Other specialty papers can be ironed onto T-shirts, are pre-scored for folding, have magnetic backing, and more.

If you like printing photos on your own printer, I strongly encourage you to buy a variety of papers and see what you like. Also fun to try is a sample pack from Red River Paper, an online paper vendor at www.redrivercatalog.com.

Printing Tips

How can you achieve the best quality prints? Along with repeated testing, try these tips for working with your photos and your printer:

◆ Use a good quality inkjet printer. Six-color printers produce better output than four-color printers, and printers designed to print photos do a better job than general-purpose printers (but may not print text as well). Also consider dye-sub printers, which are less common but which can print wonderful colors.

◆ Make sure your print head is clean and aligned. If your printouts don't look quite right, try cleaning the print head.

◆ Use good paper. Modern inkjets lay down incredibly small drops of ink, and standard paper absorbs those drops more than photo paper, blurring printouts.

◆ Make sure to print on the correct side of the paper (it's usually whiter or shinier).

◆ Don't handle the surface of the paper that will be printed on. Oils from your skin can mess up the printout.

◆ Remove each sheet from the output tray after printing, particularly with glossy films, and be careful not to touch the surface until it has dried.

◆ In the Advanced version of the Print dialog, make sure you're using the highest resolution and other appropriate settings. In particular, aim for settings that favor quality over speed.

◆ When printing black-and-white photos, make sure to print with only black ink.

◆ Make sure to crop photos to the right aspect ratio before printing or use the Zoom and Crop checkbox.

PRINTING TIPS

Setting Up an Apple ID

Before you can order anything from Apple, you must have an Apple ID with 1-Click ordering enabled. If you haven't previously set up an Apple ID to order from the iTunes Music Store or the Apple Store, you can create one within iPhoto.

To set up an Apple ID:

1. Make sure you're connected to the Internet, and click the Order Prints button to display the Order Prints window.

2. Click the Set Up Account button.

   iPhoto displays the Apple Account Sign-in dialog (**Figure 6.14**).

3. Click the Create Account button.

   iPhoto displays the first of three dialogs that collect the data necessary to create an account (**Figure 6.15**). The first asks for your email address and password, the second collects billing information, and the third garners shipping information.

4. Enter the necessary information, clicking the Step button to move through the process until you're done.

   Apple sends an email confirmation at the end of the process.

✔ Tips

- Remember that your Apple ID is always your email address.

- Choose a password that can't be easily guessed. Otherwise miscreants could go in, change your shipping settings, order prints or books with your credit card, and switch back without you realizing.

- If you have trouble with your Apple ID, visit http://myinfo.apple.com/ and confirm or re-enter your settings. You can also set up an Apple ID at this site if necessary.

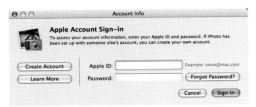

Figure 6.14 To create a new Apple ID, click the Set Up Account button in the Order Prints window to bring up the Apple Account Sign-in dialog. Then click the Create Account button.

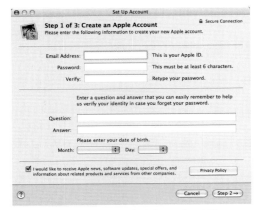

Figure 6.15 Enter your sign-in information, billing details, and shipping address in the dialogs that appear.

Strong Passwords

Apple requires that your password be at least six characters long, but you can make it stronger by ensuring that it contains numbers and punctuation along with uppercase and lowercase letters. One good strategy is to take a phrase you'll remember, like "Take me out to the ball game!" and use the first letter of each word, adding numbers where possible. The above phrase could be turned into this strong password: Tmo2tbg!

Whatever you choose, do not use a proper name or a word that will appear in the dictionary—they're too easy to guess.

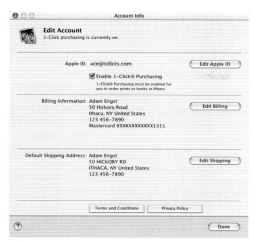

Figure 6.16 Verify and change your Apple ID settings in the Account Info dialog.

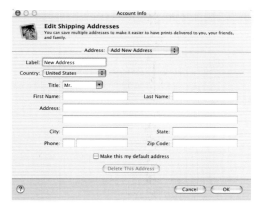

Figure 6.17 To enter a new shipping address, choose Add New Address from the Address pop-up menu, and then enter the new address in the Edit Shipping Addresses dialog.

Forgotten Passwords

If you forget your password, enter your email address in the Apple ID field in the Apple Account Sign-in dialog, click the Forgot Password button, and go through the necessary Web pages. Apple sends you an email message containing your password.

Using Your Apple ID

Once you have your Apple ID set up, you use it with Apple's ordering services. It's also useful if you want to use some of Apple's online tech support services or order from the iTunes Music Store or Apple Store. iPhoto usually remembers your Apple ID, but if not, you can always sign in manually.

To sign in using your Apple ID:

1. In one of iPhoto's Order windows (for prints, books, cards, or calendars), click either the Account Info button or the Set Up Account button to display the Apple Account Sign-in dialog (**Figure 6.14** on the previous page).

2. Enter your Apple ID and password, and then click the Sign In button.

    iPhoto displays the Account Info dialog (**Figure 6.16**).

3. If 1-Click purchasing is turned off, select the Enable 1-Click Purchasing checkbox.

4. Verify that everything else looks correct (if not, click the Edit button next to the incorrect data and make the necessary corrections), and then click Done.

✔ Tips

- You can switch between Apple IDs using the method above with two sets of email addresses and passwords. This is handy if multiple people want to order items on separate accounts.

- You can add additional shipping addresses by clicking Edit Shipping in the Account Info dialog, choosing Add New Address from the pop-up menu, and filling in the details in the dialog that appears (**Figure 6.17**). Switch between the addresses by choosing the desired one from the Ship To pop-up menu in an Order window.

Preparing to Order Prints

You will want to spend some time preparing your photos for printing by cropping them to the appropriate aspect ratios for prints. But what if you, like me, want to use the same photos for a book, which uses a 4 x 3 aspect ratio? Follow these steps for a solution.

To prepare photos for printing:

1. Make a new album, and add the photos that you want to order prints of.

2. Switch to the album, and edit each photo as desired, other than cropping.

3. In organize mode, select all the photos ([Cmd][A]) and choose Duplicate from the Photos menu ([Cmd][D]) to make copies (see "Duplicating Photos" in Chapter 4, "Editing Photos," for details).

4. Select just the copies in your album (again, "Duplicating Photos" in Chapter 4, "Editing Photos," explains this).

5. Drag them to the Source pane to create a new album of just the copies (append the word "Prints" to its name to be clear), and then return to the previous album and delete the copies from it.

    You now have two albums with identical photos; one with the originals, the other with copies. Use the original album to create your book, and crop the photos in the "Prints" album for ordering prints.

6. Go through the photos in the "Prints" album again, this time cropping each to the desired aspect ratio.

7. If you're printing photos in different sizes, manually group them by size in the album. That makes keeping track of them in the Order Prints window easier.

    Now you're ready to order the prints (see the next page).

Pixels and Prints

You may have noticed that iPhoto reports how large your photo is in pixels in the Information pane. But how does that match up with print sizes that you order? You mostly don't have to care, since iPhoto displays a low-resolution warning icon when a photo doesn't have enough pixels to print well at the desired size. For reference, here are the pixel sizes at which iPhoto starts adding the warning icon, given both in terms of the 4 x 3 aspect ratio of uncropped photos and with the appropriate cropping for the size at which you want to print.

Note that these are the *minimum* recommended resolutions. The larger your photos and the more they exceed these minimums, the better the final quality.

◆ For wallet-sized prints (about 2.4" x 3.4"), you need at least 450 x 337 pixels (when cropped to the above aspect ratio, keep the long side above 450 pixels).

◆ For a 4" x 6" print, you need at least 900 x 675 pixels (when cropped to 4 x 6, keep the long side above 900 pixels).

◆ For a 5" x 7" print, you need at least 1050 x 788 (when cropped to 5 x 7, keep the long side above 1050 pixels).

◆ For an 8" x 10" print, you need at least 1600 x 1200 (when cropped to 8 x 10, keep the short side above 1200 pixels).

◆ For 16" x 20" prints, you need at least 2132 x 1600 (when cropped to 16 x 20, keep the short side above 1600 pixels).

◆ For 20" x 30" prints, you need at least 2400 x 1800 (when cropped to 2 x 3, keep the long side above 2400 pixels).

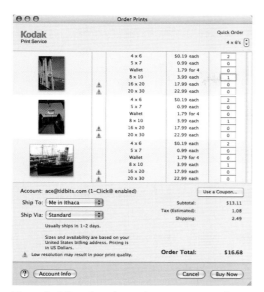

Figure 6.18 To order prints, select one or more photos, click the Order Prints button, and in the Order Prints window, enter the number of prints of each photo that you want. When you're ready, click the Buy Now button.

Ordering Prints

Once you've prepared your photos, it's time to order prints.

To order prints:

1. Make sure you're connected to the Internet, select one or more photos, and click the Order Prints button, or choose Order Prints from the Share menu.

   iPhoto opens the Order Prints window (**Figure 6.18**).

2. For each picture, enter the number of each size print you'd like to order.

   iPhoto automatically updates the total cost as you add and subtract prints.

3. Choose the appropriate shipping address and method from the Ship To and Ship Via pop-up menus.

4. Check your order carefully to make sure you're getting the right number of each print, and confirm that each photo can print at the size you've selected.

5. Click the Buy Now button.

   iPhoto uploads your pictures and alerts you when it's done.

✔ Tips

- If nothing is selected when you click Order Prints, iPhoto includes all the photos in the current album.

- Uploading takes a long time on a slow Internet connection because iPhoto uploads full-size images for best quality.

- If you want mostly 4" x 6" prints, click the Quick Order 4 x 6's arrows at the top right to increase or decrease the number of 4" x 6" prints of each photo.

- If you see a yellow warning icon next to a size you want, see "Dealing with Warning Icons" in Chapter 9, "Troubleshooting."

Shipping Details

Since the release of iPhoto 4, you can now have prints delivered not just to U.S. and Canadian addresses, but also to addresses in Japan and some European countries.

Shipping charges, at least in the United States, are now fixed at $2.49, no matter how many photos you order.

CARDS, BOOKS, AND CALENDARS

If I had to pick a single feature that sets iPhoto apart from most photo management programs, I'd choose the way iPhoto creates custom photo albums, calendars, and cards that can be professionally printed and bound. Numerous programs can help you edit and organize photos. But iPhoto is the undisputed champion of creating high-quality printed products in an easy fashion.

The beauty of iPhoto's cards, calendars, and books, apart from their quality printing on heavy, glossy paper, is that they help bridge the gap between the analog and digital worlds. Those of us who have grown up with computers are happy sharing our photos via slideshow, a digital camera hooked to a TV, or a Web page. But many people are still more comfortable with prints ensconced in acetate in a traditional photo album or appearing in a calendar or on a greeting card. Forget all the advantages of the digital world; for these people, the images somehow aren't real unless they're on paper. It's the "That's nice, dear" syndrome.

By the time you're done with this chapter, you won't have to worry about your digital photo collection being a second-class citizen when you're showing it off to a relative for whom an album is something you hold in your lap while sitting on the couch.

Similarities and Differences

Cards and calendars are new to iPhoto 6, but in designing how you work with them, Apple drew heavily on the book-creation interface. As a result, if you've created a book in iPhoto 5 or 6, you can create a card or calendar with no trouble. In the interests of avoiding needless duplication in this chapter, then, I first give the overview of creating each, followed by details that are specific to each (such as adding photos to dates on a calendar), and then I finish up with general instructions (such as how to enter and edit text) that are common to all three.

Creating Cards Overview

Of cards, books, and calendars, cards are the easiest to create, since they have room for only a single photo and minimal text. Here's the basic process:

To create a card:

1. Select the photo that you want to appear on your card.

2. Click the Card button under the display pane (**Figure 7.1**).

3. In the card design dialog, choose Greeting Card or Postcard from the pop-up menu and select one of the theme previews (**Figure 7.2**).

    iPhoto creates your card (**Figure 7.3**).

4. For the front of the card, choose the desired background and design from the Background and Design pop-up menus (see the facing page), and add and format text as desired to the back or inside of the card (flip forward a few pages for instructions on different ways to format text).

5. When you're done, click the Buy Card button, and run through the process of ordering your card.

✔ Tips

- If you're not sure which of several photos you might want to use, you can select multiple photos before creating the card, and then drag different photos into the photo slot on the front of the card to see how they look.

- Greeting cards are 5" x 7" with a picture on the outside and text on the inside; postcards are 4" x 6" with a picture on the front and room for text or text and an address on the back.

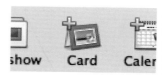

Figure 7.1 Click the Card button with a photo selected to make a card from that photo.

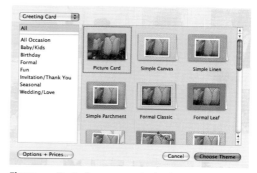

Figure 7.2 Next, choose your desired card type from the pop-up menu and pick a theme from the scrolling list of themes.

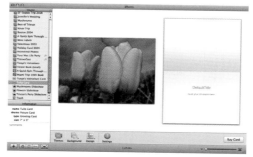

Figure 7.3 iPhoto creates the card in the Source pane to the left, showing the front and inside of the card in the display pane.

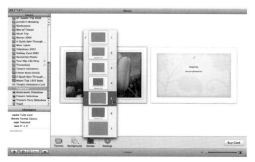

Figure 7.4 Choose a design from the Design pop-up menu to change the look of your card.

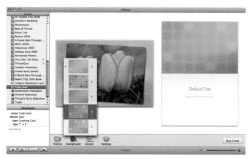

Figure 7.5 Choose a color from the Background pop-up menu to change the color of your card.

Designing Your Card

iPhoto provides only a few ways you can change the design of your card, making it extremely easy to come up with a sleek greeting card or postcard.

To design a card:

1. Select the front of your card by clicking it.

2. From the Design pop-up menu, choose a design (**Figure 7.4**). Repeat as necessary until you've found the design you like.

3. Select the back/inside of your card by clicking it in the display pane.

4. From the Design pop-up menu, choose a design. Repeat as necessary until you've found the design you like.

5. If you don't like any of the designs, click the Themes button and choose a new theme from the card design dialog.

6. From the Background pop-up menu, choose a background color (**Figure 7.5**).

7. Enter text in the provided text boxes and, if you don't like the default text formats, reformat it as desired.

✔ Tips

- In general, I recommend sticking with the fonts that Apple's designers chose for each design. Otherwise, you risk picking a font that won't print well or may not look as you expect on the finished card.

- You can enter text only in the provided text boxes. Different themes may offer additional places to enter text, but in general, text options are limited with cards.

- With postcards, the back of the card can accept either a design that provides room for general text or a design that provides space for an address and a stamp.

Creating Calendars Overview

Calendars are a bit more involved to create than cards, though less so than books. Here's the basic process:

To create a calendar:

1. Select the photos that you want to appear in your calendar.

2. Click the Calendar button under the display pane (**Figure 7.6**).

3. In the calendar design dialog, select a theme from the list of themes. Note the preview of each theme (**Figure 7.7**).

4. iPhoto then displays the calendar options dialog; set the options for when to start the calendar, how many months it should contain, and what holidays and calendar events should be included on it automatically (**Figure 7.8**).

   After informing you of how to add photos to the calendar pages, iPhoto creates your calendar (**Figure 7.9**).

5. For each calendar page, set the number of photos and the design using the Layout and Design pop-up menus. Drag photos from the vertical unplaced photo list to slots in the calendar page or to particular dates in a month. You can drag photos from slot to slot or date to date to move them around, or off the page entirely to put them back in the unplaced photo list.

6. When you're done, click the Buy Calendar button and run through the process of ordering your calendar.

✔ Tip

- You might be able to save some time placing photos if you arrange the photos in an album before selecting the entire album and clicking the Calendar button.

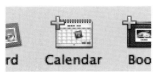

Figure 7.6 Click the Calendar button with photos selected to make a calendar from those photos.

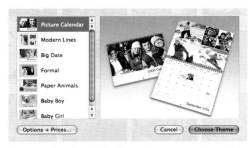

Figure 7.7 Next, select a theme from the scrolling list of themes.

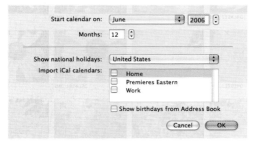

Figure 7.8 Set the options for your calendar.

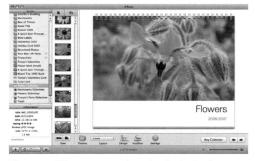

Figure 7.9 iPhoto creates the calendar in the Source pane to the left, showing the cover in the display pane, with the unplaced photos to the left.

Click to view page layouts.

Click to view unplaced photos.

Click to view one page at a time.

Click to view two pages at once.

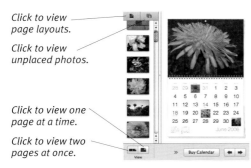

Figure 7.10 Use the buttons above the vertical list to switch between showing calendar pages and unplaced photos (showing above). Use the buttons below the list to switch between showing both calendar pages (top and bottom, showing above) and just the top or the bottom page in the display pane.

Drag to reposition the photo.

Drag to zoom in on the photo.

Click to include a caption.

Enter your caption here.

Click to select the caption location.

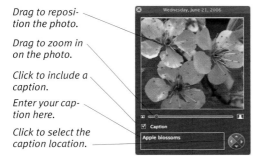

Figure 7.11 Double-click a photo on a date to zoom in, reposition it within the square, add a caption, and position the caption location.

Enter custom text for a particular date under the date number.

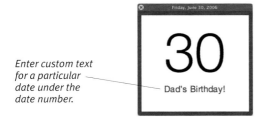

Figure 7.12 Click a date to open a panel in which you can enter custom text. You can apply font styles and colors to the custom text, but not to the date number.

Designing Calendar Pages

Depending on the theme you select, there may be quite a few design options for individual calendar pages. Follow these steps:

To design a calendar page:

1. Select a page by clicking it in the display pane or in the vertical list (**Figure 7.10**).

2. From the Layout pop-up menu, choose a page type, which generally involves the number of photos on the top page.

3. From the Design pop-up menu, choose a design (most themes have only a few).

4. If you don't like any of the designs, click the Themes button and choose a new theme from the calendar design dialog.

5. Drag photos from the unplaced photo list to photo slots on the top page or to individual dates on the bottom page. Move or delete photos until the page looks the way you want.

6. Double-click photos on dates to zoom and position them, and to add captions (**Figure 7.11**).

7. Enter text in any provided text boxes, and add text to individual dates by clicking a date and typing the text in the pop-up panel (**Figure 7.12**).

✔ Tips

- When viewing calendar pages in the vertical list, you can click the top or bottom page of the thumbnail to select it (use the controls explained in **Figure 7.10**), which helps when choosing page designs.

- Some themes offer independent designs for the top and bottom pages; others apply the design to both pages at once.

- Captions can appear only in cells adjacent to their pictures.

Creating Books Overview

Because books offer the most flexibility, they require the most effort to create. But fear not; iPhoto still makes the process far more simple than laying it out by hand would be. Here's my recommended process:

To create a book:

1. Make a normal album with the photos you want in your book (see "Creating Albums" and "Adding Photos to Sources" in Chapter 3, "Organizing Photos").

2. Arrange the photos in the album in the rough order you want them to appear in the book (see "Sorting Photos" in Chapter 3, "Organizing Photos"). Make sure no photos are selected when you're done.

3. Click the Book button under the display pane (**Figure 7.13**).

4. In the book design dialog, choose a book size from the Book Type pop-up menu and select a theme from the list of themes. The dialog shows a preview of each book size and theme (**Figure 7.14**).
   After informing you of how to add photos to the book, iPhoto creates your book.

5. For each book page, set the number of photos and the design using the Page Type and Page Design pop-up menus, and add text as desired. You can drag photos from slot to slot to move them around or off the page entirely to put them back in the unplaced photo list.

6. When you're done, click the Buy Book button, and run through the process of ordering your book.

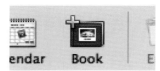

Figure 7.13 To make a book from an album, select it and click the Book button.

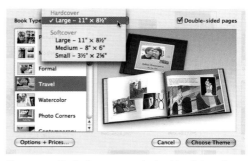

Figure 7.14 Next, choose your desired book type from the Book Type pop-up menu and pick a theme from the scrolling list of themes.

Avoid Autoflow!

Should you let iPhoto lay out your book automatically via the Autoflow button later on? Only if you're particularly short on time and want a quick result. It's much harder to re-arrange photos on pre-built pages (so use automatic layout only if your photos are already in the correct order). Also, iPhoto can't guess how many related photos you've given it or which photos are likely to look good together in a two-page spread, so expect to spend time fixing every page.

There's no harm in trying an automatic layout, but if you don't like it, delete the book and start over, rather than trying to fix each page. I never use the Autoflow button.

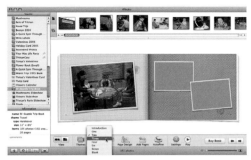

Figure 7.15 Choose the number of photos you want to appear on the page from the Page Type pop-up menu.

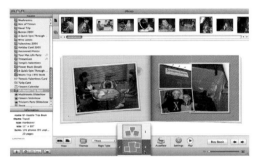

Figure 7.16 Next, choose a design from the Page Design pop-up menu.

✔ More Tips

- The page designs assume an aspect ratio of 4 x 3, so if you use a non-standard cropping ratio, photos may not line up as you expect (see "Cropping Photos" in Chapter 4, "Editing Photos"). A different page design or photo arrangement might help, or you may have to zoom in on the photo and drag it within the slot frame.

- At any time, you can click the Autoflow button to have iPhoto lay out the rest of the photos in the unplaced photo list automatically. I recommend against it.

Designing Book Pages

If you choose to lay out your photos on pages manually (and you should), you need to make a number of choices about how each page will look.

To design a page:

1. Select a page by clicking it.

2. From the Page Type pop-up menu, choose either the page type (Introduction, One, Two, etc.) or the number of photos you want to appear on the page (**Figure 7.15**).

   iPhoto changes the design of the selected page, pushing already placed photos up to the unplaced photo list if you reduced the number of available photo slots.

3. Add, remove, or rearrange photos within the available slots.

4. From the Page Design pop-up menu, choose a design (**Figure 7.16**).

5. Repeat steps 2–4 until you have the page looking exactly as you want.

✔ Tips

- Each theme offers different page design possibilities, ranging from none (Picture Book) to some that vary primarily by background color (Watercolor, Crayon). Spend some time looking at the page designs in each theme to get a feel for which ones you like the most.

- If you want your cover image to appear inside the book as well, you must duplicate it (see "Duplicating Photos" in Chapter 4, "Editing Photos").

- After the cover page, which is required, the other page designs are optional.

- The more photos in a page design, the smaller they appear on the page.

Adding, Deleting, and Moving Book Pages

No matter how many photos you use to create a book, iPhoto creates the book with 20 blank pages (10 if single-sided). You should fill up those pages, since you'll pay for blanks, but what if you need more, or what if you find yourself with extras at the end?

To add a page or page spread:

◆ Click the Add Pages button or choose Add Page from the Edit menu.

iPhoto adds either one page, if you're viewing a single page at a time, or a two-page spread, if you're viewing page spreads, to the right of the currently selected page or page spread, and fills the new page or pages with photos from the unplaced photo list (**Figure 7.17**).

To delete a page:

◆ While viewing pages (not unplaced photos) in the scrolling list, select a page, choose Remove Page (Delete) from the Edit menu, and click Delete when iPhoto asks if you want to delete the page.

To move a page or page spread:

◆ While viewing pages (not unplaced photos) in the scrolling list, drag a page or page spread (it depends on your current view) from one position in the scrolling list to another position (**Figure 7.18**).

iPhoto rearranges the pages in the book to match.

✔ Tip

■ Remember that you can choose Undo (Cmd Z) from the Edit menu if you add or delete pages by mistake.

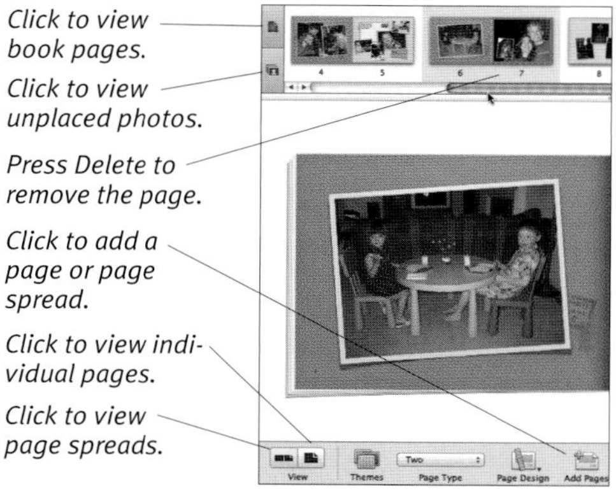

Click to view book pages.
Click to view unplaced photos.
Press Delete to remove the page.
Click to add a page or page spread.
Click to view individual pages.
Click to view page spreads.

Figure 7.17 Use the controls in book mode to set whether you're seeing pages or unplaced photos in the scrolling list, to set whether pages appear by themselves or as two-page spreads, and to add new pages.

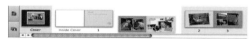

Figure 7.18 To rearrange pages, drag them from position to position in the scrolling list.

Arrangement Tips

Think carefully about the best arrangement of photos and pages in your book. A chronological layout may work well for vacation photos, whereas mixing shots of people might make more sense for party photos.

For the best layouts, pay attention to the photos that will appear on the same page to make sure they aren't overlapping and have compatible colors, consider not just one page at a time but the entire two-page spread, and think about the direction people are facing when placing multiple photos on a page (Control-click a photo and choose Mirror Image to make people face the opposite direction).

Note that page designs can change when you swap landscape and portrait photos.

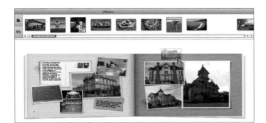

Figure 7.19 To add a photo to a page, creating a new slot in the process, drag a photo to a blank portion of the page, as I'm doing on the right-hand page.

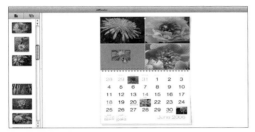

Figure 7.20 To add a photo to an existing slot, drag it to the destination slot, as I'm doing to the lower left corner slot in this calendar page.

Working with Photos on Pages

There are a few things you can do after clicking a photo to select it. All these actions use the same commands you'd use in organize or edit mode but are active when creating books, calendars, and cards.

◆ You can rotate the photo.

◆ You can duplicate the photo.

◆ You can revert to the original version of the photo.

◆ You can set the title of one or more photos using the Information pane or the Batch Change command.

◆ You can see more information about the photo.

Arranging Photos on Book and Calendar Pages

As you design pages in books and calendars, you must arrange photos so they appear in the right order.

To arrange photos on pages:

◆ To change the number of photo slots on a page, choose a different page type from the Page Type (book) or Layout (calendar) pop-up menu.

If the new page type has fewer slots, iPhoto pushes already placed photos back into the unused photo list.

◆ To add a photo to a page manually, drag it from the unplaced photo list or from another page to a blank portion of the page (**Figure 7.19**).

◆ To remove a photo from a photo slot, drag the photo from the slot to the area outside the page, or to the unplaced photo list.

iPhoto removes the photo from the slot, putting it either at the beginning of the unplaced photo list or where you dropped it. The slot may or may not disappear, depending on the number of remaining slots.

◆ To add a photo to a slot, drag it either from the unplaced photo list or from another visible slot, to the desired slot (**Figure 7.20**).

If the destination slot is empty, iPhoto assigns the photo that slot. If the destination slot is already occupied, iPhoto swaps the two photos.

◆ To change how a photo overlaps with an adjacent photo, (Control)-click it and choose Move to Front or Send to Back from the contextual menu that appears.

Editing Photos on Pages

While you're laying out and arranging photos in cards, books, and calendars, you may discover that a particular photo would look better if it were cropped more heavily or otherwise edited. You can easily make non-permanent crops (zooming into a photo) or switch to edit mode for other changes.

To zoom and center photos:

1. Double-click a photo to reveal the zoom slider above the image (**Figure 7.21**).

2. Drag the slider to the right to zoom into the image, essentially cropping it further without actually changing the original.

3. Drag the image itself within the photo slot to center the photo within its frame.

4. Click anywhere outside the photo when you're done.

To edit photos:

1. [Control]-click a photo and choose Edit Photo from the contextual menu that appears (**Figure 7.22**).

2. Make your changes, and when you're done, either click the Done button or double-click the photo to return.

✔ Tips

- In certain cases, you may need to re-center photos within their frames even if you haven't zoomed; certain page designs cut off the edges of photos.

- To fit a photo within its frame (after you've zoomed, or if it's wrong to start with), [Control]-click it and choose Fit Photo to Frame Size from the contextual menu that appears.

- An editing shortcut: double-click the photo when the zoom slider is showing to switch to edit mode.

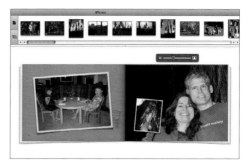

Figure 7.21 To zoom into a photo, double-click it, drag the zoom slider to the right, and then drag the photo around to re-center it, as I've done in the large picture on the right-hand page above.

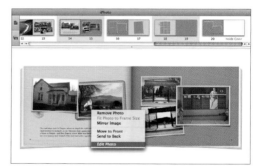

Figure 7.22 To make other editing changes, Control-click the photo and choose Edit Photo. When you're finished, click the Done button to return to the book, card, or calendar that you're creating.

Zooming Is Cool!

I adore iPhoto's zooming and centering capabilities, since many photos look better on card, book, and calendar layouts when they're zoomed further than they were cropped initially. Although zooming acts like cropping, and may cause a yellow warning icon to appear if there isn't enough data in the zoomed portion to print well, it's entirely non-destructive and doesn't affect the original file.

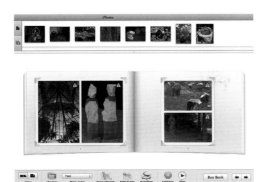

Figure 7.23 When a page design calls for a photo to be printed larger than its resolution allows, iPhoto places a warning icon on the offending image.

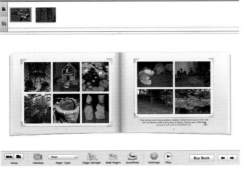

Figure 7.24 To make the warning icon disappear, change the page design so the printed size better matches the resolution of the image. Adding more photos decreased the size of each photo to the point where they would print at a decent quality.

Text Warning Icons

If you see a small, yellow, triangular warning icon next to a text box while designing pages (**Figure 7.24**), it's because the text doesn't fit in the box. The font size is predetermined by the theme, but you can switch to a different font or shorten the text.

Dealing with Warning Icons

One problem that can appear any time you print a digital photo is poor quality, or rather, your inability to predict the quality of a print. Numerous variables can play a part in reducing the quality of a printed image, but iPhoto tries to help prevent one of the most common—printing an image at a size larger than is appropriate for the image's resolution. When you have an image that's too low resolution for the proposed size, iPhoto displays a triangular warning icon to alert you to the problem (**Figure 7.23**).

Ways to deal with a low-resolution warning icon:

◆ Choose a different page design so the photo with the warning icon shrinks small enough that the icon disappears (**Figure 7.24**).

◆ Move the image to a different location on the current page or another page where it will appear at the necessary smaller size.

◆ Cropping a photo or zooming it makes it more likely that the image won't be large enough to print properly. To remove cropping, select the image, and from the Photos menu choose Revert to Original. Remember that this will remove all your changes, not just the cropping. Try again after cropping the image less heavily.

◆ If you run into this problem regularly, make sure your camera is set to take pictures at its highest resolution.

◆ If you decide to live with a low-resolution warning icon, note that the icon won't appear on the printed page.

Entering and Editing Text

Once you have laid out all your pages to your satisfaction, you can enter or edit the text that appears with the photos.

Ways to enter or edit text:

◆ Click a text box and either enter new text or edit the existing text. While you're editing, iPhoto displays a selection rectangle around the text box (**Figure 7.25**).

◆ You can use all the standard editing techniques and commands that you've become accustomed to as a Mac user—commands like Cut, Copy, and Paste, not to mention double- and triple-clicking.

◆ You can check the spelling of your text. See "Checking Spelling as You Type," in this chapter.

✔ Tips

■ If you leave iPhoto's placeholder text alone, those text boxes won't appear in the final book. Photos don't take over the empty space; it just prints blank.

■ iPhoto can pick up existing album names, titles, and comments for books if Automatically Enter Photo Information is selected in the settings dialog.

■ Changes you make to titles and comments no longer propagate to other modes, as they did in previous versions of iPhoto.

■ iPhoto no longer tries to simplify editing by zooming in on the page in the display pane so the text displays larger. Now you must zoom in manually, using the main size slider (**Figure 7.26**).

■ If you copy and paste text, the font-related information of the copied text accompanies the pasted text, which may not be desirable.

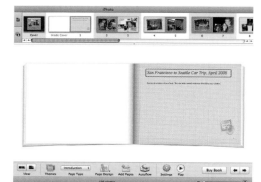

Figure 7.25 To edit or enter text, click a text box and enter new text or edit the existing text. If there is too much text in the text box, a warning icon appears to alert you when you click out of the box. No scroll bars will appear; you must edit the extra text blindly.

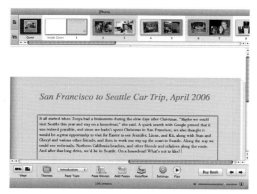

Figure 7.26 It's helpful to zoom in using the size slider so you can see what you're typing.

Typing Text "Correctly"

You're going to zoom into your photos perfectly and arrange them just so—are you then going to write text that looks downright trashy? Follow a few simple rules to make sure your text looks as good as your pictures and iPhoto layouts (if you don't believe me, compare the example captions to the left). For details, snag a copy of Robin Williams's classic book *The Mac is not a typewriter.*

Rules for classy looking text:

◆ Put only one space after periods, commas, question marks, parentheses, or any other punctuation.

◆ Use true quotation marks (" ") instead of double hash marks (" "). To get them, type [Option][[ ] and [Option][Shift][[ ].

◆ Use true apostrophes (' ') instead of hash marks (' '). To get them, type [Option][ ]] and [Option][Shift][ ]].

◆ Punctuation goes inside quotes.

◆ Instead of double hyphens (--), use an em dash (—). Press [Option][Shift][-].

◆ If you want to put a copyright symbol (©) in your book instead of (c), get it by typing [Option][G].

◆ To make a list, use bullets (·) rather than asterisks (*). To type a bullet, press [Option][8].

◆ In text boxes that have relatively long lines of text, edit to prevent the last line from containing only a single word.

◆ Avoid underlining text. Instead, use italics, which may require that you select an italic version of the font you're using.

◆ Use uppercase sparingly, and only in titles. Uppercase text is hard to read.

The Wrong Way

Here it's a cold afternoon in March. Mary is gazing out over the GRAND CANYON at sunset--check out the sweater Grandma Bunny actually <u>knitted</u> for her. The other folks in this picture are:

* My friend Samuel from work.

* Mary's cousin JoAnn.

* JoAnn's husband, who goes by "Chuck".

Copyright (c) 2006 Joe Schmoe

The Right Way

Here it's a cold afternoon in March. Mary is gazing out over the Grand Canyon at sunset—check out the sweater Grandma Bunny actually *knitted* for her. The other folks in this picture are:

· My friend Samuel from work.

· Mary's cousin JoAnn.

· JoAnn's husband, who goes by "Chuck."

Copyright © 2006 Joe Schmoe

Changing Fonts, Styles, and Sizes Globally

Although Apple hired professional designers to create the card, calendar, and book templates, iPhoto makes it possible to change the font, style, and size of text for different categories of text. Be careful modifying these defaults, though, because Apple's font choices are highly intentional, and if you change them too much, the results may not look as elegant as you'd like.

To change fonts, styles, and sizes:

1. When creating a card, calendar, or book, click the Settings button to bring up the settings dialog (**Figure 7.27**, **Figure 7.28**, and **Figure 7.29**). For calendars, click the Fonts tab, if necessary.

2. To change the look of different classes of text, choose from the various pop-up menus to change the font and style, and enter new sizes in the size fields.

3. Click OK to apply your changes.

✔ Tips

■ The classes of text often change for different themes.

■ If you muck up the text settings badly, click Restore Defaults to reset them.

■ Using certain Type 1 PostScript fonts can cause your book order to be cancelled. For more information, see http://docs.info.apple.com/article. html?artnum=300964.

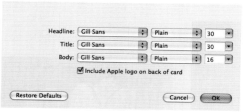

Figure 7.27 Cards have relatively little text, and thus provide only a few categories you can modify. Deselect the Include Apple Logo on Back of Card checkbox if you don't want to advertise Apple's role in making your gorgeous card.

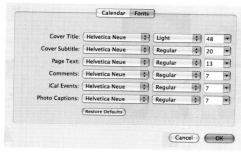

Figure 7.28 Calendars offer quite a few more categories of text to modify. Be careful, because some caption and event text is very small, and not all fonts work well at small sizes.

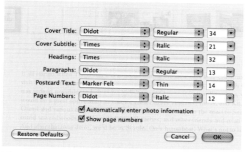

Figure 7.29 Along with a number of categories of text, books offer the option to include photo titles and comments automatically, and to turn page numbers on and off.

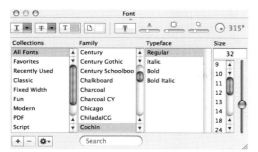

Figure 7.30 Select the font, style, and size from the Family, Typeface, and Size columns in the Font palette.

Changing Fonts, Styles, and Sizes per Text Box

iPhoto also provides several ways to modify the font, style, and size of selected text.

To change fonts, styles, and sizes:

1. Select the text you want to change.

2. Open the Font palette by choosing Show Fonts ((Cmd)(T)) from the Edit menu's Font menu.

3. In the Font palette, you can choose a font from the Family column, a style from the Typeface column, and a size from the Size column (**Figure 7.30**).

   iPhoto changes the currently selected text to match your choices.

To change just styles:

◆ Select some text, and from the Edit menu's hierarchical Font menu, choose Bold ((Cmd)(B)) or Italic.

◆ (Control)-click the selected text, and choose Bold, Italic, Underline, or Outline from the contextual Font menu.

✔ Tips

■ Bold and Italic are dimmed in the menus if the current font has no Bold or Italic typeface. Check the Font palette to verify.

■ iPhoto does not provide keyboard shortcuts for Italic, Underline, or Outline.

■ The Restore Defaults button in the settings dialog also overrides any individual font changes you've made.

■ Be judicious in your changes; excessive use of fonts and styles generally looks lousy, and I strongly encourage you to print a page or two on your own printer before buying a card, calendar, or book whose fonts you've changed.

Copying Font and Style Information

If you've set the font, style, and size for one piece of text, you can copy that to any other bit of selected text easily.

1. Select the text whose settings you want to use elsewhere.

2. Choose Copy Style from the Edit menu's hierarchical Font menu.

3. Select the text whose settings you want change.

4. Choose Paste Style from the Edit menu's hierarchical Font menu.

   iPhoto changes the currently selected text to match the font, style, and size of your original selection.

Changing Text Color

Although it's not obvious, iPhoto provides controls to change the color of text as well.

To change colors:

1. To open the Colors palette, [Control]-click a text box and choose Show Colors from the Font menu (**Figure 7.31**).

   or

   In the Font palette, click the text color button.

   iPhoto opens the Colors palette (**Figure 7.32**).

2. Select the text to which you want to apply a color, and click a color in the color wheel.

   iPhoto changes the color of the text.

✔ Tips

- You can apply color only to selected text, not to classes of text in the settings dialog.

- To copy a color from elsewhere on the screen to the color box, click the magnifying glass icon, and then click a color anywhere on the screen.

- Drag the color box to one of the cells of the color swatch collection to save it for repeated use. Clicking one of the color swatches applies it to the selected text.

- Copying fonts also copies colors.

- Use color carefully and sparingly—it's too easy to make a book garish by applying too much color. You don't want your text to compete with your photos.

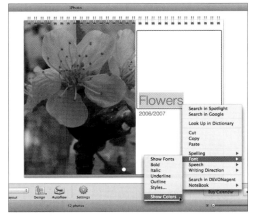

Figure 7.31 To open the Colors palette, Control-click a text box, and from the hierarchical Font menu, choose Show Colors.

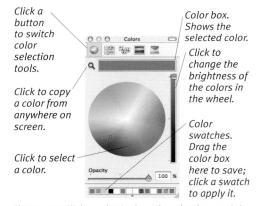

Click a button to switch color selection tools.

Click to copy a color from anywhere on screen.

Click to select a color.

Color box. Shows the selected color.

Click to change the brightness of the colors in the wheel.

Color swatches. Drag the color box here to save; click a swatch to apply it.

Figure 7.32 Click a color in the color wheel to put it in the color box and apply it to the selected text.

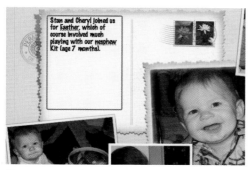

Figure 7.33 Note how iPhoto has underlined the misspelled words in red.

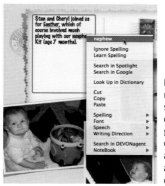

Figure 7.34 To replace a misspelled word with one of iPhoto's guesses, Control-click the word and choose a guess from the contextual menu.

Checking Spelling as You Type

You won't be typing much in iPhoto, but since its editing environment is crude, typos are likely. The last thing you want in a beautifully designed card, calendar, or book is a glaring typo, so I recommend you use Mac OS X's built-in spell checker to verify the spelling of your titles and captions as you type them.

To check spelling as you type:

1. Click a text box, and from the Edit menu's Spelling menu, verify that Check Spelling As You Type has a checkmark next to it.

2. Type your text in any text box.

    iPhoto displays a red line underneath any words that aren't in the system-wide Mac OS X spelling dictionary (**Figure 7.33**).

3. Control-click a word with a red underline to display a contextual menu that enables you to replace the word with one of iPhoto's guesses, ignore the misspelling for this launch of iPhoto, or learn the spelling by adding it to your system-wide Mac OS X dictionary (**Figure 7.34**).

✔ Tips

- Happily, after four broken versions, Apple *finally* fixed Check Spelling As You Type in iPhoto 6 so that it's on by default and stays on all the time.

- Be sure to click every text box before ordering to look for red underlines, since iPhoto won't mark misspellings until you click the text box that contains them.

- Ignore Spelling isn't particularly worthwhile—iPhoto forgets ignored text between launches.

Talking Captions

For longer spans of text, select all the text (Cmd A), Control-click it, and from the Speech menu, choose Start Speaking. iPhoto will read your text to you, which can help identify mistakes.

Printing on Your Own Printer

iPhoto makes it easy to print a card, calendar, or book on your own printer, which is certainly faster than waiting for Apple to deliver the finished product, though books and calendars lack bindings, of course.

To print on your own printer:

1. While in a card, calendar, or book, choose Print from the File menu (Cmd P).

    iPhoto displays the standard Print dialog (**Figure 7.35**).

2. If desired, click Advanced, choose the options you want, and click the Print button.

✔ Tips

■ I like printing individual pages from a book layout to mix photos and text on a single page.

■ I also particularly like printing the date pages from calendars for posting in schools or other organizations.

■ It's difficult to print cards, since you need to print one page, wait for the ink to dry, and then flip the paper and print the second page on the other side, and the two sides may not match up. Test before assuming it will work!

■ Click the Preview button in the Print dialog to see what your output will look like before printing. I strongly recommend that you do this, especially since it simplifies printing only selected pages.

■ Choose Save As PDF from the PDF dropdown menu to generate a PDF instead of printing. It's a nice way to share a calendar or photo layout with a friend since you can send it to them via email or by posting it on the Web.

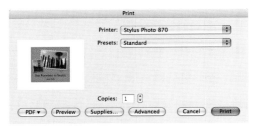

Figure 7.35 To print a book on your own printer, choose Print from the File menu. For additional options, such as a custom page range, click the Advanced button.

Printing Selected Pages

If you want to print just a few pages in your book, you may find it difficult to figure out exactly which page numbers to enter into the Print dialog. That's because iPhoto doesn't assign a page number to the cover, and the inside cover is never printed. Follow these steps for a more obvious approach:

1. Choose Print from the File menu (Cmd P) to bring up the Print dialog.

2. Click Preview to make iPhoto create a PDF and automatically open it in Apple's Preview application.

3. In Preview, review exactly which pages you want to print, paying attention to the page numbers in the page drawer.

4. In Preview, choose Print from the File menu and enter the appropriate page numbers in the Pages fields. Set any other printing options you want, such as number of copies or print quality.

5. Click Print to send your pages to the printer.

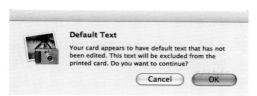

Figure 7.36 If you haven't edited some of iPhoto's default text, it warns you with a dialog like this.

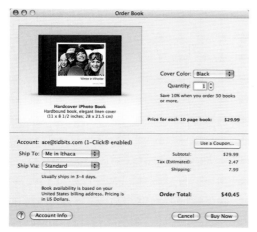

Figure 7.37 Convey the details of your order to Apple in the Order window.

Pricing and Shipping Details

Prices vary by style, size, and number of pages; read Apple's pricing page at www.apple.com/ilife/iphoto/features/pricing.html for details.

Shipping costs vary by the number of items you order and the type of item, but note that per-item shipping costs are less for subsequent items (in other words, if you buy two copies of a book, you'll pay only a little more to receive the second one, instead of double the normal shipping charge).

Ordering Cards, Calendars, and Books

Once you've designed a card, calendar, or book, ordering it from Apple is easy.

To order a card, calendar, or book:

1. Select the item you want to order, and verify that each page looks right.

2. Make sure you're connected to the Internet, and click the Buy button.

   iPhoto assembles the print job, warning you if some photos won't print well, if some default text hasn't been edited (**Figure 7.36**), if other text doesn't fit, or if a book or calendar isn't complete.

   iPhoto then opens the Order window (**Figure 7.37**).

3. For hardcover books only, choose a cover color from the Cover Color pop-up menu.

4. Enter the number of items you want to order in the Quantity field.

   iPhoto automatically updates the total cost as you add and subtract items.

5. Choose the appropriate shipping address and method from the Ship To and Ship Via pop-up menus.

6. Click the Buy Now button.

   iPhoto uploads your pictures and alerts you when it's done.

✔ Tips

- Uploading takes a long time on a slow Internet connection because iPhoto uploads full-size images for best quality.

- If you're warned about low-resolution images, see "Dealing with Warning Icons" in Chapter 9, "Troubleshooting."

SHARING PHOTOS

8

In earlier editions of this book, the "Sharing Photos" chapter covered all of iPhoto's "sharing" tools, including printing, creating slideshows, making Web pages, and more. But iPhoto provides so many ways of sharing photos that I now devote entire chapters to displaying photos onscreen; to printing; and to cards, calendars, and books.

So what's left? Plenty. This chapter focuses on how you can share actual photo files with other people. For instance, you might want to share photos with a family member who also uses your Mac, or a roommate whose Mac is on your network. Or maybe you want to send photos to friends via email or on a CD or DVD. iPhoto can help in all of these situations and more. I've organized this chapter in roughly that order; think of it as near (sharing on your Mac) to far (sending a CD to a Windows-using relative).

It's worth keeping in mind that although Apple has provided various different tools for sharing these original photos, there are usually trade-offs. For instance, it's trickier to burn a CD of photos for someone who uses Windows than for someone who uses iPhoto on the Mac. And to share photos via photo-casting requires a .Mac account. And Apple still hasn't made it easy for people on the same Mac to share an iPhoto Library folder.

Sharing a Library via iPhoto Library Manager

Mac OS X is a multi-user operating system, so it's common for people who share a Mac each to have an account. But what if you want to share the same iPhoto Library among multiple users on the same Mac? You can use Brian Webster's $19.95 shareware iPhoto Library Manager utility, available from http://homepage.mac.com/bwebster/iphotolibrarymanager.html.

To share your library among users:

1. With iPhoto *not* running, rename your iPhoto Library folder to Shared iPhoto Library (to avoid confusion) and move it from the Pictures folder to the Shared folder at the same level as your user folder (**Figure 8.1**). The Shared folder may or may not contain other items.

2. Open iPhoto Library Manager, and drag the Shared iPhoto Library folder from the Finder into the iPhoto Library Folders list in iPhoto Library Manager.

3. Select the Shared iPhoto Library folder in the list, click the Options button, choose Read & Write from each of the three Permissions pop-up menus, and select the three checkboxes underneath.

   These settings cause iPhoto Library Manager to fix the permissions on the Shared iPhoto Library folder whenever necessary (**Figure 8.2**).

4. For each user, log in and repeat steps 2 and 3.

5. From now on, each user on your Mac should launch iPhoto by clicking the Launch iPhoto button in iPhoto Library Manager.

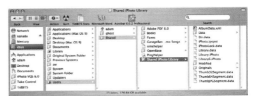

Figure 8.1 Store your iPhoto Library folder in the Shared folder at the same level as your user folder, preferably with a slightly different name to avoid confusion in iPhoto Library Manager.

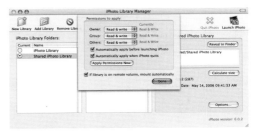

Figure 8.2 Set the permissions properly for shared iPhoto Library folders in the Options dialog in iPhoto Library Manager.

Permissions Problems

You must jump through these hoops to share an iPhoto Library folder because of how iPhoto assigns permissions to thumbnails in the Data folder.

iPhoto Library Manager works around the problem by fixing permissions constantly. The techniques on the opposite page have similar effects: turning on Ignore Ownership on This Volume for an external drive ignores permissions entirely, and the issue disappears with network volumes because each user can log into a shared account, thus ensuring that all newly imported photos are written with the same ownership.

For more on this, including yet another technique, see the article I wrote on the topic for Macworld Magazine at www.macworld.com/2006/05/secrets/junedigitalphoto/.

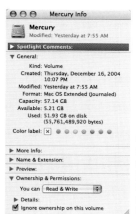

Figure 8.3 To use another hard drive to store a shared iPhoto Library folder, you must select the Ignore Ownership on This Volume checkbox.

Choosing Network Sharing Approaches

iPhoto's official method of sharing photos over a network is discussed on the next page, "Sharing Photos via iPhoto Sharing." What's the difference between that approach and the shared volume method discussed on this page?

Use the shared volume method to share an entire iPhoto Library folder and have each person make changes that are seen by every other person. This method lets you share the work of editing photos, making albums, and assigning keywords.

Use iPhoto's photo-sharing approach to let other people see and potentially copy your photos without making any other changes. This approach works best when each person has their own primary collection of photos but wants to access a few photos from other people.

Neither approach is "better," and which you choose depends mostly on whether you consider photos community property or personal property that can be shared.

Sharing a Library via a Shared Volume

There's another trick you can use to share photos among multiple users of the same Mac, and it also works for sharing an iPhoto Library folder across a network.

This technique requires a "shared volume," which is either another hard drive or a Mac with Personal File Sharing turned on in the Sharing preference pane. If you're using a network, it must be at least 54 Mbps AirPort Extreme, or preferably 100 Mbps Ethernet; anything else will be too slow.

To share your library among users:

1. If you are using another hard drive as your shared volume, select it in the Finder, choose Get Info (Cmd I) from the File menu, and under Ownership & Permissions in the Get Info window, select the Ignore Ownership on This Volume checkbox (**Figure 8.3**).

2. With iPhoto *not* running, copy your iPhoto Library folder from the Pictures folder to where you want to store it on the shared volume.

3. Rename the iPhoto Library folder in your Pictures folder to "Old iPhoto Library."

4. For each user (whether on the same Mac or over your network), open iPhoto while holding down Option, click the Choose Library button, and select the iPhoto Library folder on the shared volume.

   Option-launching iPhoto and selecting a library teaches iPhoto to use the selected library instead of the default.

5. From now on, each user should be able to use iPhoto normally, although only one person may use the shared iPhoto Library folder at a time.

Sharing Photos via iPhoto Sharing

iPhoto enables you to share all your photos (but not movies!), or just individual albums, with other iPhoto users on your network. iPhoto sharing is easy to turn on and use.

To share photos among Macs:

1. From the iPhoto menu, choose Preferences ([Cmd][,]) and click the Sharing tab.

   iPhoto displays the Sharing preferences (**Figure 8.4**).

2. Select Share My Photos, and then select either Share Entire Library or Share Selected Albums.

3. If you selected Share Selected Albums, select the albums you want to share in the list below (**Figure 8.5**).

4. In the Shared Name field, enter a name for the shared folder under which your photos will appear for other users on your Mac and network.

5. If you want to restrict access to your shared photos, enter a password in the Require Password field. You'll then have to give that password to approved users (**Figure 8.5**).

6. Close the Preferences window.

✔ Tips

- Amazingly, iPhoto cannot share movies you take with your camera via network sharing. They simply don't show up.

- iPhoto sharing also works between users of the same Mac, when both are logged in via Fast User Switching.

- iPhoto automatically selects the Require Password checkbox when you type the password for the first time.

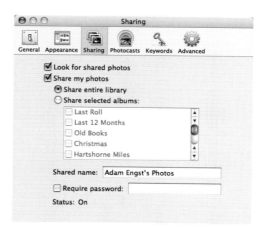

Figure 8.4 Turn on photo sharing in the Sharing pane of iPhoto's Preferences window.

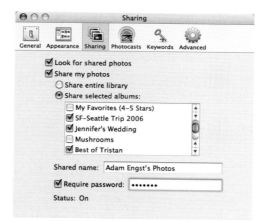

Figure 8.5 You can restrict shared photos to specific albums, and you can require that users enter a password to access your shared photos.

Turning Off Sharing

To turn off photo sharing, simply deselect the Share My Photos checkbox in the Sharing pane of iPhoto's Preferences window. If anyone is currently connected to your photos, iPhoto asks if you're sure you want to turn off photo sharing first.

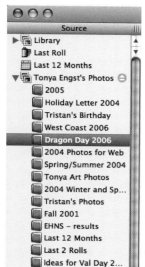

Figure 8.6 You access shared photos in the Source pane; click the shared photo folder to load it, and click the expansion triangle to the left to display its albums.

Actions Allowed for Shared Photos

Just because you can see shared albums in your Source pane doesn't mean you can do everything with their contents that you can do with your own photos.

You *can* copy shared photos and albums to your Library or albums, print shared photos, play a basic slideshow with shared photos, send shared photos to others via email, and upload shared photos to .Mac Slides.

You *cannot* edit shared photos in any way, assign keywords and ratings, get photo info, make a new album on the remote Mac, use a shared album to create a book, put shared photos on your Desktop or use them as your screen saver, make an iDVD slideshow, burn them to disc, send them to iWeb, or export them in any way.

Basically, you can only view shared photos; for any action that requires making changes, you must first copy the photos to your Mac.

Accessing Shared Photos

Working with shared photos is similar to using an iPhoto disc (see "Importing from an iPhoto Disc" in Chapter 2, "Importing and Managing Photos").

To access shared photos:

1. Make sure the Mac with the shared photos has iPhoto launched and photo sharing turned on.

2. On the Mac from which you want to access the shared photos, launch iPhoto, and from the iPhoto menu, choose Preferences ([Cmd], [,]) and click the Sharing tab.

   iPhoto displays the Sharing preferences.

3. Make sure Look for Shared Photos is selected (**Figure 8.4**; opposite).

4. Close the Preferences window.

   In the Source pane, iPhoto creates a shared folder for the shared photos.

5. Click the shared folder to load it. If the shared photos are protected by a password, enter it when prompted.

   iPhoto loads the shared photos, displaying individual albums underneath the shared folder when you click its expansion triangle (**Figure 8.6**).

✔ Tips

- If more than one copy of iPhoto on your network is sharing photos, iPhoto creates a Shared Photos folder and puts all the albums for shared photos inside it.

- To disconnect from a shared photo album, click the little eject button next to its name in the Source pane.

- To import all the photos in a shared album, drag it to another spot in the Source pane.

Sharing Photos via Photocasting

iPhoto 6 introduced an innovative new way to share photos with friends and relatives over the Internet: photocasting. In essence, photocasting involves iPhoto automatically uploading all the photos in an album to .Mac and keeping the online version in sync as you make changes to that album. Creating a photocast requires a .Mac account (see "Setting Up a .Mac Account" in Chapter 5, "Showing Photos Onscreen"), but accessing one doesn't.

To create a photocast:

1. Create an album or smart album containing the photos you want to photocast (see "Creating Albums" and "Creating and Editing Smart Albums" in Chapter 3, "Organizing Photos").

2. With your new album selected, choose Photocast from the Share menu or click the Photocast button, if it's showing.

    iPhoto displays the Publish a Photocast dialog (**Figure 8.7**).

3. Choose the size at which you want your photos uploaded, check the Automatically Update When Album Changes checkbox if you want to update the photocast on changes, and select Require Name and Password (and fill in a name and password) if you want to restrict access to your photocast.

4. When you're done, click Publish.

    iPhoto uploads the photos, displaying a progress pie chart as it goes. When it's done, iPhoto displays the URL to your photocast and offers to announce it via email (**Figure 8.8**).

5. To create an email message with the photocast's URL, click Announce Photocast.

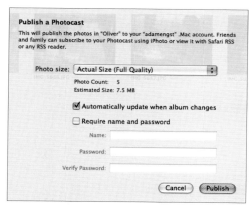

Figure 8.7 Choose the size of photos to publish, and decide whether you want the album to update automatically, and if you want to restrict access.

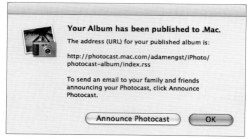

Figure 8.8 When iPhoto is done uploading, it gives you the option of announcing your photocast via email; it's a good way to get the URL where you can copy it.

✔ Tips

- Photocasts cannot contain movies.

- The Actual Size option recompresses photos to make them smaller, so the photos aren't as high quality as the originals.

- To stop publishing a photocast (and remove the photos from your .Mac account), select the album, choose Photocast from the Share menu, and click Stop Publishing when prompted. You can also delete the album.

- On your iDisk, photocasts are stored in folders within Web/Sites/iPhoto/.

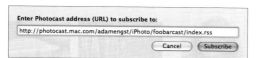

Figure 8.9 To subscribe to a photocast in iPhoto 6, choose Subscribe to Photocast from the File menu, then enter the photocast's URL in the dialog that appears.

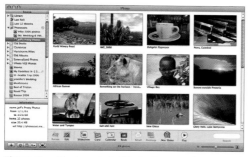

Figure 8.10 Photocasts in iPhoto 6 appear in a special Photocasts folder in the Source pane and can be used almost like any other photo in iPhoto.

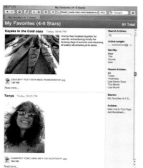

Figure 8.11 Photocasts in Safari use Safari's RSS interface; click a thumbnail to display a larger version of the image.

Other RSS Readers

Those using Windows (or at least not using iPhoto 6), can use the following RSS readers to view iPhoto 6's photocasts:

◆ Bloglines (works in any Web browser): www.bloglines.com

◆ Sage (for the Firefox Web browser; replace "photocast" in the URL with "web"): http://sage.mozdev.org/

Accessing Photocasts

Although creating a photocast requires a .Mac account, subscribing to one does not. The subscriber needs iPhoto 6, Apple's Safari Web browser, or another photo-capable RSS reader on any platform.

To subscribe to a photocast:

1. Receive a photocast URL in email, or find one posted on the Web. Copy it to the clipboard.

2. In iPhoto 6, choose Subscribe to Photocast ([Cmd][U]) to open a dialog into which you can paste the photocast URL (**Figure 8.9**). In Safari, choose Open Location ([Cmd][L]) from the File menu. (Other RSS readers will have a command along the lines of Subscribe or Open.)

3. Paste the photocast URL and press Return.

   iPhoto, Safari, or the RSS reader subscribes to the photocast and downloads all the photos contained within it (**Figure 8.10** and **Figure 8.11**).

✔ Tips

- You can use photocast images like other photos. However, you cannot burn discs with them or photocast them yourself without copying them to a local album.

- Photocasts are stored like film rolls within the Originals, Modified, and Data folders in your iPhoto Library folder, but oddly, they don't appear in your Library.

- To update a photocast manually, click the little circling arrows icon next to the Photocasts folder.

- To unsubscribe from a photocast, delete the photocast album. When you do, iPhoto prompts you to import the photos, because otherwise you'll lose them.

Exporting Files

iPhoto's export capabilities are fairly limited, but they should suffice for most situations.

To export files:

1. Select one or more photos.

2. Choose Export from the File menu ([Cmd][Shift][E]).

    iPhoto displays the Export Photos dialog (**Figure 8.12**).

3. If it's not already selected, click the File Export tab.

4. Choose the format for the exported photos from the Format pop-up menu, select an image scale, and select how you want them named. Then click the Export button.

5. iPhoto displays a Save dialog. Navigate to your desired folder and click OK to save your images.

✔ Tips

- iPhoto can export into only JPEG, TIFF, and PNG formats. For other formats, use a tool like GraphicConverter; see the sidebar to the right.

- Only JPEG files can be scaled to a different size; if you save in TIFF or PNG format, you're stuck with the full image size.

- When iPhoto scales an image, it does so proportionally with the limits you set.

- The point of the Original item in the Format pop-up menu is to enable you to export a RAW file, GIF file, or other file format that iPhoto would have converted to JPEG when it was edited.

- If you export only a single image, iPhoto gives you a chance to rename the image manually before saving (**Figure 8.13**).

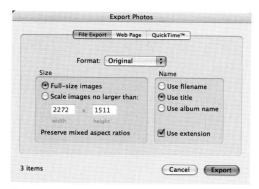

Figure 8.12 Use the File Export pane in the Export Photos dialog to choose the format, scale, and name for your exported images.

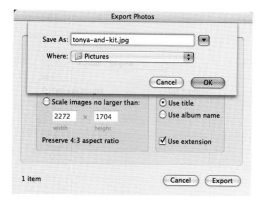

Figure 8.13 If you export only a single image, iPhoto lets you name it from within a dialog.

Use GraphicConverter

If you want to do anything more than basic exporting of files, try the $30 shareware GraphicConverter, available at www.lemkesoft.com/en/graphcon.htm. GraphicConverter is far better at converting images between formats, resizing them, and performing many other useful tasks, a number of which can be done in batch mode on an entire collection of images.

EXPORTING FILES

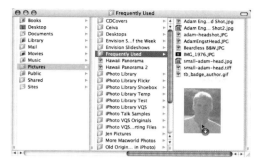

Figure 8.14 For a quick export without any chance to reformat, rename, or resize the exported photos, just drag one or more to the Finder.

Exporting Files by Dragging

If you just want copies of a couple of photos and don't need to reformat or resize them, you can just drag the files to the Finder.

To export multiple files:

◆ Select one or more photos and drag the selection to a folder in the Finder (**Figure 8.14**).

iPhoto saves the files where you drop them, using each file's original name.

✔ Tips

■ When you drag photos to export them, you aren't given the opportunity to change their scale or image format.

■ You can also drag photos to other photo-related programs. So, for instance, you could maintain another photo catalog in a program like iView MediaPro by dragging photos from iPhoto into iView MediaPro's window. This is not actually exporting, since the other programs are working with the same file as iPhoto. Because of this, don't drag files to image-editing programs and make changes, because iPhoto won't be able to track those changes. And definitely don't delete photos from those other programs!

■ If you want to export photos in order to burn them to a CD-R disc for a person who doesn't use iPhoto, your best bet is to drag photos from iPhoto to folders in the Finder, and then burn those folders. Watch out for the rotation problem; see the sidebar to the left.

■ Unfortunately, you can't drag an album to the Finder to create a new folder containing the album's photos.

Exported Photos May Not Be Rotated

If you export a photo you've edited only by rotating it, the exported file isn't rotated if you use the drag-to-the-Finder method of exporting. This error happens because iPhoto rotates only the photo's thumbnail initially, rotating the actual photo only if necessary.

You can work around this problem in two ways. First, use the Export Photos dialog instead of dragging to the Finder. Second, make another editing change to the photo before dragging the photo to the Finder. Any editing change other than rotation forces iPhoto to modify the photo's file instead of just the thumbnail, which sets the rotation properly as well.

Emailing Photos

For many people, email is the preferred method of receiving photos from friends.

To configure iPhoto for email:

◆ In the General pane of iPhoto's Preferences window, choose your email program from the Email Photos Using pop-up menu (**Figure 8.15**).

iPhoto changes the Email button's icon to match your email program.

To send photos via email:

1. Select the photos you want to send.

2. Choose Email from the Share menu, or click the Email button.

iPhoto displays a dialog with options for your photos (**Figure 8.16**).

3. Choose the maximum size you want the photos to appear from the Size pop-up menu, and, if you want to include titles and comments, select their checkboxes.

4. Click the Compose button.

iPhoto exports the pictures (converting them to JPEG), creates a new message, and attaches the photos, which appear inline only in Apple's Mail (**Figure 8.17**).

✔ Tips

■ If you send too many photos, or don't shrink their sizes enough, your message may be too large to be delivered.

■ You can also drag photos from iPhoto into some email programs, but that sends the photos at full size.

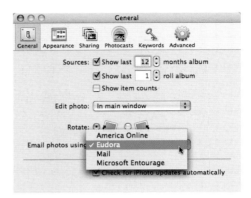

Figure 8.15 In the General pane of iPhoto's Preferences, choose your email program from the Email Photos Using pop-up menu.

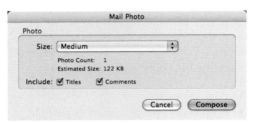

Figure 8.16 Make sure to set a reasonable size for your photos before sending them via email or they'll take too long to transfer for you and your recipient.

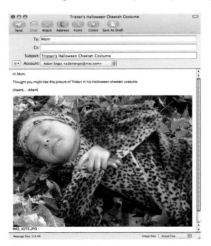

Figure 8.17 Here's what the message looks like in Mail. You don't get much control over the layout, but don't worry, because there's no way of telling what it will look like on the receiving end anyway.

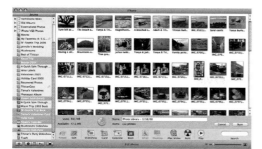

Figure 8.18 To get started, select the items you want to burn in the Source pane, choose Burn from the Share menu, and then insert a blank disc.

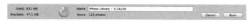

Figure 8.19 Once you've inserted the disc, iPhoto lets you name your disc and gives you information about how much data will be burned to it.

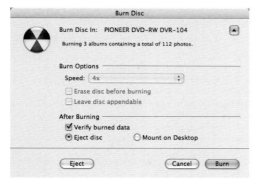

Figure 8.20 iPhoto verifies that you really want to burn a disc with one last dialog that also provides additional burn options if you click the button in the upper-right corner.

Receiving an iPhoto Disc

If someone sends you an iPhoto disc, you can browse the photos on it directly; to import them see "Importing from an iPhoto Disc" in Chapter 2, "Importing and Managing Photos."

Sharing Photos on Disc with iPhoto Users

Email is fine for a few photos, but if you want to share a lot of photos, burning a CD or DVD to send to your recipient works better.

To burn an iPhoto disc:

1. Select the items you want to burn, which is best done by selecting entire film rolls in the display pane, or folders, albums, books, or slideshows in the Source pane (**Figure 8.18**).

2. From the Share menu, choose Burn or click the Burn button, insert a blank disc if prompted, and click OK.

   Below the display pane, iPhoto shows the name of the disc and information about how much data will be burned to the disc (**Figure 8.19**). The disc icon will be red if it can't hold the selected photos.

3. Select fewer or more photos to use the space on your destination disc as desired.

4. Change the name of the disc if you want.

5. When everything looks right, click the Burn button (next to the disc name) to start the burn, and when iPhoto asks you to confirm one last time and lets you set additional burning options, click Burn (**Figure 8.20**).

   iPhoto creates a disk image, copies the selected photos to it, and burns the disc.

✔ Tips

- If you select albums to burn, the iPhoto disc will retain those album references. Film roll information is lost, however.

- Your disc name appears in both iPhoto and in the Finder.

- On the disc, your photos are stored in an iPhoto Library folder like the main one.

Sharing Photos on Disc with Windows Users

Alas, not everyone uses a Mac, and not even all Mac users use iPhoto, and for these people using an iPhoto disc is difficult, since they must sort through the iPhoto Library folder's directory structure to find the photos you've sent them (though the new iPhoto 6 structure is easier). Follow these steps instead.

To burn a disc for use by non-iPhoto users:

1. Insert a blank CD or DVD, choose Open Finder from the Action pop-up menu (**Figure 8.21**), and then give your disc a name like any other volume.

2. In iPhoto, select a group of photos you want to burn and export them to the just-inserted disc (see "Exporting Files," earlier in this chapter). If you wish, when saving the exported photos, click the New Folder button to create a new folder and store those photos in it.

3. Repeat step 2 until you've exported all the photos you wish to burn.

4. In the Finder, select the disc icon on the Desktop or in a Finder window's sidebar, choose Burn Disc from the File menu, and verify the disc name and burn speed before clicking Burn (**Figure 8.22**).

   The Finder proceeds to burn the disc (**Figure 8.23**).

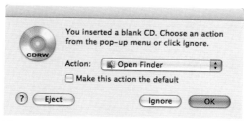

Figure 8.21 Choose Open Finder from the Action pop-up menu after you insert the blank disc.

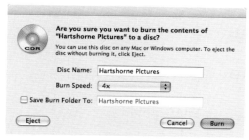

Figure 8.22 The Finder verifies the name and burn speed before burning.

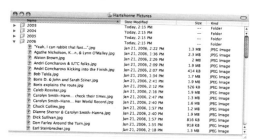

Figure 8.23 You end up with a simple hierarchy of photos on the disc, easily usable in any computer and with any program.

Setting CD/DVD Actions

If the Finder doesn't ask how you wish to handle a blank disc when you insert it, open the CDs & DVDs preference pane in System Preferences and set the Insert a Blank CD/DVD pop-up menus to Ask What to Do.

9

TROUBLESHOOTING

The Trouble with Bugs

Many iPhoto problems that I've seen people report seem to be specific to their photos, a particular iPhoto Library folder, their Mac, or the phase of the moon, and I have been unable to reproduce them. I still include here the potential problem and any solutions I've heard of or can think of, but this uncertainty makes it impossible for me to say when or if Apple has fixed the incorrect behavior. As such, some of the problems and solutions listed in this chapter may no longer apply to iPhoto 6; there's simply no way to tell.

I continue to include these suggestions even when I can't verify them because bugs are slippery, and just because I can't reproduce a particular problem in this or any other version of iPhoto doesn't mean that you won't experience it. And then one of the suggestions in this chapter may save your bacon (or at least your photos).

Also keep in mind that updates to iPhoto very well may eliminate even those problems I've confirmed in iPhoto 6, so be sure to use Software Update to check for new versions on a regular basis.

The world of iPhoto is no more a perfect place than the real world. No one, iPhoto's developers least of all, wants problems, but bugs are a fact of life, and you may have a problem with iPhoto at some point.

One advantage iPhoto has in this respect is that it runs only under Mac OS X, which boasts a feature called protected memory. That means that if one program, such as iPhoto, crashes, no other program should be affected. Also on the positive side is the fact that iPhoto saves your changes frequently and automatically, so you're unlikely to lose much work even if it crashes. Put simply, if iPhoto crashes, just relaunch the program and pick up where you left off. If the crashes happen regularly, you may need to do some troubleshooting. One way or another, keep good backups! (See "Backing Up Your Photos" in Chapter 2, "Importing and Managing Photos.")

Of course, most of the problems you might encounter won't result in a crash. It's more likely you'll have trouble importing photos from an unusual camera, printing a photo at the exact size you want, or dealing with thumbnails that don't display properly. Those are the sorts of problems—and solutions—I'll focus on in this chapter.

General Problems and Solutions

Some problems you may experience in iPhoto aren't related to particular activities. Others are, and subsequent pages in this chapter will address issues with importing, editing, slideshows, printing, and more.

Performance Problems

If you find iPhoto slow to perform certain operations, try these tricks. Some are obvious (if expensive); others less so:

◆ Turn off title, rating, and keyword display using the View menu.

◆ Shrink thumbnails to a smaller size.

◆ Use the triangles next to film rolls to hide thumbnails you don't need to see.

◆ Quit other programs that are running. In my experience, there is usually one culprit (likely the Classic environment), which you can identify by launching Activity Monitor from your Utilities folder and clicking the %CPU column title to see which applications are using the most processor time.

◆ Restart your Mac by choosing Restart from the Apple menu. Restarting is especially helpful if you don't have much free disk space, which cramps Mac OS X's virtual memory techniques.

◆ Check your disk with DiskWarrior (www.alsoft.com/DiskWarrior/); sufficient disk corruption can cause huge performance problems on startup.

◆ Add more RAM to your Mac. iPhoto works with 256 MB of RAM, but it likes a lot more, and RAM is cheap. I always recommend at least 512 MB.

◆ Buy a faster Mac. That's always fun.

Photos Disappear

Some people report having troubles with photos disappearing from iPhoto's display pane, even when the files are still present in the iPhoto Library folder (see "iPhoto Directory Structure" in Chapter 2, "Importing and Managing Photos"). Try the following procedure to fix the problem, keeping in mind that you may lose your albums, keywords, and titles. Follow these steps after backing up your iPhoto Library folder:

1. Hold down Cmd Option while clicking the iPhoto icon in the Dock to launch it. This causes iPhoto to display the Rebuild Photo Library dialog.

   Try each of the options, quitting and relaunching in between attempts, and see if one of them fixes the problem. If not…

2. Drag your corrupt iPhoto Library folder to the Desktop, and launch iPhoto to create a new iPhoto Library.

3. Option-drag the Library6.iPhoto file, and the Modified and Originals folders into the new iPhoto Library folder to copy them into it. Launch iPhoto with Cmd Option and select the first two checkboxes to rebuild all the thumbnails. If that doesn't help…

4. Repeat step 2 to create yet another new iPhoto Library folder, and then manually drag the year folders contained in the Originals folder into iPhoto to import them. If you want, repeat with the contents of the Modified folder, but don't import any exact duplicates.

Unfortunately, I can't figure out any way to trick iPhoto into connecting the modified versions of photos to the originals you restored in step 4, so you'll have to sort out which version of each modified photo you want to keep.

Flaky Behavior or Crashes

Sometimes iPhoto just acts strangely, and I've come up with a few ways of dealing with weird behavior (make sure you have a backup before deleting any files!):

◆ Quit iPhoto and relaunch it.

◆ Restart your Mac by choosing Restart from the Apple menu.

◆ Quit iPhoto. From the Preferences folder inside your user's Library folder, drag the file com.apple.iPhoto.plist to the Desktop and launch iPhoto again.

◆ Hold down Cmd Option while clicking the iPhoto icon in the Dock to launch it. In the Rebuild Photo Library dialog, try each of the options, quitting and relaunching in between attempts, and see if one of them fixes the problem.

◆ Use iPhoto Library Manager's Rebuild Library command, which uses the AlbumData.xml file written by iPhoto to recreate the library, which is a completely different method from what iPhoto uses.

◆ Quit iPhoto. From the iPhoto Library folder, drag the files Thumb32.data, Thumb64.data, ThumbJPGSegment.data, and AlbumData.xml to the Desktop and launch iPhoto again. Don't touch any other files in the iPhoto Library folder, especially Library6.iPhoto!

◆ Run Disk Utility and use the buttons in the First Aid tab to verify and repair both permissions and the disk.

◆ Reinstall a fresh copy of iPhoto, deleting the old one first.

◆ Try creating a new iPhoto Library folder and re-importing your photos from the Originals and Modified folders.

Other Problems

Here are a few other general problems and their solutions:

◆ If other iApps can't see your photos, or if some photos or albums are missing, quit all the iApps, drag the file AlbumData.xml from the iPhoto Library to the Desktop, launch iPhoto, create a new album, quit iPhoto, and try the other programs again.

◆ If you have trouble with iPhoto's photo sharing or the sharing tools that upload data, shut off or bypass your firewall to see if it's blocking necessary ports.

◆ If iPhoto complains about being unable to establish a connection when uploading to .Mac, make sure the date is set correctly in the Date & Time preference pane in System Preferences.

◆ If mailing a photo in Apple's Mail doesn't result in an enclosure, and another user on the Mac has successfully attached a photo in the same session, restart the Mac and try again.

◆ If you've ended up with duplicate photos for some reason, you can delete them with the iPhoto Diet utility from http://pages.cpsc.ucalgary.ca/~fuhrer/personal/freestuff/. Make sure iPhoto Diet has been updated for iPhoto 6 (it hadn't as of press time) and make a backup before running it!

Report Your Problems!

Report any problems you may have by choosing Provide iPhoto Feedback from the iPhoto menu and then filling in Apple's Web-based feedback form.

Importing Problems and Solutions

I've had little trouble importing photos into iPhoto. However, because importing involves interacting with an unpredictable outside world of cameras, card readers, and files of varying formats, problems can occur.

Camera or Card Reader Isn't Recognized

Mac OS X and iPhoto support many common digital cameras and card readers, but not all of them. And sometimes iPhoto may not recognize specific memory cards, even if it recognizes the card reader in general. Try the following tips:

◆ Make sure the camera is turned on, in review mode, and plugged in via USB properly. I know it seems obvious, but we've all made this mistake before.

◆ Use Software Update, accessible in System Preferences, to make sure you have the latest version of Mac OS X, since Apple continually adds support for more digital cameras and card readers.

◆ If your camera is incompatible with Mac OS X and iPhoto, buy a card reader that supports the memory card used by your camera.

◆ If your user account can run only certain applications, that may prevent you from importing in iPhoto. The only fix is for an administrator-level user to increase the capabilities of your account by changing your account limitations in the Accounts preference pane.

◆ Some cameras must be placed in Picture Transfer Protocol mode to communicate with iPhoto. And if that doesn't work, try other modes. Check the manual for help.

◆ iPhoto has had trouble with some large memory cards. People have resolved the issue by reformatting the card in the camera, using a memory card reader, or using smaller cards.

◆ If you have two cameras connected at once, or a camera and a scanner, iPhoto may become confused about which device to use. Connect only one device at a time if this causes trouble for you.

◆ If you haven't yet purchased a camera or card reader, check the compatibility list Apple publishes at www.apple.com/macosx/upgrade/cameras.html.

Nothing Appears after Import

If nothing appears in iPhoto after you import files from your hard drive, try these solutions:

◆ If the files you imported were located in the iPhoto Library folder, iPhoto assumes they've already been imported and won't do so again. To solve the problem, move the files out of the iPhoto Library folder and try again.

◆ Instead of using the Import to Library command in the File menu, drag the images (or a folder containing them) onto iPhoto's display pane. This technique works better on occasion.

◆ Like all Mac OS X applications, iPhoto is sensitive to proper permissions. So, if you've moved your iPhoto Library folder and are trying to import from another user, verify in the Finder's Get Info window for the iPhoto Library folder and all enclosed folders that the appropriate user has Read & Write permissions.

◆ The photos might be duplicates, which iPhoto imports only if you tell it to do so. See Chapter 2, "Importing and Managing Photos."

Damaged Photos Warning Appears during Import

Sometimes when you import photos, you may see an error dialog complaining about unreadable photos. It can occur for a variety of reasons:

◆ You're accidentally importing non-graphic files, such as aliases to photos, HTML documents, or other data files.

◆ The image files may actually be damaged. See if you can open them in Preview or GraphicConverter. If so, you may be able to convert them to another format and eliminate the corruption.

◆ If your files are in an unsupported format, try using GraphicConverter to convert the images to JPEG. Similarly, if RAW images from your camera aren't supported by iPhoto, see if your camera manufacturer makes a utility that will convert them to a supported format.

◆ Sometimes the problem may relate to a communications failure between your camera or card reader and your Mac. Try plugging the camera or card reader directly into one of the Mac's USB ports rather than into the keyboard's USB port or a port on a USB hub.

◆ iPhoto can display the damaged photo error message if your hard disk is full. Since iPhoto duplicates every photo when importing from files, if you're importing hundreds of megabytes of photos from files, it's by no means unthinkable that you could run out of disk space. Clear some space and try importing again.

◆ Photos taken with Apple's QuickTake 100 and QuickTake 150 digital cameras must be converted from the special format Apple used into the JPEG format.

Other Importing Problems

Here are a miscellany of importing problems and solutions that don't fit larger categories:

◆ iPhoto may crash if you disconnect your camera while photos are transferring.

◆ If iPhoto fails to warn you about duplicates, it may be because the date and time on your camera are wrong.

◆ Make sure there are no aliases among files you are importing; they can cause crashes.

◆ iPhoto 2 won't recognize discs burned in iPhoto 4 through iPhoto 6, although the later versions can recognize older discs.

◆ If iPhoto 6 complains about not being able to upgrade your library on the first launch, the problem is related either to incorrect permissions or to locked files. For instructions on solving this problem, see http://docs.info.apple.com/ article.html?artnum=303232.

◆ If you import a file that is misnamed— a TIFF file with a .jpg filename extension, for example—iPhoto may display the picture strangely when editing, refuse to let you order prints, or even crash. Delete the misnamed picture from your Photo Library; then rename it appropriately in the Finder before importing it again.

◆ If you have erased your camera and need to recover the original photos, check out the $29 PhotoRescue (a free version will tell you if it's going to work). Learn more at www.datarescue.com/photorescue/. Also try the $39.95 ImageRecall from www.flashfixers.com/software/.

Editing Problems and Solutions

Most photo editing problems stem from using another program to edit the photos.

Photos Don't Open in an External Program

Although it is unlikely that you'll run into this problem, it could be frustrating. Here are a few reasons it could happen:

◆ If you have changed the name of the photo's file in the Finder, it may not open when double-clicked in iPhoto. The solution? Change the filename back to what iPhoto expects, and don't mess with any filenames within the iPhoto Library folder. It's a bad idea!

◆ Double-check to make sure iPhoto's preferences are set to open photos in an external program, that the program is present on your hard drive, and that you can launch it and open photos normally.

iPhoto Crashes When You Double-Click Photos

There are a few reasons iPhoto might crash when you double-click a photo to edit it within iPhoto:

◆ Changing the photo's filename in the Finder can cause this problem. Don't do it!

◆ A corrupted photo can cause iPhoto to freak out. Editing and saving the original file in another application might eliminate the corruption, or you could delete the corrupt photo and import it again, assuming you have another copy.

iPhoto Doesn't Allow Editing

Some people have reported importing images from a CD that they later couldn't edit in iPhoto. As a workaround, convert the images in GraphicConverter from JPEG to TIFF, for instance, and see if you can import and then edit those versions.

Also verify that the permissions on the files allow your user to write to the files. To check, select them in the Finder, choose Get Info from the File menu ([Cmd][I]), and look in the Ownership & Permission area.

Revert to Original Dimmed

You may see the Revert to Original command in the File menu dimmed after you've made a change. This can happen if you drag a photo from iPhoto to another program to edit the photo. If you do that, iPhoto will be unable to track changes you've made and Revert to Original will be dimmed. There's no workaround, other than making sure to open photos for editing in external applications properly from within iPhoto.

Thumbnails Are Corrupted or Cause Crashes

If a thumbnail doesn't reflect edits, is entirely black, or causes iPhoto to crash, hold down [Cmd][Option] while clicking the iPhoto icon in the Dock to launch it. In the Rebuild Photo Library dialog, select the first two checkboxes to rebuild all thumbnails.

Beware of Too Much Editing

One quick warning about editing. iPhoto saves edited photos using the lossy JPEG compression format, which throws away information in the image to keep file sizes small. That's no problem in normal usage, but an excessive number of edits could cause a slight degradation in image quality.

RAW File Facts

Apple's support for RAW files in iPhoto has caused some confusion. The following facts may shed some light on it for you:

◆ RAW files are considered to be "digital negatives" that aren't to be modified, so changes you make are always saved to a secondary file. As a result, on import, iPhoto converts the RAW file to JPEG and stores the RAW file itself in the Originals folder. Alternatively, you can set iPhoto to save edited RAW files as 16-bit TIFFs.

   You never work on the RAW file directly, only on its JPEG or TIFF stand-in. If you wish to throw out your edits and start a new copy from the RAW file again, use Revert to Original.

◆ Because of the large size of uncompressed RAW files and the JPEG conversion that occurs during import, the import process takes a long time with RAW files.

◆ The first time you edit a RAW file, iPhoto displays a RAW badge in the lower right corner of the window.

◆ Scrolling may seem slower when browsing through large thumbnails of RAW files. The problem is that when you're using a thumbnail size larger than the actual thumbnails, iPhoto must load the original photo to create the thumbnail. That's a slower process. To speed up scrolling, press 2 while in organize mode to zoom to thumbnail size (press 0 to zoom to the smallest size and 1 to zoom to the largest size).

◆ To export a RAW file in RAW format, choose Original from the Format pop-up menu in the Export Photos dialog.

◆ For more info, see `http://docs.info.apple.com/article.html?artnum=300879`.

Slideshow Problems and Solutions

Slideshows can run into a variety of problems; try these solutions:

◆ Some transitions, like Cube and Flip, may not work on older Macs with less capable video cards.

◆ Music purchased from the iTunes Music Store and used in a slideshow can be heard only on authorized computers. Either pick different music or convert tracks (burn to CD and re-import into iTunes) for use on other computers.

◆ If slideshows look wrong, try switching to "Thousands" of colors in the Displays preference pane.

◆ If a slideshow takes a long time to start, it may be because of a very large music file you've set to play. Pick a smaller file to speed start time.

◆ If slideshow transitions are slower than you've set, it may be because your photos are too large or your screen resolution is too high. Setting a lower resolution in the Displays preference pane or using smaller photos should speed transitions.

◆ If you can't see your iTunes music library when selecting music for a slideshow, open each iLife application in this order: iTunes, iPhoto, iMovie, and then iDVD.

◆ If you can't play music purchased from the iTunes Music Store, upgrade to the latest version of QuickTime. Get it from `www.apple.com/quicktime/download/`.

◆ If a Windows user sees error -8992 when trying to play your QuickTime movie, have them turn off DirectDraw Acceleration in the Video Settings screen of the QuickTime Settings control panel.

RAW FILES AND SLIDESHOWS

Printing Problems and Solutions

Many printing problems you'll experience will be specific to your particular printer and setup, so read your printer manual carefully and be sure to test before printing at the highest quality on expensive paper.

Prints Don't Appear Correctly on the Paper

You may have trouble getting prints to show in exactly the right location on the paper. Try these solutions to the problem:

◆ Set the paper size appropriately in the Paper menu in the Print dialog. This is essential for unusual paper sizes.

◆ Make sure the margins are set correctly for your printer and paper combination.

◆ Verify that you load paper into your printer properly. This solution helps particularly with unusual paper sizes.

Photos Print at Incorrect Sizes

Even if you ask iPhoto to print a standard size print, the image that comes out of the printer might not be the size you want. This can happen for a few reasons:

◆ Make sure your image is cropped to the appropriate aspect ratio. Otherwise, iPhoto shrinks the image proportionally to make it fit, adding borders in one dimension to accommodate the size change.

◆ Changing the layout to print multiple pages per sheet of paper in the Advanced options of the Print dialog will likely result in unpredictable photo sizes.

◆ Changing the scale in the Page Setup dialog has no effect.

Poor Print Quality

The main complaint with printing occurs when print quality doesn't meet your expectations. Here are a few suggestions for addressing print quality problems:

◆ Make sure your inkjet cartridges aren't clogged. Once my black ink cartridge clogged and it took me an hour to figure out that the clog caused color photos to print oddly. Your printer manual should tell you how to clear clogs.

◆ Change your ink cartridges. It's possible that one is low on a specific color and not yet reporting the problem.

◆ Use different paper. You'd be amazed how much better print quality is on paper designed for photo printing.

◆ Make sure your paper is loaded correctly to print on the printable side. It's usually whiter or glossier than the other side.

◆ Make sure you select the appropriate settings in the Print dialog for your printer to use high-quality mode.

◆ If iPhoto put a low-resolution warning icon on the picture in the Print dialog's small preview, there isn't enough data in the image to print at the size you requested. Print at a smaller size. See "Dealing with Warning Icons," later in this chapter.

◆ CMYK files, which you can create in some programs (but won't come from a standard digital camera), may not print correctly in iPhoto. Try converting them to RGB.

◆ Verify that the problems aren't inherent to the original image. If so, you may have to edit the image in another program to correct the issue.

Print and Book Problems and Solutions

A few common problems have cropped up when working with prints and books.

Can't Enable 1-Click Ordering

A number of people have reported problems with enabling 1-Click ordering within iPhoto, even though they have a 1-Click account with Apple that works on Apple's Web sites. A lot of the early problems seemed to happen to people who had joined the Apple Developer Connection (ADC), and it's unclear if that particular issue has been completely addressed. To fix the problem, try one of these solutions:

◆ Connect to http://store.apple.com/, click the Sign In link, and log in to your Apple Store account. Click the "Change Apple ID or Password" link, sign in again, and then change your password (changing other data wouldn't hurt either). The goal here is to force the Apple database to update so you can connect to it via iPhoto. (If changing your account on the Apple Store doesn't have the desired effect, try running through the same procedure at http://myinfo.apple.com/.)

◆ Follow the above procedure, but instead of clicking "Change Apple ID or Password," click "Change 1-Click Settings." Again, make some changes and toggle 1-Click via the Web to see if that enables iPhoto to connect.

◆ If you can set up a new email address easily, create it and then add a new Apple ID that uses the new email address. This generally seems to work, but isn't an ideal solution, since then you have to keep track of an extra email address.

Errors during Ordering

You may encounter a few problems during the process of ordering items from Apple:

◆ If you see an error dialog complaining that a network connection could not be established, verify that your Internet connection is working by loading a page in a Web browser or by checking your email.

◆ You may see a confusing error message that says, "The changes to your account information could not be saved." Ignore the message, and enter your credit card information again, making sure the card hasn't expired. If that doesn't work, try a different credit card.

◆ If you see an alert that your password is invalid, but it works fine in the Apple Store, change your password to be less than 30 characters. The Apple Store allows 32-character 1-Click passwords, whereas iPhoto allows only 30-character 1-Click passwords.

◆ Different aspects of iPhoto may request access to your password keychain during ordering. That's totally fine.

◆ If you have a firewall that blocks port 80, try turning your firewall off, or allowing data to pass through on port 80, to solve upload errors.

Photos Don't Upload

Some people have had trouble uploading photos to Apple's servers to have them printed or turned into a book or other item. Here are a few things to try:

◆ Try again later. Many Internet problems come and go, so a second try an hour or a day later may succeed.

◆ If possible, see if the problem occurs when uploading to .Mac Slides as well. If not, the problem may be limited to the specific servers used for prints or other printed items.

◆ If possible, verify that you can upload a large file using a different program. If that fails, the problem is likely with your Internet connection. If it works, the problem is probably in iPhoto.

◆ If iPhoto complains about an error while accessing your account information, make sure the date and time on your computer are set properly in the Date & Time preference pane. It's a good idea to select "Set Date & Time Automatically" in that preference pane to eliminate the problem in the short term. If your Mac is several years old and loses track of the date and time regularly, you need to buy it a new clock battery.

◆ Contact Apple via the Web forms available from www.apple.com/support/iphoto/customerservice/.

Apple Has Trouble Processing Your Book or Photos

There are several problems that can prevent Apple from printing photos you've uploaded, the two most common of which are damaged files and files that contain a question mark in the filename. You should receive email telling you about the problem, but a few common issues include:

◆ If a photo has a ? in the filename, it won't print. Export the photo, change the filename, reimport, and delete the original.

◆ Damaged photos may not print. To identify damaged photos, connect to Apple's Web site at www.apple.com/internetservices/yourorderstatus/, where you can look for missing or partial thumbnails for the order in question. Once you've identified the damaged files, try exporting them, opening them in another application, saving a copy of each, and re-importing the copies to eliminate the corruption.

◆ If you order a print of an image that indicates it may be subject to another person's copyright, Apple puts your order on hold pending verification that you have the right to make a copy of the photo. You must complete and submit an iPhoto Print Consent form; Apple will tell you how to do this when you're contacted.

◆ Using certain Type 1 PostScript fonts can cause your book order to be cancelled. For more information, see http://docs.info.apple.com/article.html?artnum=300964.

◆ If over half of the page numbers in a book are hidden by photos, Apple may cancel your order. It's easiest to deselect the Show Page Numbers checkbox in the Settings dialog before placing the order, although you could also change the theme or page design to one in which photos don't cover the page numbers.

◆ If you receive email from Apple saying your order can't be processed, you can wait for Apple to contact you with details, or you can try to figure out what went wrong, cancel the order, and then resubmit it. Apple gives you up to 90 minutes to cancel the order yourself; do this by logging in with your Apple ID to www.apple.com/internetservices/yourorderstatus/ and clicking the Cancel Order link.

Prints or Books Aren't What You Expect

It's highly frustrating to order (and pay for) prints or books that aren't of the quality you expect. Follow these tips to avoid common problems:

◆ Prints ordered via iPhoto often come back darker than is ideal. This may be because Mac and PC monitors have different color contrast settings, something called *gamma*. Macs usually use a gamma of 1.8, whereas PCs use a darker gamma of 2.2. The belief is that Kodak serves more PC customers and has thus tweaked its equipment so PC users don't think their prints look washed out.

   You can adjust your monitor to use PC gamma settings when working with photos. In the Color pane of the Displays preference pane, click the Calibrate button to run the Display Calibrator Assistant. Then work through the Display Calibrator Assistant, picking 2.2 Television Gamma in the third screen. When you're done, save the profile you created, and select it in the Color pane of the Displays preference pane.

◆ Prints use a three-color process whereas books use a four-color process. Because black is added to photos in books, they can appear slightly darker in books than when ordered as prints.

◆ If prints in your order from Apple are garbled, the problem may be that the photos were modified in another application (like Photoshop) to use CMYK or grayscale format. To fix the photos, use another application to change the color space to RGB, which Apple requires for ordered prints and books.

Order Doesn't Arrive or Is Damaged

There are several ways to learn more about your orders and to contact Apple if you experience problems with your order:

◆ Check the status of your order at www.apple.com/internetservices/yourorderstatus. You need your Apple ID and password to sign in.

◆ Contact Apple via the Web forms available from www.apple.com/support/iphoto/customerservice/. Be sure to include the text of the confirmation message Apple sent you so they have your order details.

PRINT AND BOOK PROBLEMS AND SOLUTIONS

Dealing with Warning Icons

Let's say you want to print a photo in a card, calendar, or book, on your printer, or via Apple's online print service, but iPhoto is displaying a warning icon on the page thumbnail, on the preview in the Print dialog, or next to a specific size you want in the Order Prints window. What can you do to resolve this situation?

Ways to handle warning icons:

◆ You can simply print at a smaller size. When printing photos and ordering prints, try a smaller size (**Figure 9.1**); with a card, calendar, or book, choose a different page design or rearrange the photos so the offending one prints at a smaller size (**Figure 9.2**). Or, don't zoom into it as far.

◆ If the photo is too small because you cropped it, you can select it, choose Revert to Original from the Photos menu, and crop it again to a larger size. I recommend this procedure primarily if you think you're right on the edge of receiving the warning icon.

◆ You can also increase the size of your image using GraphicConverter or Adobe Photoshop. The way these programs scale the photo up might look better than iPhoto's method, though it's harder.

✔ Tips

■ For exact details about how many pixels photos must have to print at different sizes, see "Preparing to Order Prints" in Chapter 6, "Printing Photos."

■ To learn how image resolution relates to what comes out of a printer, take a look at "Understanding Resolution" in Appendix A, "Deep Background."

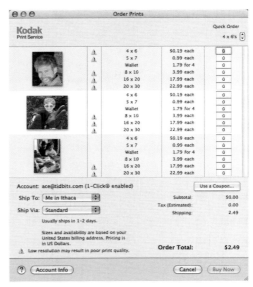

Figure 9.1 Note how the three images showing here have warning icons applied to different print sizes. The first (heavily cropped) image can print well only at wallet size. The second (slightly cropped) won't print well at 8" x 10" or larger. The third image (uncropped) drops out at 16" x 20".

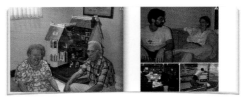

Figure 9.2 Note how all these photos, which were taken with my old QuickTake 100 at 640 x 480 pixels, show low-resolution warning icons except the two smaller photos in the three-up page design. A 640 x 480 image must be quite small to print acceptably.

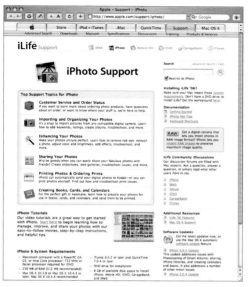

Figure 9.3 Start with Apple's iPhoto support pages for general help and pointers to other resources.

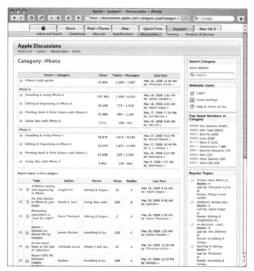

Figure 9.4 If all else fails, ask for help on Apple's iPhoto discussion boards.

Help Resources

I'm sure other problems and solutions will become known after I finish writing. Along with iPhoto's online help (choose iPhoto Help from the Help menu), a variety of Internet resources provide assistance.

Places to look for more help:

◆ Check Apple's iPhoto support pages at www.apple.com/support/iphoto/ (**Figure 9.3**) and www.apple.com/support/iphoto/customerservice/.

◆ Search in Apple's Knowledge Base using the Search field on the pages listed above. Narrow your search by adding terms, so if you're having trouble importing RAW files, search for "import RAW" or something similar.

◆ Try asking a question on Apple's iPhoto Web-based discussion forums linked at http://discussions.info.apple.com/ (**Figure 9.4**). In my experience, these discussions are good for straightforward questions; harder questions tend to go unanswered. When posting, state your problem clearly and include relevant information while at the same time keeping the question concise.

◆ For order-related problems, contact Apple via the Web forms available from www.apple.com/support/iphoto/customerservice/. Make sure you have your order details at hand.

◆ Check out *TidBITS*, the free weekly newsletter I publish. It contains tons of useful information on all sorts of topics, including digital photography. Visit www.tidbits.com and search on "iPhoto" or "photography" to see relevant articles. You can also subscribe to receive issues in email.

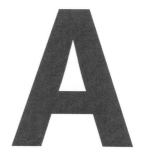

DEEP BACKGROUND

Right off the bat, let me say that you don't need to read this appendix. It's deep background, the kind of detail that you might wish to delve into when you're attempting to understand how iPhoto works, perhaps because you've just printed a photo and you're unhappy with the results.

The following pages contain "Understanding Aspect Ratios," "Understanding Resolution," and "Understanding Color Management." Each of these discussions examines an aspect of digital photography from which iPhoto, for the most part, tries to shield you. That's great most of the time, but if you're trying to understand how cropping removes information from a photo, thus making it print at a lower quality, you'll want to come here for the explanation.

Lastly, although I've called this appendix "Deep Background," these topics are so complex that entire books have been written about each one. If these discussions leave you with more questions, I'd encourage you to visit a library or bookstore and browse its collection of books on photography, digital imaging, and pre-press. I especially recommend *Real World Scanning and Halftones, Third Edition,* by David Blatner, Conrad Chavez, Glenn Fleishman, and Steve Roth.

Understanding Aspect Ratios

iPhoto makes it easy to select and crop a portion of a photo using a specific aspect ratio, but why is this important? It matters because aspect ratios differ between traditional and digital photos.

An aspect ratio is the ratio between the width of the image and its height, generally expressed with both numbers, as in the line from Arlo Guthrie's song "Alice's Restaurant Massacree" about "Twenty-seven, *eight-by-ten*, color glossy photographs with circles and arrows and a paragraph on the back of each one."

The aspect ratio of 35mm film is 4 x 6 (using the standard print size rather than the least common denominator of 2 x 3) because the negative measures 24mm by 36mm. Thus, traditional photographs are usually printed at sizes like 4" x 6", 5" x 7", or 8" x 10", all of which are close enough to that 4 x 6 aspect ratio so photos scale well. When there's a mismatch between the aspect ratio of the original negative and the final print, either the image must be shrunk proportionally to fit (producing unsightly borders) or some portion of the image must be cropped. (The alternative would be to resize the image disproportionally, which makes people look like they're reflected in a fun-house mirror.)

The equivalent of film in digital photography is the *CCD* (charge-coupled device), which is essentially a grid of many light-sensitive elements that gain a charge when exposed to light. Through much digital wizardry, the camera translates those charges into the individual dots (called *pixels*) that, put together, make up the image. Zoom in on a picture all the way, and you can actually see these pixels. So if your digital camera uses a CCD that can capture a picture composed

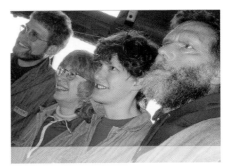

Figure A.1 This is a 4 x 3 image with a 4 x 6 landscape selection. A bit of the bottom of the image would be lost, which is fine.

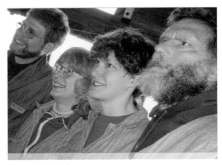

Figure A.2 This is a 4 x 3 image with a 5 x 7 landscape selection. Very little of the bottom of the image would be lost to cropping.

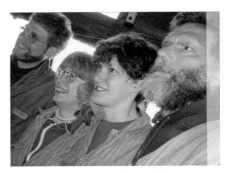

Figure A.3 This is a 4 x 3 image with an 8 x 10 landscape selection. Losing the right side of the image would be somewhat problematic.

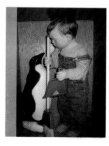

Figure A.4 This is a 4 x 3 portrait image with a 4 x 6 portrait selection. A bit on the left would be lost, which is fine (a better crop would take some from the left, the right, and the top).

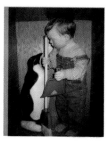

Figure A.5 This is a 4 x 3 portrait image with a 5 x 7 portrait selection. A very small amount on the left would be lost, which is fine.

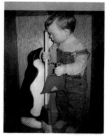

Figure A.6 This is a 4 x 3 portrait image with an 8 x 10 portrait selection. As with the landscape image on the previous page, the aspect ratios match badly for this image, since the selection cuts off the top of Tristan's head.

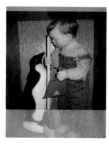

Figure A.7 This is a 4 x 3 portrait image with a square selection. As you can tell, the square selection is a lousy choice for this image.

of 1600 pixels wide by 1200 pixels high, basic math shows that your photos will have a 4 x 3 aspect ratio.

Why did digital camera manufacturers choose a 4 x 3 aspect ratio when 4 x 6 is the 35mm film standard? It matches the aspect ratios of most computer monitors. Whether your monitor runs at 640 x 480, 800 x 600, or 1024 x 768, division reveals that it has a 4 x 3 aspect ratio. Displaying a photo at full screen size without cropping thus requires a 4 x 3 aspect ratio. (And why do computer monitors use a 4 x 3 aspect ratio? Because that's the aspect ratio used by televisions. However, since HDTV uses a 16 x 9 aspect ratio, some monitors now use that or 16 x 10.)

Hopefully the choices in iPhoto's Constrain pop-up menu make more sense now. If you're starting from a photo with a 4 x 3 aspect ratio, and you want a 20" x 30" print (a 4 x 6 aspect ratio), there's no way to print that photo without adding borders or cropping because of the mismatch in aspect ratios. The same applies to other standard print sizes—they don't match the 4 x 3 aspect ratio of most digital photos. Rather than suffering borders or automatic cropping, it's better to crop the image yourself so you can be sure the important parts are retained. **Figures A.1** through **A.7** show how cropping a 4 x 3 image at the other common aspect ratios works for two sample images (results will vary by image).

The 4 x 3 aspect ratio plays an important role in output too, since iPhoto's book designs all assume images in the 4 x 3 aspect ratio. The books vary the final image size depending on the page design, and you can zoom in and re-center the image to crop temporarily, but as long as the aspect ratio of your images remains 4 x 3, the layout will work as Apple intended. You can use different aspect ratios in a book, but the layout may not work well.

UNDERSTANDING ASPECT RATIOS

Understanding Resolution

Understanding how the dimensions of a digital photo relate to what comes out of a printer is hard. That's why iPhoto merely alerts you with a warning icon when a photo won't print well at a specific size. Read these two pages to learn why iPhoto displays warning icons; "Dealing with Warning Icons" in Chapter 9, "Troubleshooting," offers help.

Pixels and Dots

Every digital photo is made up of a rectangular grid of points, called pixels, each of which can display one of sixteen million colors or several hundred shades of gray. For instance, photos from one of my cameras are 1600 pixels wide by 1200 pixels high. Monitors also display rectangular grids of pixels, often 1024 pixels wide by 768 pixels high.

Not all of a 1600 x 1200 photo can fit on a 1024 x 768 monitor when every pixel in the image is mapped to a pixel on the monitor. To display a photo so it fills a monitor, iPhoto removes pixels on the fly, a process called *downsampling*.

You can't perform the same one-to-one mapping when it comes to print, though, because most printers (which have only four or six colors) can't display a pixel's exact color in a single dot. Instead, they use collections of single-colored dots to fool the eye into seeing that color. For this reason and other more complex ones, the main fact to grok is that, in general, the more pixels in the image, the better it will look printed.

This fact is particularly relevant when you're printing images at large sizes. For instance, why does an image that looks fine when printed at 4" x 6" appear fuzzy at 8" x 10"?

Imagine a knitted blanket. If you stretch it to make it larger, you can see through the holes between the strands of yarn. Expanding a

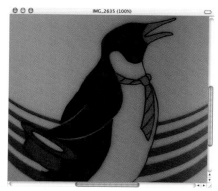

Figure A.8 The original image at 100 percent.

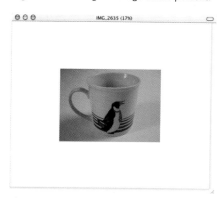

Figure A.9 Shrink the image to 17 percent of original size and the loss of detail caused by downsampling makes it hard to see the stripes on the penguin's tie.

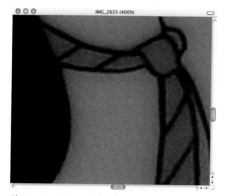

Figure A.10 Expand the image to 400 percent of the original and the fuzziness added by interpolation becomes evident.

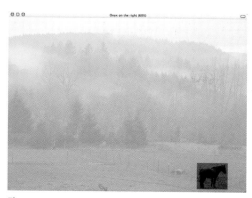

Figure A.11 The original 1600 x 1200 pixel image, with a small area to crop selected.

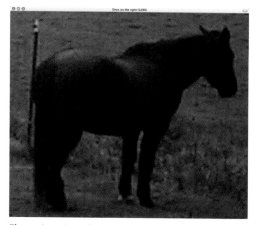

Figure A.12 Crop the image to 206 x 183 pixels and you can see how the horse looks much fuzzier due to all the interpolation necessary to expand it to the desired size.

photo to print at a larger size works similarly, except the printer fills in each hole with dots of roughly the same color as the dots surrounding the hole, a process called *interpolation*. The more pixels in the image, the smaller the holes that need to be filled, and the less interpolation is necessary.

Downsampling vs. Interpolation

Downsampling onscreen works well, since it's easy to remove similarly colored pixels without changing the image much. Even though the photo loses pixels and thus some detail, quality doesn't suffer too much (**Figure A.8** and **Figure A.9** on the previous page). Along with the fact that onscreen images are extremely bright because monitors *emit* light, whereas paper *reflects* light, minimal downsampling helps explain why photos look good on monitors at full size.

Interpolation, particularly on a printer, is different. There's no way to avoid the fact that expanding a photo requires adding dots that didn't exist before, and because those dots exist only by virtue of the dots around them, they make the image look fuzzier (**Figure A.8** and **Figure A.10** on the previous page). Interpolation simply cannot add details to the image that weren't originally present. Scale an image too large, and iPhoto warns you that so much interpolation will be needed that you won't like the result.

Cropping Implies Interpolation

Cropping exacerbates the problem because it removes pixels, making the photo smaller and requiring more interpolation to expand the image back up to the desired size.

To see this, compare the original image in **Figure A.11** with **Figure A.12**, which shows a heavily cropped version of the same image, displayed at the same size as the original. Notice how the cropped horse is fuzzier.

Understanding Color Management

iPhoto 5 first introduced tools for manually adjusting color saturation, temperature, and tint. Why did it take Apple so long to add these tools? Color correction of any sort is devilishly difficult to do right (and as you may have noticed, even the automatic Enhance tool can get it wrong at times). Color correction suffers from two basic problems: the fact that color is highly perceptual and the fact that different devices render color in different ways.

Color Perception

Everyone sees color in different ways. My wife and I, for instance, frequently disagree on whether a given color is green or blue, and the fact that my opinion generally seems to match what others think as well doesn't change the fact that she is perceiving a different color. Add that to the fact that at least 10 percent of the population suffers from some level of color blindness.

The conditions in which color is perceived also make a huge difference, as you've probably realized if you ever purchased a shirt in a store lit with fluorescent lights and were surprised by how the shirt looked when you tried it on at home under incandescent lights. Similarly, when painting a room, you have to consider how the color will look in sunlight during the day and with artificial lighting at night. The differences can be striking.

The lesson here is that you cannot define color objectively—there is no right answer. Always keep that in mind and it will remove some of the stress about achieving the "perfect" color in your photos.

Rendering Color

Digital cameras, computer monitors, inkjet printers, and commercial photo processing equipment all use different methods of rendering color. Even with monitors, there's little common ground between normal CRT-based monitors and the increasingly popular LCD flat-panel monitors.

When you take a picture with your camera, look at it on your Mac, print a copy on your printer, and order a large print of the image from Kodak, you would like the colors in the image to match closely at each step. The engineers designing these devices have managed to make the color produced by each one match fairly well, but not perfectly. Here's how it works.

Imagine a three-dimensional graph, with the X-, Y-, and Z-axes representing the amount of red, green, and blue in every possible color. (Don't worry about this turning technical; that's as bad as it gets.) Now imagine an amorphous blob in the graph that represents the specific set of colors any given device can capture (for digital cameras) or display (for monitors or printers). That blob is called the *gamut,* and every device has a gamut that's at least slightly different.

The problem with matching color across completely different devices is that each device can render only colors in its gamut. When a color, say a specific light green, falls into an area where there's overlap between gamuts, each device does the right thing and renders the exact same light green. However, when a color falls outside the set of colors a device can render, it's a problem. The device cannot render a color outside its gamut, so it makes an educated guess about what color to render instead.

Color-Matching Systems

Many efforts have been made to address this problem, but the one you're most likely to have heard about, being a Mac user, is Apple's ColorSync technology. The particular approach it uses to make educated guesses about which colors to render on different devices is immaterial; suffice to say that its goal is consistency. In theory, if you have chosen or set up a ColorSync profile for your monitor and your printer, for instance, it should help ensure that the colors you see on your monitor match those printed by your printer.

Without getting into too many details, you can calibrate your monitor by choosing System Preferences from the Apple menu, clicking the Displays preference pane, clicking the Color tab, and clicking the Calibrate button to run and work through the Display Calibrator Assistant. Then, when you're printing, look for a ColorSync setting in the Color Management panel of the Print dialog. Whether it's present or not depends on your printer driver, but if the setting is present at all, it's usually the default. That's all there is to basic use of ColorSync, and on the whole, it works pretty well.

You may not be limited to ColorSync's educated guesses about how to render color (my Epson's Photo-Realistic mode sometimes produces better results), and in fact, none of the commercial photo processing companies, including Kodak, use it. Why not? Two reasons.

First, photos are displayed on monitors and on paper totally differently. Monitors *emit* light, causing photos to be extremely bright. Paper *reflects* light, so unless you shine a floodlight on a photo, you can't come close to the amount of light emanating from a monitor.

Second, color is highly perceptual, and Kodak and other photography companies have done incredible amounts of research to determine not so much how to match colors exactly, but how to print photographs that meet people's expectations.

In the end, the problem of matching color perfectly among devices is just too hard. Even with technologies like ColorSync, the differences between a photo on a light-emitting monitor and light-reflecting paper mean that the photo processing companies have a better chance of satisfying customers if they concentrate more on producing a photograph that looks desirable than on matching colors perfectly in an imperfect world where everyone sees color differently.

Should You Correct Colors?

Color correction is complex, and the necessary tools are also usually complex. Apple did a fairly good job with giving iPhoto basic color-correction tools in the Adjust window, and many photos can be improved with judicious color correction. Of course, iPhoto's tools are still limited in comparison to those in programs like Adobe Photoshop; in particular, iPhoto's tools always affect the entire image, rather than letting you select a portion of the image to correct.

Now that you know how hard it is to achieve reliable, predictable results, should you color correct your photos using iPhoto or another program? It depends on how much you want to play. For those who don't like to fuss, don't bother. If you like fiddling with your photos so you can make them just right, go ahead. And for the majority of us who fall between those two poles, I recommend doing manual color correction only on those images you like the most and that will benefit from it the most. Remember, the "right" color is the one that looks right to you.

TAKING
BETTER PHOTOS

B

iPhoto and your digital camera will make you a better photographer, for the simple reason that the best way to improve a skill is constant practice. Thanks to iPhoto, it's easier to take and review photographs than ever before.

But you need not discover all the ways you can take better photos on your own. Having the best equipment for the kind of photos you want to take will help, as will learning some of the basics of different types of photography. This appendix offers that advice, ranging from choosing the best camera for your needs to tips on how to take great pictures of kids. (Hint: The posed portrait is unlikely to work.)

So skim these few pages to find tips that you can use to create better photos with minimal extra effort.

What Kind of Photographer Are You?

When choosing the camera that will help you take the best photos, it's important to choose one that matches the kind of photos you actually take. But, what sort of photographer are you? In one way of thinking, there are two types of photographers: artistic and documentary (and as is usually the case, most people overlap somewhat).

You're an artistic photographer if:

◆ You care more about the overall look of a photo than the subject of the picture (**Figure B.1**).

◆ Objects and landscapes fill many of your photos and stand alone as aesthetic representations of your reality.

◆ Display and print quality is of the utmost importance. You regularly print and display your best photos.

◆ You're willing to take time to set up the perfect shot, and you do things because they give you photo opportunities.

You're a documentary photographer if:

◆ Who or what appears in the photo is more important than the overall look (**Figure B.2**).

◆ The most common subjects of your photos are people and places, and they usually fit into and support a larger story.

◆ You're willing to trade quality for convenience, ease of use, or speed of shooting.

◆ You don't have the free time or patience to set up shots, and you prefer to snap a few pictures quickly, hoping that at least one will turn out well. You carry your camera to record events or in the hope of getting a good shot.

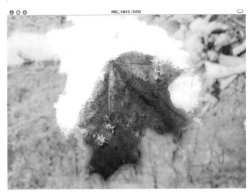

Figure B.1 There's not much of a story in this photo—I was just intrigued by the color of the leaf underneath the new-fallen snow. We're definitely looking at an artistic photograph here.

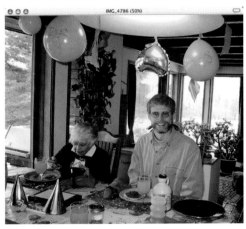

Figure B.2 In contrast, here we have a picture of me and my grandmother at my 35th birthday party. Whether or not it's a good photo is almost immaterial—what's important is that it reminds me of a special meal with my family. It's a pure documentary photograph.

Choosing a Camera

Once you've determined what sort of photographer you really are (and that may be different from the type of photographer you'd like to be in an ideal world), working through the variables that differentiate digital cameras becomes significantly easier.

Form Factor

Digital cameras come in a wide variety of sizes, and for documentary photographers, small size can be important so the camera fits in a pocket and so the fact that you're taking pictures doesn't overwhelm the event. In contrast, artistic photographers are often willing to carry larger cameras because of their increased quality and flexibility. Most cameras fall in a middle ground, so it's best to hold the camera to see how it feels in your hand before buying it.

Megapixels/Quality

Within the form factor that matches your shooting style, you should usually try to get the most megapixels (larger cameras have larger CCDs and can thus capture more pixels). But lens quality makes a difference too, and the best way to determine lens quality is to read detailed camera reviews. Artistic photographers need to pay the most attention to quality issues.

Lens Capabilities

For documentary photographers, this mostly comes down to whether or not the camera has a decent optical (ignore digital) zoom for capturing far away events. For artistic photographers, zoom capabilities are important for those times when you simply can't (or shouldn't) get close enough to the subject (such as a grizzly bear). Also important are macro capabilities for stunning close-ups of flowers, insects, and other small objects.

Extra Features

Extra features may be important: documentary photographers may appreciate a short movie capability, whereas artistic photographers might look for the capability to use an external flash or different lenses. Also pay attention to factors like the camera's battery type. AA batteries are cheap and easily found, and you can buy good rechargeable batteries, but the smallest cameras generally have their own battery packs and chargers.

Price

Everyone has a budget, and here's where you must decide how much to pay. Documentary photographers will pay more for truly tiny cameras with decent quality, whereas artistic photographers pay more for quality, manual controls, and support for additional lenses. Although more money will buy a better camera, you can take good pictures with almost any camera.

Interface

Some cameras are easier to use than others, which is important for documentary photographers who need to be able to set options quickly before missing a particular shot. Artistic photographers care more about control, so the camera interface should help them twiddle manual settings easily.

Speed

Digital cameras can be quite slow, with a few seconds to start up, a lag between when you press the shutter release and when the picture is taken, and a few-second lag between shots. Documentary photographers in particular should look for faster cameras, so as to avoid missing that perfect shot due to camera lag. Artistic photographers interested in action shots should also pay attention to speed or risk losing great photos.

Where to Read Camera Reviews

After you've determined roughly what kind of camera you want, you have a few choices. You can go to a store and buy whatever the salesperson recommends after hearing your story. You can depend on a friend who has already researched a similar type of camera. Or you can do the research yourself. Be forewarned—if you're not a camera buff, you may find reading numerous camera reviews overwhelming, thanks to the incredible detail provided. I've found the sites below useful for reviews, buyer's guides, news, discussions, and other digital photography information.

Camera review sites:

◆ *Digital Photography Review* has an especially detailed tool for comparing the specs on different cameras, along with a buying guide.
Find it at: www.dpreview.com

◆ *Digital Camera Resource Page* offers an extensive camera database through which you can search to find cameras with your desired specifications.
Find it at: www.dcresource.com

◆ *Imaging Resource* stands out from the pack with its Comparometer, which lets you compare sample photos taken with different cameras. The site also offers a simple camera shopping guide.
Find it at: www.imaging-resource.com

◆ *Steve's DigiCams* offers detailed reviews that are unfortunately broken into multiple pages, making reading clumsy.
Find it at: www.steves-digicams.com

A Better Starting Point

Honestly, camera reviews make me crazy, since I don't have a background in traditional photography to help me understand all the jargon. I've tried to lay out the basics here, but if you want more information about how to think about the right camera for your needs and how to understand the camera reviews, I recommend Larry Chen's *Take Control of Buying a Digital Camera*, one of the Take Control ebooks. Larry also provides advice on evaluating image quality and gives you a camera comparison worksheet to help you track the different models you're considering. Read more about it at www.takecontrolbooks.com/buying-digicam.html.

Camera Accessories

Although all you need to take good photos is a camera, there are some accessories that can help at times.

Bigger Memory Card

Most cameras ship with small memory cards, and you may feel as though you should shoot at a lower resolution to save space. Don't do it—just buy a larger memory card. Visit www.dealram.com to compare prices at multiple vendors for the type of memory card your camera uses.

USB Card/PC Card Reader

If you have friends with digital cameras, a USB or FireWire (much faster) card reader that accepts all the types of memory cards can make it easy to share photos of an event on the spot, without having to mail them around later. Folks with PowerBooks might also look for a PC Card adapter that lets you plug your memory card right into the laptop.

Also consider an iPod with an attachment like Apple's iPod Camera Connector, the Belkin Digital Camera Link, or the Belkin Media Reader; they let you offload photos from your camera to your iPod. Search for "iPod camera" in Google to learn more.

Monopod/Tripod

In low-light situations, if you don't use the flash, you risk your photos coming out blurry. The solution? Attach the camera (most have the appropriate threaded mount) to a monopod or a tripod. Documentary photographers are less likely to want to use even a monopod (which is smaller and faster to use than a tripod) because of it getting in the way, whereas artistic photographers are more likely to accept a little extra annoyance in exchange for the highest quality photos. Either way, make sure it's easy to use.

Extra Batteries

It's unfortunately common to run out of power at a bad moment, particularly if you're using your camera's flash or LCD display a lot. Avoid missing great photos because your camera is dead by carrying an extra battery pack or set of batteries. Proprietary battery packs tend to be expensive, but my experience is that it's worth buying the camera vendor's battery rather than one from an independent manufacturer. Other cameras take standard AA batteries; you can use any normal battery, but it's cheaper and more environmentally friendly to use rechargeable batteries, such as those available from Quest Batteries; visit www.questbatteries.com.

Lens Cleaning Kit

Those of us who have used only digital cameras may not realize that it's well worth getting a special lens cleaning kit that can remove dust and dirt from your lens and LCD (and for cameras with removable lenses, the CCD inside). Normal cloth might cause scratches. Any camera store should be able to recommend a lens cleaning kit.

Printer

With iPhoto, you can always order prints from Apple. But you may want to print them yourself, perhaps for instant gratification, greater control, or privacy reasons. For that you'll need a color printer. There are a number of different technologies, such as inkjet, laser, and dye-sublimation. Inkjet printers are the most common (buy a six-color printer for the best photo quality) and offer excellent quality, but have high per-print materials costs. Dye-sublimation printers have the best quality for photos, but are more expensive. And color laser printers are the cheapest to run for many prints. You can learn more at camera review sites, which also often review printers.

General Photo Tips

No matter what type of photos you take, a few general tips will take you a long way.

- Consider the Rule of Thirds. Divide the image into a 3 x 3 grid and try to position the main subject of the photo where the lines intersect (**Figure B.3**). If your photo will have strong horizontal (as in a horizon) or vertical lines (as in a building), try to keep them on the horizontal or vertical lines. Centering can work, but tends to be a bit dull for anything but portraits.

- Pay attention to where the light comes from and try to avoid shooting into strong light. It's better to shoot with light at your back (make sure your subjects aren't squinting) or to one side whenever possible. If you have to take a picture of people who have the sun behind them, turn on your flash to light up their faces, which will otherwise be too dark.

- Don't be afraid to shoot from odd angles or unusual heights. Digital cameras encourage experimentation, and playing around can produce some great shots.

- Avoid a busy background that will distract the eye from the subject of the photo (**Figure B.4**).

- Keep the camera steady, particularly when you're shooting in low light without the flash. The beauty of the LCD screen on the camera is that you can set the camera on a solid object to shoot, even when it's not at a comfortable height.

- Remember that the flash on most small digital cameras works well only to about 10 feet. Relying on room light is tricky, but the more light you can throw on the subject in a normal room, the better.

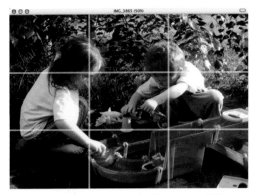

Figure B.3 Note how the heads of Tristan and his cousin Madeline are at the intersections of the grid, increasing visual interest and emphasizing their interaction.

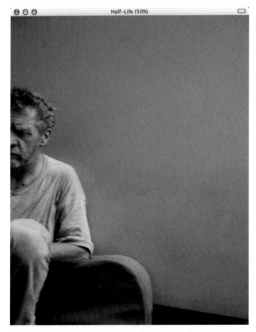

Figure B.4 This photo shows the value of an uncluttered background—the blank wall helps the eye focus on the man in the scene. Note too that the fact that he's only half in the frame increases the power of the photo. Sometimes in photography, as in graphic design, some "white space" can improve the image.

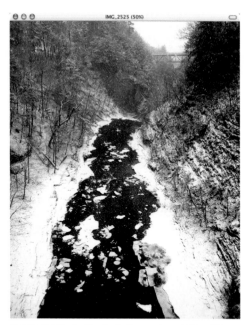

Figure B.5 Portrait orientation makes all the difference for this picture of the long, deep gorge that runs through Cornell University.

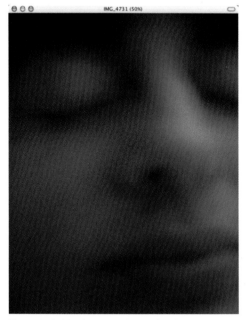

Figure B.6 This close-up of my wife's face works in large part because it's so close and out of focus.

More General Photo Tips

Here are a few more tips that can help.

◆ Try to match the orientation of the subject to the orientation of the photo (**Figure B.5**). Landscape orientation, where the photo is wider than it is tall, usually works best for landscapes (with specific exceptions, such as the gorge in **Figure B.5**), whereas portrait orientation, where the photo is taller than it is wide, works best for people. Computers and TVs use landscape orientation, so keep that in mind if you plan to do a lot of slideshows.

◆ Try to avoid posing your subjects. Most people aren't very good at describing exactly what they want the person in the photo to do, and most people aren't good at adopting a specific pose without it looking forced. Give it a try and you'll appreciate how hard professional photographers and models work.

◆ Figure out exactly what interests you about a scene before shooting. That helps you set up the shot and find different ways of emphasizing the subject.

◆ Take lots of photos—they don't cost anything. This is especially important when the scene is changing, but even with shots you set up, it's worth taking a couple, just in case one shot works better than another.

◆ As a corollary, try alternative ways of taking a given picture, such as with and without the flash. Do this enough and you'll start to figure out when to use certain settings for your desired effect.

◆ Don't be afraid to get close and fill the frame with the subject, even when it means cutting off parts of people's bodies or faces (**Figure B.6**).

Portrait Photo Tips

For many of us, pictures of people make up the bulk of our photo collections. Use these tips to improve your portraits of family and friends in the future.

◆ Get closer. A lot of portraits are taken from too far away, lessening the impact of having that particular person in the photo. Of course, since getting closer isn't always feasible, a good zoom lens can help.

◆ When you're taking pictures of traveling companions, break the previous rule a bit so you can add context to the shot. Signs work well for reminding you of where and when a picture was taken, particularly if they're in other languages.

◆ For candid snapshots, which are often the best kind, make sure you have enough light and just point the camera in the right direction and shoot from the hip (**Figure B.7**). Lots of these shots will be terrible, but the effort of tossing them is well worth the occasional amazing shot you'll get.

◆ Don't warn people in advance that you're going to take a photo unless you want forced smiles. If you need people to look at you, pre-focus your camera by pressing the shutter release button halfway, then say something to get their attention. As soon as they look at you, and before they realize you're taking a picture, press the button the rest of the way down.

◆ In group photos, make everyone crunch together and overlap. The presentation is much more interesting than if everyone just lines up by height (**Figure B.8**).

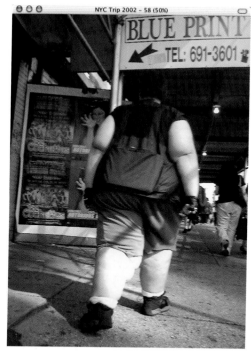

Figure B.7 I took this photo while holding the camera at my waist and walking normally down the street.

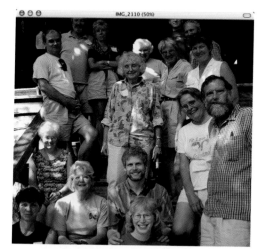

Figure B.8 This group photo from my family reunion works well because the different levels provided by the stairs help everyone overlap neatly.

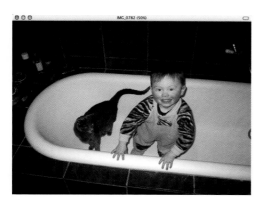

Figure B.9 Getting a cat and a child both looking photogenic at the same moment can be tricky unless you're willing to take lots of shots.

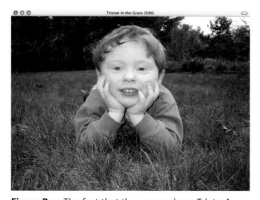

Figure B.10 The fact that the camera is on Tristan's level, about a foot off the ground, provides a good perspective.

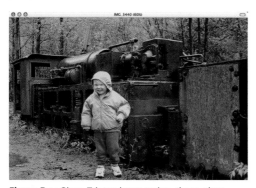

Figure B.11 Since Tristan loves trains, these abandoned mine trains at the Last Chance Basin Mining Museum in Juneau, Alaska, were a big hit. He asked me to take this photo and even agreed to pose in it.

Child and Pet Photo Tips

People may be the most common subjects of photos, but I'll bet most of those photos are pictures of children. And those folks who don't have children around often seem to replace kid photos with pet photos. Children and pets require similar shooting styles.

◆ Adults are usually capable of at least that oh-so-familiar forced smile, but kids often don't want to participate, and it's almost impossible to convince pets to pose. Give it up and shoot surreptitiously.

◆ When kids or pets are playing, they may not notice you, so work fast and take lots of pictures, perhaps with your camera's burst mode (**Figure B.9**). Try to avoid calling out names, since that will almost certainly break the spell.

◆ If the kids or pets realize what you're doing, just be patient and stay prepared in case you get another chance.

◆ If you plan to take pictures of children, encourage them to wear brightly colored clothing. Lots of color can make your photos more eye-catching.

◆ With both kids and pets, get down on their level (**Figure B.10**). Otherwise you end up shooting the tops of their heads.

◆ At zoos or similar attractions, try to photograph the child reacting to, or interacting with, the animals.

◆ It can be great fun to involve kids in the decisions about what pictures to take, particularly if you're on a trip. Ask them what they'd like you to take pictures of, and let them set the scene (**Figure B.11**).

◆ Outdoor photos often work the best, perhaps because it's easier to get good, uncluttered backgrounds.

Landscape Photo Tips

There are places where it seems almost impossible to take a bad photo (glaciers and mountain vistas, for instance), but a few tips can help improve other landscape pictures.

◆ Take advantage of the long light early in the morning (less haze) or just before dusk (sunset colors), since you get more interesting shadows and interplay between light and dark. Try to keep the sun at your back or your side.

◆ Try to keep the horizon level, although iPhoto can straighten photos if an otherwise good photo is marred by a bit of skew (**Figure B.12**).

◆ Keeping the Rule of Thirds in mind, if the land is the subject of your photo, make two-thirds of the photo be land, with one-third sky. If the sky is the focus of the photo (sunset photos can produce the most amazing colors), then reverse those proportions so the sky fills most of the frame.

◆ Try to include an object in the foreground to catch the eye, rather than leaving the entire landscape in the far distance (**Figure B.13**). A foreground object has the added advantage of indicating the magnitude of the scenery.

◆ When possible, eliminate distracting elements, such as telephone poles or electric lines. Otherwise, try to use them in the composition of the photo.

◆ Try using reflections in water or windows for interesting effects and perspectives (**Figure B.14**).

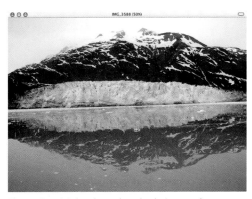

Figure B.12 It's hard to take a bad picture of a glacier... unless you can't hold the camera straight. iPhoto's Straighten tool can fix this shot.

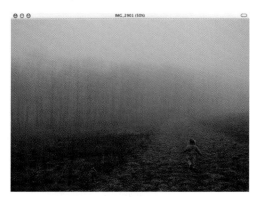

Figure B.13 The misty woods in the background evoke a mood, but Tristan running away from the camera down the mown strip in the field lends focus.

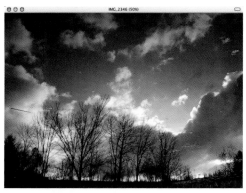

Figure B.14 This picture, although seemingly a normal landscape of trees and the sky, is actually a reflection in a pond, giving the scene added depth.

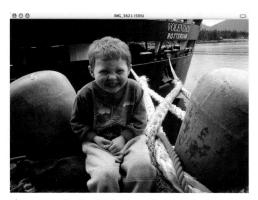

Figure B.15 Having Tristan pose in front of our cruise ship, with its name visible in the background (though hard to read at this size), made for a perfect travel picture.

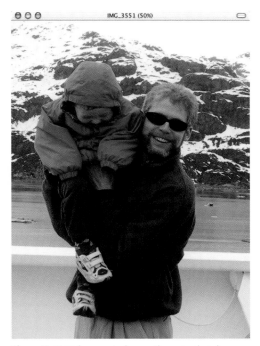

Figure B.16 Make sure to have other people take pictures of you. You'll especially appreciate having done this if you decide to make a book of your trip in iPhoto.

Travel Photo Tips

Although the tips for landscapes and portraits apply equally as well when you're traveling, a few special tips can help improve your vacation photos.

◆ Include your traveling companions in the shots when possible, because without them, you could just buy a postcard.

◆ Take photos that remind you of an area or event. Shoot details such as buildings, signs, or natural landmarks, but take them from your perspective and, when possible, with your traveling companions (**Figure B.15**).

◆ Don't get sucked into the trap of posed shots of your companions in front of whatever the local attraction may be. Have some fun and keep it light, partly so you get better shots, and partly so your traveling companions don't get sick of your camera.

◆ Ask one of your companions, or a passer-by, to take pictures that include you. Otherwise it may seem as though you weren't along on the trip (**Figure B.16**).

◆ Take pictures of the people you meet (it's best to ask for permission first), and make notes so you remember each person later.

◆ Plan ahead so you can take lots of photos. That may entail carrying an extra memory card or two, bringing an iPod with a camera adapter or a rechargeable digital wallet drive to store photos, or lugging a laptop along (at which point you can post Web pages of your travel photos for friends and family back home). It's also worth doing a bit of culling every night to free space used by bad shots.

INDEX

INDEX

INDEX